Effective Language Learning

MODERN LANGUAGES in PRACTICE

The **Modern Languages in Practice Series** provides publications on the theory and practice of modern foreign language teaching. The theoretical and practical discussions in the publications arise from, and are related to, research into the subject. *Practical* is defined as having pedagogic value. *Theoretical* is defined as illuminating and/or generating issues pertinent to the practical. Theory and practice are, however, understood as a continuum. The Series includes books at three distinct points along this continuum: (1) Limited discussions of language learning issues. These publications provide an outlet for coverage of actual classroom activities and exercises. (2) Aspects of both theory and practice combined in broadly equal amounts. This is the *core of the series*, and books may appear in the form of collections bringing together writers from different fields. (3) More theoretical books examining key research ideas directly relevant to the teaching of modern languages.

Series Editor
Michael Grenfell, *Centre for Language in Education, University of Southampton*

Editorial Board
Do Coyle, *School of Education, University of Nottingham*
Simon Green, *Trinity & All Saints College, Leeds*

Editorial Consultant
Christopher Brumfit, *Centre for Language in Education, University of Southampton*

Other Books in the Series
Cric Crac! Teaching and Learning French through Story-telling
    ROY DUNNING
The Good Language Learner
    N. NAIMAN, M. FRÖHLICH, H. H. STERN and A. TODESCO
The Elements of Foreign Language Teaching
    WALTER GRAUBERG
Inspiring Innovations in Language Teaching
    JUDITH HAMILTON
Le ou La? The Gender of French Nouns
    MARIE SURRIDGE
Target Language, Collaborative Learning and Autonomy
    ERNESTO MACARO
Validation in Language Testing
    A. CUMMING and R. BERWICK (eds)

Please contact us for the latest book information:
Multilingual Matters Ltd, Frankfurt Lodge, Clevedon Hall,
Victoria Road, Clevedon, England BS21 7SJ

MODERN LANGUAGES IN PRACTICE 6
Series Editor: Michael Grenfell

Effective Language Learning

Positive Strategies for Advanced Level Language Learning

Suzanne Graham

MULTILINGUAL MATTERS LTD
Clevedon • Philadelphia • Toronto • Adelaide • Johannesburg

For Edward

Library of Congress Cataloging in Publication Data

Graham, Suzanne
Effective Language Learning: Positive Strategies for Advanced Level
Language Learning/Suzanne Graham
Modern Languages in Practice: 6
Includes bibliographical references and index
1. Language and languages–Study and teaching. I. Title. II. Series.
P51.G67   1997
418'.007–dc21   96-48702

British Library Cataloguing in Publication Data

A CIP catalogue record for this book is available from the British Library.

ISBN 1-85359-380-X (hbk)
ISBN 1-85359-379-6 (pbk)

Multilingual Matters Ltd

UK: Frankfurt Lodge, Clevedon Hall, Victoria Road, Clevedon BS21 7SJ.
USA: 1900 Frost Road, Suite 101, Bristol, PA 19007, USA.
Canada: OISE, 712 Gordon Baker Road, Toronto, Ontario, Canada M2H 3R7.
Australia: P.O. Box 6025, 95 Gilles Street, Adelaide, SA 5000, Australia.
South Africa: PO Box 1080, Northcliffe 2115, Johannesburg, South Africa.

Typeset by Archetype, Stow-on-the-Wold
Printed and bound in Great Britain by WBC Book Manufacturers Ltd.

Contents

Foreword by Dr Bob Powell vii
Preface ix
Acknowledgements x

1   Introduction 1

2   Bridging the Gap: Language Learning Difficulties 10
      Introduction 10
      Communicative Competence 11
      Practical Implications 14
      Proficiency at Advanced Level 16
      Key Findings 20
      Gender Differences 28
      Implications for the Classroom 30

3   Learning Strategies: Processing Language and Managing Change . 37
      Introduction 37
      The Good Language Learner Revisited: Beginnings 38
      Recent Developments in Learning Strategy Research 40
      Investigating Learning Strategies: Methods and Approaches 43
      Key Findings 48
      Gender Differences in Strategy Use 81
      Implications for the Classroom 83
      Conclusion 91

4   Affective Concerns and the Question of Gender 92
      Introduction 92
      Attitudes and Motivation 96
      Gender 99
      Key Findings 103
      Implications for the Classroom 116
      Conclusion 122

5   The Role of the Teacher: Teaching Language or Teaching
     Learning? 124
         Introduction 124
         Key Findings: Easing the Transition 127
         Teachers' Views of Learning and Learners 137
         Implications for the Classroom 139

6   Students in the Round: Looking at Individuals 147
         Introduction 147
         Student M (Female) 147
         Student P (Female) 151
         Student F (Male) 154
         Student H (Male) 157

7   Conclusion 162
         Introduction 162
         The Way Forward 168
         Final Thoughts 171

Appendices 172
     Appendix A.1 Glossary 172
     Appendix A.2 Definitions of Learning Strategies Used by Students 175
     Appendix B: Research Instruments 184
     Appendix C: Materials Used in the Think-Aloud Interview . . . 196
     Appendix D: Subjects Involved in the Study 202
     Appendix E: Tables of Results 205
References 216
Index 226

Foreword

Language teachers frequently claim that language teaching differs enormously from the teaching of other subjects. They do this with some justification. Modern methods, as well as placing great demands on the physical resources of the teacher and emphasising the importance of careful sequencing of activities, insist on extremely high levels of grammatical knowledge, cultural awareness and oral proficiency.

Similarly, it must be acknowledged that communicative approaches to teaching languages have also added to the strains of being a student of a foreign language. Not only do language learners have to take a much more active part in the proceedings with all the risks that that might entail, they also have to demonstrate their competence and performance in many more ways than previously demanded through tests and examinations.

Research into foreign and second language acquisition during the 1970s and 1980s generally concentrated more on pedagogy than learning processes. It is only relatively recently that the focus has shifted, rightly in my view, to take account of the interaction between teacher and learner from the perspective of the learner. Some academics still tend to underestimate the complexity of the language learning process, reducing it to the mere development of 'practical' skills which, when rehearsed with sufficient frequency, will enable any reasonably intelligent person to communicate. However, Suzanne Graham recognises the need to understand more fully the challenges facing foreign language students, especially as they embark upon on a more advanced course of study. Her motivation to investigate these difficulties and the strategies which are employed by teachers and learners to overcome them derives from first-hand experience. But she has also been at pains to underpin her study with detailed and critical analysis of current theories. It is this blend of theoretical perspectives and the working through of concrete problems that characterises her writing.

The context of the research which is presented in this book may be specific to a particular phase in the English educational system but the methodology and the insights gained thereby are relevant to anyone seeking to improve the quality of teaching and learning. The key research questions are set out in the introductory chapter. These questions also address important features or variables which have been neglected in the research to date, such as sex differences and learner anxiety. In the approach Dr Graham has adopted to investigating language learning strategies through think-aloud techniques, she has made advances in research methods by re-defining and refining existing taxonomies and by transcript processing. Her research also shows the value of learner diaries as a research tool.

Within each subsequent chapter, following discussion of the central issue to be addressed and the research procedures selected, the implications for classroom practice are highlighted and clear recommendations are made to teachers for enabling their students to become more effective learners by, for example, reducing their anxiety, teaching them a wider range of language processing strategies and, generally, helping them to become more reflective and self-critical in their approach to learning. The main message to teachers is unequivocal: understanding *how* their students are learning is as important as being aware of *what* they are learning. In short, to espouse an educational philosophy which places learner auton-omy at the centre of all the planning is insufficient if one fails to prepare students for this new found independence and one remains ignorant of the strategies they are using.

The penultimate chapter brings us into direct contact with four of the students who were at the centre of the research project. Their particular strengths and weaknesses are illustrated and discussed. These case-studies provide an apposite context for offering suggestions for enhancing all language students' repertoire of learning strategies and skills. The final chapter then offers a coherent synthesis of the project outcomes and sets out a practical action plan for teachers.

On a personal note, I have known the author for several years. I have watched her grow in confidence and experience through her initial teacher training, her first teaching post and then the doctoral research which has provided the core material for this volume. More recently, she has been an indispensable colleague on a number of research projects. It is not often in the world of education that one has the privilege of developing a professional relationship with so gifted, yet so modest a person. Her analytical skills and practical common sense combine admirably in this book to produce a most readable study and useful guide.

Dr Bob Powell
Director of the Language Centre
University of Warwick

Preface

In writing this book I have had two aims, both of equal importance. The first is to provide insights into some of the learning processes of students of French and German as they begin language learning at Advanced Level (A-level). It is hoped that by focusing the attention of teachers and others concerned with A-level language learning on aspects of the classroom that previously may not have received full consideration, the needs of students will become clearer and easier to meet. With this in mind, the book looks at the following areas: learners' perceptions of the difficulties they experience at this stage of their language learning; the learning strategies they employ to overcome such difficulties; the relationship between these learning difficulties and learning strategies and such factors as gender, motivation and anxiety; teachers' perceptions of their students' difficulties, and the measures they take to ease the transition to A-level language study.

The second aim follows on very closely from the first. By looking at how successful and unsuccessful language students learn, the book seeks to illustrate how all learners at this level can become more proficient in their language learning. While most students use a broad range of learning strategies, these are not always implemented in the most appropriate manner. A recurring theme throughout the book is that many of the difficulties experienced by students can be mitigated by more explicit teaching of the effective use of learning strategies. Above all it argues for the need to encourage greater reflection among students about their own learning behaviour, in order to promote learning that is truly self-directed and hence more fulfilling.

Acknowledgements

I should like to express my gratitude to several people who helped in various ways in the production of this publication: to Bob Powell and Carol Morgan for their sound advice and encouragement during the initial research project; to the students and teachers who talked to me and allowed me into their classrooms; to Simon Green, for his helpful comments during the writing of the book; and most of all to my parents and husband Alan, for their unfailing support throughout.

Thanks are due to the following publishers and authors for permission to include copyright material in the text:

BBC (No date) *Voix de France: Les Français et leurs vacances*. London: BBC.

Northern Examinations and Assessment Board. (1989) *General Certificate of Education. French Advanced Paper II. Friday 9 June 1989*. Manchester: Northern Examinations and Assessment Board.

O'Malley, J.M. and Chamot, A.U. (1990) *Learning Strategies in Second Language Acquisition* (pp. 44–5; 137–9). Cambridge: Cambridge University Press.

It has not been possible to trace the following copyright holders and I would be grateful to hear from them:

Oxford, R. (1985) *A New Taxonomy of Second Language Learning Strategies*. Washington, DC: ERIC Clearinghouse on Languages and Linguistics.

Oxford, R. (1986) Development and psychometric testing of the strategy inventory for language learning. Army Research Institute Technical Report. Alexandria, VA: US Army Research Institute for the Behavioural and Social Sciences.

Text from University of Oxford Delegacy of Local Examinations (1989) *Advanced Supplementary Level Summer Examination, May 1989. French. Paper I: Ville Pratique. Jeunes Rennais — Un Coup de Pouce Pour Vos Vacances*.

1 Introduction

The impetus to this book comes from personal experience as a practising teacher, working to a large extent with students of French and German who were preparing for Advanced Level (A-level) — the examination generally taken by language students in England, Wales and Northern Ireland at 18 years of age.[1] At the time of my first teaching appointment, in September 1988, students entering into A-level language programmes were the first to have previously taken the 'intermediate' examination, the General Certificate of Secondary Education (GCSE)[2] in Modern Foreign Languages, with its greater emphasis on communicative skills as compared to previous examinations in the UK at that level.

This personal experience was revealing in a number of aspects. First, it was evident that, although there had been a considerable growth in the number of pupils choosing to pursue a foreign language to an advanced level, the disparity between the A-level candidate figures for girls and those for boys was still marked.

Second, students seemed to come to A-level with a large amount of enthusiasm, having in the main enjoyed GCSE work and gained a high grade in the examination. Thus prior to the advanced course most were quite confident in their abilities in the foreign language. Third, and in contrast to the positive note of the last observation, it appeared that many students were finding the transition from GCSE to A-level very difficult, especially with regard to the manipulation of language and structure, the acquisition of higher level vocabulary, written accuracy and the analysis of complex written texts (including literature). As later chapters will make clear, GCSE aims to develop in students practical skills of communication in tasks typically including role-play, general conversation about prescribed topic areas, and comprehending relatively short written and oral texts of a largely factual nature. Students are assessed principally on the ability to transmit a message rather than on linguistic accuracy. A-level, on the other hand, while similarly emphasising the importance of communication, further requires students to use language accurately, often within tasks such as essay writing, translation or the discussion of more abstract

themes. Coping with these new demands can adversely affect the motivation and self-confidence of some students who, prior to A-level, have
probably only known success in foreign language learning.

These personal observations were borne out by those made by colleagues in my own and other schools: while welcoming the higher level of
oral fluency the GCSE examination had encouraged in students, many
teachers expressed concern about helping students to attain the degree of
grammatical awareness and accuracy required at A-level. Moving from
anecdotal to more concrete evidence, it seems in retrospect that these
observations coincided with those emerging from certain research projects,
such as the NEEDS Project (reported in Crossan (1992), and Low (1991)).
This followed 100 UK students through the two years of A-level study
(1989–1991) in either French, history or physics. It found that in the foreign
language, learners experienced difficulties in extensive reading, writing
accurately and at length, using grammar correctly, vocabulary acquisition,
listening comprehension and oral discussion work and adopting effective
study skills and time management. Low (1991) writes of the 'culture shock'
experienced by such students at the point of transition from GCSE to
A-level. Similarly, the difficulty often experienced by learners at this stage
is echoed in the title of a text aiming to help teachers adapt learners to more
advanced work — *Bridging the Gap: GCSE to 'A-level* (Thorogood & King,
1991).

In many discussions the tension between students' ability to communicate fluently and their difficulties with precision and accuracy is
underlined. In the Examiners' Report on the 1991 A-level examination in
French set by the Northern Examining Board (NEAB), concern is expressed
about declining levels of accuracy and attention to detail, matched,
however, by 'evidence of greater freedom and confidence in the use of
language, and a desire to communicate a wide variety of feelings and ideas'
(NEAB, 1992: 19, 29). Hurman (1992), in a survey of oral examiners' views
on the performance of candidates in A-level French, German and Spanish
examinations, comes to similar conclusions.

A review of such observations, however, leaves one with the sense that
our knowledge of the *precise* character of beginning A-level learners'
difficulties is essentially limited. Within the UK at least, earlier research into
foreign language learning at this level, such as the 1985 HMI report, *Modern
Languages in the Sixth Form*, was in general restricted to the teaching
methods and materials employed, without reference to the behaviour of
learners themselves. The NEEDS project mentioned earlier has gone some
way to illuminate our perceptions of students' experiences of the transition

to A-level work, but a more detailed insight into the problem is required if we are to propose a remedy for it.

With these thoughts in mind, a research project was undertaken in the period 1991–93, under the aegis of the University of Bath. The first aim of the study was to examine the precise nature and extent of the difficulties perceived by learners as they make the transition to A-level work. Furthermore, in view of the growing international interest in language and gender, particularly within the classroom (summarised in Holmes, 1991), it seemed appropriate to investigate whether there is any difference in the learning difficulties experienced by male and female students at this level. Research into gender differences in British foreign language learners has so far concentrated on younger pupils (e.g. Batters, 1988; Powell, 1986a).

Second, it was difficult to ignore the observation frequently made by teachers that while some students continue to experience great difficulties throughout the two years of an A-level course, others adapt far more easily and successfully to the demands made upon them. This prompts the question as to why learners who embark on a programme of study with largely the same level of competence in terms of previous examination grades should display such different types of learning behaviour. In short, what makes a good language learner at this level and can we help less successful learners become more like their more successful classmates by identifying the learning strategies of the latter? Are there any differences in the strategies used by males and those used by females? While most teachers have some idea of what their students find difficult, very few, it is supposed, have any real knowledge of what students themselves do in order to try to overcome their difficulties. It may be that in searching for a solution to the problem of transition we are best advised to turn to those who do in fact cope with the change. This project was undertaken in order to address this gap in our awareness of what our students are experiencing. Furthermore, while the research was carried out within the UK, the answers it offers to the questions posed here are of relevance to language learning within a wider context.

The nature of language learning strategies will be considered in greater detail in Chapter 3, but here we might define learning strategies in general as the thoughts and behaviours 'students use to comprehend, store, and remember new information and skills' (Chamot & Küpper, 1989: 13). As such, learning strategies are at the core of a model of language acquisition that begins with the assumption that it is just another complex cognitive task, no different from any other kind of learning. This view departs radically from theories which attribute an identity to language and linguistic processes which is separate from general learning. It further suggests that differences in the level of proficiency language learners achieve arise from differences in learning behaviour, strategies or mental processes, rather than learner characteristics such as motivation — although certain learner characteristics *may* affect the efficiency of these mental processes.

To many language teachers, dismissing the importance of learners' individual characteristics may seem at odds with what they instinctively feel about how their students vary in their approach to language learning. Likewise, Spolsky (1989: 3) argues that one of the main aims of research into language learning is to illuminate the question of 'who learns how much of what language under what conditions'. Other models of second language acquisition[3] (e.g. Gardner, 1985) which emphasise the importance of more personal characteristics such as aptitude and the learner's attitude to the foreign language and its speakers might thus seem more plausible. Indeed, the influence of certain learner variables, including motivation (Gardner & Lambert, 1972) and anxiety (Gardner et al., 1976) has been highlighted by empirical research. Thus in the present study it was felt important to pay attention to the affective or emotional responses of learners, an area that previous investigations of advanced learners have tended to pass over.

A further question that needs exploration is the relationship between these factors and learning strategy use. For while a view of language learning that focuses on cognitive processes might be criticised for underestimating the effect of personal characteristics on the level of language proficiency achieved, models which emphasise these characteristics or individual differences seem lacking in the view they give of the actual learning processes that occur within the language student. What one might call 'individual differences models' generally aim to describe, as Spolsky (1989: 120) points out, 'a set of facts about language that will account for observable utterances without postulating a method of storage, or production, or comprehension of those utterances'. On the other hand, a 'cognitive' approach tries to do many of these things without taking into consideration social psychological factors. Many observers of language learning (e.g. Stern, 1983) would argue that it is influenced by a number of closely interwoven factors and that to take an exclusively cognitive or social psychological approach is to ignore many important elements involved in language learning. Hence in the present study the aim was to consider the process from both perspectives. That is, individual differences in language learning were at the centre of the investigation, with explanations for them sought through an examination of the various affective and cognitive variables that students bring to the learning situation — in particular, those relating to anxiety, motivation, gender and learning strategies.

A further influence considered worthy of investigation was the role played by the teacher in advanced language learning. More precisely, it was felt imperative to gain a clearer insight into teachers' perceptions of the problems arising at the point of transition to A-level study, in order to substantiate the anecdotal evidence referred to in earlier paragraphs. This area is of particular importance in so far as major discrepancies between the difficulties reported by students and those perceived by their teachers are likely to exacerbate the problems of transition at this level.

Finally, before any suggestions can be made as to how teachers might help students to adapt more successfully to their new courses, we need detailed information on what teachers are doing at present, both in terms of the teaching strategies they themselves apply and any training they give their pupils in developing effective learning strategies.

There are of course other factors which could be considered in an examination of the process of transition to A-level work. These include: the effect of different course materials used and the syllabus followed (particularly concerning whether literature or topics are studied); teaching styles in different establishments; and the nature of the establishment in which students are working (for example, school or college). Languages other than French or German might also be considered. It was not, however, possible to investigate all areas relating to the theme of A-level language learning, and so five main questions were selected for more detailed consideration:

(1) What difficulties are faced by A-level learners within the foreign languages classroom?
(2) What are the learning strategies employed by students to overcome the difficulties they experience?
(3) How do these learner difficulties and learning strategies relate to gender and affective factors, such as anxiety and motivation?
(4) How do teachers perceive their students' learning difficulties and what steps do they take to resolve them?
(5) What are the implications of the above for teaching and learning in the foreign languages classroom?

The project thus adhered more to a descriptive, interpretative research model than to a confirmatory, hypothesis-testing type (cf. the research approaches discussed by Anderson & Burns (1989). Or, to borrow the terminology employed by Larsen-Freeman and Long (1991), and Skehan

(1989, 1991), to the 'research-then-theory', rather than the 'theory-then-research' format. While the latter allows the researcher, working from a set of initial hypotheses, to concentrate on certain key areas of the problem in hand, it is possible that such an approach may cause other arguably important factors to be overlooked, a danger that is less likely in the research-then-theory approach. This, in its turn, however, brings with it the problems of an unwieldy amount of data and a lack of focus (Skehan, 1991). Of course, as Skehan suggests, it is possible, and arguably desirable, for a research project to combine elements of both approaches and indeed this was the course generally adopted in the present project. Skehan (1991) advocates studies which, while focusing on a small area of language acquisition, simultaneously make reference to a larger theoretical framework of past research into the field as a whole.

The 'dual perspective, between the macro and the micro' (Skehan, 1991: 292) was followed in this study to the extent that while learner difficulties and learning strategies were the chief areas of investigation, this was carried out with constant reference to findings in the field of language learning as a whole. Furthermore, the guiding focus for the project was the fifth research question, concerning the implications of the key findings for the classroom. Hence it was decided that the research methodology used to investigate the areas outlined should be as close to the classroom experiences of learners as possible; that is, it should use largely 'idiographic' techniques (Cohen & Manion, 1989: 9) which look at learning from the point of view of the individual and are qualitative rather than quantitative in nature. On the other hand, both the initial question concerning the extent of learners' perceptions of their language learning difficulties, and that investigating teachers' perceptions of and reactions to those difficulties, demanded an element of quantification. It seemed appropriate to seek answers to these questions initially from a wide population (600 students, 100 teachers), and then carry out a follow-up study among a smaller group (24 students, nine teachers). With these aims in mind the research model shown in Figure 1 was devised.

The implications that the project's findings have for the classroom equally guide the structure the discussion will take in subsequent chapters. The four initial questions outlined in Figure 1 will be taken in turn, beginning with a brief examination of the issues underlying the area of concern and, where appropriate, setting it against what we know already from previous studies. Then, the key findings from the investigation will be outlined. The chief focus of the chapter, the implications of these findings for the classroom, will then follow.

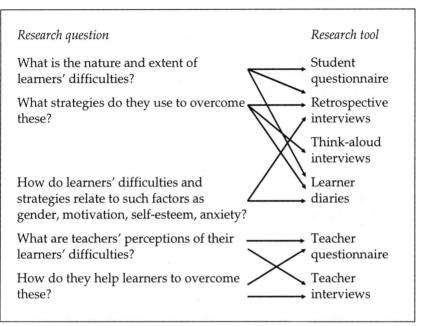

Figure 1. Research model

Working within this framework the outline of the book is as follows.

Chapter 2: Bridging the Gap: Language Learning Difficulties. As the background to a discussion of language learning at A-level, this chapter begins by discussing what is meant by the term 'proficiency' and how our understanding of it has evolved over the years, leading to the present concern with communicative competence.

The influence of current notions of proficiency on our expectations of advanced learners is then considered, leading to what the research project discovered from learners themselves about their difficulties in making the transition to A-level language work. The focus is on difficulties of a cognitive nature within the chief skill areas (listening, reading, writing and oral work, mastering vocabulary and grammar, topic and course work).

These findings then lead to a detailed discussion of the need to reassess how we present language to learners at A-level, and what we expect of them at this stage of their learning.

Chapter 3: Learning Strategies: Processing Language and Managing Change. After a review of what previous research has taught us about learning strategies, this chapter reports on the strategies used by learners as they try to cope with the difficulties outlined in Chapter 2. In particular, learning strategies as employed on think-aloud tasks are analysed, highlighting any differences in strategy use attributable to gender or learner effectiveness.

The lessons to be learnt from the strategies used by effective learners are then discussed, together with a consideration of how these strategies might be taught to other students.

Chapter 4: Affective Concerns and the Question of Gender. Here the emphasis is on the part played in language learning by factors such as motivation, anxiety and gender. Findings from the research project regarding students' difficulties associated with poor motivation and low self-esteem are presented. This is followed by a look at how students claim to deal with these problems, again examining more closely any differences attributable to gender or learner effectiveness.

How the difficulties outlined in the chapter might be resolved is then considered, suggesting positive classroom strategies in such areas as oral work and self-assessment.

Chapter 5: The Role of the Teacher: Teaching Language or Teaching Learning? This reports on information gathered from teachers in different schools and colleges regarding their perceptions of their learners' strengths and weaknesses, how they felt they helped students to make the transition to more advanced language work, and how far they encouraged learners to adopt effective learning strategies.

Recommendations arising from these observations are then presented, including suggestions for teaching strategies and good practice in the key areas of language learning at A-level. Particular emphasis is placed on the need for the effective teaching of learning strategies and further suggestions as to how this might be achieved are made.

Chapter 6: Students in the Round: Looking at Individuals. The overall learning approach of four students is examined in detail, as examples of the ways in which problems in cognitive and affective areas can come together. Suggestions are then made as to how such students can be helped to become more effective learners.

Chapter 7: Conclusion. The main findings and arguments presented in previous chapters are drawn together. A seven-point plan is outlined for tackling some of the problems highlighted by the study.

The materials and results from the study are given in the appendix together with a glossary of some of the technical terms.

Notes

1, 2. In view of the context in which the research project took place, the terms 'GCSE' and 'A-level' have been used throughout the book. Students taking the first of these examinations at 16 years of age have generally been studying the foreign language for two to five years, and are expected to have developed practical skills of communication, largely within topics of a concrete, factual nature, such as personal and social life. Candidates for the A-level examination will have studied the language for two additional years and will have reached a higher level of competence, involving the ability to discuss orally and in written form a much wider range of intellectual issues with greater precision and linguistic accuracy (both examinations are described in further detail in the Glossary, Appendix A.1). It is intended, however, that the arguments presented in the book will be of relevance to language learning beyond the GCSE/A-level framework, for example, in other contexts where learners are initially encouraged to concentrate on practical communication and are then required to develop rapidly greater linguistic awareness and skills of argumentation.

3. The closely allied terms 'second language' and 'foreign language' are often used interchangeably in the literature. In the present study, 'foreign language' is generally preferred, given the context of the investigation. Where, however, the alternative term is deemed to be more appropriate, for example, when referring to the established research field of second language acquisition, this has been employed.

2 Bridging the Gap: Language Learning Difficulties

Introduction

It has sometimes been observed that 'success' in foreign language learning eludes many of those who embark upon the task; Stern, for example, remarks that everyone interested in the study of a second or foreign language

> 'faces the problem of inadequate knowledge and frequent failure. Success in second language learning is not the rule. Moreover, failure can be accompanied by a sense of isolation or alienation, by dissatisfaction, and an awareness of one's own inadequacy.' (Stern, 1983: 340)

Admittedly, Stern was writing more than a decade ago and his remarks may seem unduly pessimistic when set against the evident success of many students in today's classrooms in terms of their ability to communicate in a foreign language. Yet personal experience suggests that at certain stages of a student's language learning career the task may indeed seem a very difficult one, particularly if the expectations of the learner suddenly shift as he or she 'progresses' to a higher level of instruction.

But before we look in detail at what the nature of students' difficulties and achievements in A-level language learning might be, it is important to begin with an outline of the objectives or standards against which their progress is to be measured. In the introductory chapter it was suggested that today's foreign language teachers, while often concerned about their students' difficulties in the areas of grammatical accuracy, recognise the advantage these learners have over their forebears in terms of their readiness to communicate (especially orally). This facility is sometimes referred to as 'communicative competence', a term which is not, however, always used with precision. The following sections aim to outline exactly what is meant by communicative competence and to examine its influence on current forms of assessment at A-level. In order to set the scene for the research project described later on in the chapter, the chief focus will be assessment in England and Wales; it is however intended that comments made regarding the tension that may arise between communicative fluency and grammatical precision can be applied to language learning in other contexts.

Communicative Competence

In many respects our view of what it means to know a foreign language has evolved along with our understanding of how such a language is acquired and how it should be taught. At the beginning of this century the 'grammar–translation' method of teaching still held sway in most schools, in most countries, although questions concerning its appropriateness had been raised since the 1850s. It placed emphasis on imparting a knowledge of the foreign language as a grammatical system, with the mother tongue used as a point of reference to aid the learning of the second language. As such, proficiency or achievement was judged to consist of a thorough knowledge of the formal aspects of the language, often tested by means of grammar-based exercises and translation to and from the target language. Little value was placed on using the language in its spoken form and limited travel abroad, together with more restricted foreign trade than there is today, meant that there was no social or economic pressure for language proficiency to have a communicative element.

During the Second World War and after, however, the advantages of being able to communicate with other nations became more widely recognised. In the United States, for example, large numbers of service personnel needed to be trained in foreign languages, for whom the grammar-translation approach was thought to be inappropriate. Hence in part the emergence of the audiolingual method (taking a similar form in the UK but known there as the 'audiovisual' approach), with its emphasis on spoken language but generally in the form of responses to stimuli, fostered by the inculcation of the 'habits' of the foreign language. This approach was influenced by the behaviourism movement in the field of psychology, which held that all human behaviour, language learning included, is essentially a series of habits acquired in response to stimuli. In language learning, errors were regarded as interference from the habits of the native language and thus to be eliminated as soon as they surfaced. From a proficiency point of view, achievement was assessed according to learners' control over a 'system of habits of communication' (Lado, 1961:

22), rather than their ability to communicate in authentic situations. Testing was essentially a means of finding out whether correct 'habits' had been formed.

The behaviourist view of learning, however, did not go unchallenged, most notably in the work of Chomsky. A full discussion of his ideas is beyond the scope of this chapter but certain key elements may be outlined. In several publications Chomsky argued that language is not a set of acquired habits or a series of abstract rules but a unique, innate human function. Within the human mind, it is posited, exists a 'universal grammar' made up of a set of general principles that govern all languages. Yet individual languages have their own particular parameters (or variations) within the framework of the universal principles. From the evidence of linguistic input learners receive, they must set the parameters that apply to their mother tongue. Children thus internalise a knowledge of the grammar of their native language (gaining what Chomsky calls 'competence'), which allows them to develop language use ('performance'; Chomsky, 1965: 4). It is further suggested that certain features of the native language are acquired before others and that this natural order of acquisition is impervious to external influences such as instruction. This last point has had a particular impact on theories of second language acquisition, for example, that of 'interlanguage', a term first used by Selinker (1972). Again, this is a complex theory but in its essence it suggests that learners pass from one transitional stage of competence to another while acquiring the target language; this 'interlanguage' is based on the target language but is incomplete and unstable, and errors have a natural place within it.

One result of these and similar discussions about the nature of language acquisition was to draw a distinction between abstract knowledge of a language and the ability to *use* that language in real situations. This is seen in Chomsky's reference to 'competence' and 'performance' mentioned earlier. The social embeddedness of language is heavily emphasised in views of language competence that emerged at the end of the 1970s and early 1980s, most notably in the case of communicative competence. The term is developed most fully in the work of Canale & Swain (1980). There, it does not, as is sometimes believed today, refer solely to oral fluency but has a far wider application. Canale and Swain have formulated a three-part definition, consisting of grammatical, sociolinguistic and strategic competence. *Grammatical competence* includes knowledge of lexical items, rules of morphology, syntax, semantics and phonology. Canale & Swain reject the notion that emphasis on language use for meaningful communicative purposes leaves no place for grammar; they argue that it contributes to the effectiveness of communication, allowing learners to express themselves more fully and with greater precision, and as such should be developed by being taught and assessed within the context of meaningful communication.

Sociolinguistic competence is essentially concerned with being able to produce and comprehend language which is appropriate to certain social situations and which observes the conventions of politeness of those situations. This involves knowledge of the sociocultural rules of language use, for example, the use of different registers or forms of address (e.g. the appropriate use of the 'vous' form in French). Sociolinguistic competence also implies knowledge of the rules of discourse, which govern the way in which language structures can be combined to produce unified texts in different modes — for instance, speeches, academic articles, or operating instructions. More specifically, these rules cover the way in which grammatical links bind language together (cohesion) and the appropriate combination of utterances (coherence). In a later version of the definition of communicative competence, Canale (1983) separates out discourse competence as an individual factor, rather than just a sub-section of sociolinguistic competence.

Strategic competence refers to 'verbal and non-verbal communication strategies that may be called into action to compensate for breakdowns in communication due to performance variables or to insufficient competence' (Canale & Swain, 1980: 30). That is, it describes the ability to get one's message across successfully even if, for example, there are gaps in one's foreign language vocabulary; mime or gestures might be used to communicate, or a paraphrase of the intended sentence given instead.

In a more recent contribution to the debate, Bachman (1990) argues for the use of more precise terminology if we are to understand fully the nature of language proficiency. He prefers the term 'communicative language ability' (CLA), claiming that the term communicative competence fails to distinguish between competence or knowledge, and performance, indicating the ability to use this knowledge in communication. With this in mind, Bachman defines CLA as both 'knowledge, or competence, and the capacity for implementing, or executing that competence in appropriate, contextualised communicative language use' (Bachman, 1990: 84). CLA has three components — language competence, strategic competence and psychophysiological mechanisms — which are in turn subdivided into smaller parts.

Briefly, *language competence* consists of (1) *organisational competence*; this is made up of grammatical competence, i.e. knowledge of vocabulary, syntax or the rules that govern how words are arranged in phrases or sentences, and textual competence, i.e. knowledge of the conventions for joining pieces of language together to form a cohesive whole); and (2) *pragmatic competence* (made up of illocutionary competence, i.e. the ability to use language to perform different functions, and sociolinguistic competence, i.e. sensitivity to the conventions for using language appropriately in different cultures and circumstances).

Strategic competence in this model differs from Canale & Swain's (1980) definition of the term as the ability to compensate for breakdowns in communication. Bachman sees it instead as 'a general ability, which enables an individual to make the most effective use of available abilities in carrying out a given task' (Bachman, 1990: 106). It is thus closely allied to the effective and flexible use of strategies of learning and communication — something which, it will be argued in later chapters, is a central factor in determining how effectively students cope with the challenges of advanced language learning.

Finally, *psychophysiological competence* refers to auditory, visual and neuromuscular skills used to receive and produce utterances on a concrete level.

Practical Implications

For all their differences, both Canale and Swain's, and Bachman's view of communicative competence/performance go beyond the level of 'survival' language use which is sometimes associated with the term (see Mitchell, (1988) who found that some language teachers interpreted it thus). An awareness of grammatical appropriateness and sociolinguistic nuances clearly has an important place within communicative competence. It further extends beyond spoken language; Canale (1984: 111) defines communication as 'the exchange and negotiation of information between at least two individuals through the use of verbal and nonverbal symbols, oral and written/visual modes, and production and comprehension processes'.

If we turn to the influence such views have had on the assessment of foreign language learning, then elements of the theoretical perspectives outlined in the last few pages can be traced in the development of assessment in the last 15 years or so. This is not merely the case in the United Kingdom but is true of language learner in other contexts. For example, the emphasis on language as a communicative tool is reflected in syllabuses constructed according to a notional/functional approach such as the Council of Europe's 'Threshold Level' for English as a Second Language (van Ek, 1979). There the aim is the development of practical skills for communication within social and commercial settings. Within this framework, proficiency is viewed as the completion of communicative tasks, within a clearly defined range of functions (e.g. socialising, getting things done), notions (e.g. expressions of size, quantity), topics (e.g. free time and entertainment), settings (e.g. travel and transport) and language forms that the learner will be expected to use.

Syllabuses for learners have taken similar forms in England and Wales in the form of the GCSE. In the document outlining the principles of language assessment at this level, the *National Criteria* for French (Department of Education and Science/Welsh Office, 1985) (its recommendations were to apply to all languages), one of the main aims of the GCSE examination is stated as the development of 'the ability to use French effectively for purposes of practical communication' (Department of Education and Science/Welsh Office, 1985: 1). Tasks are set within specified topic areas and typically include role-playing based on a stimulus, general conversation on a range of prescribed topic areas, responding to short spoken and written texts. While some expression of opinions in the target language is required, this applies generally only to higher levels and again is within prescribed topic areas. More specific assessment objectives place emphasis firmly on the successful completion of tasks, rather than on a demonstration of linguistic knowledge. Communicative ability is to be largely assessed globally according to the overall effectiveness of the candidate's responses.

Many of the aims of the GCSE have been preserved with the introduction of the National Curriculum for foreign languages in England and Wales. The authors of the report on which the final National Curriculum proposals have been based, acknowledge, for example, 'the importance of the immediate goal of communication'. Importantly, however, they go on to argue that the pursuit of this goal 'has led to some neglect of awareness of structure as an aid to language learning' (Department of Education and Science/Welsh Office, 1991: 6), later underlining the importance of linguistic knowledge in 'ensuring progress in the longer term and as a basis for continued study at higher levels' (Department of Education and Science/Welsh Office, 1991: 6).

Nevertheless, in practice it still seems that at GCSE level grammar is sometimes viewed as an optional extra to communication, rather than being the integral feature which it is in theoretical discussions of communicative competence. For example, in many GCSE foreign languages syllabuses it is stated that for higher level written tasks, scripts will be assessed on the one hand for 'communication', on the other, for accuracy or 'quality of language'.

Proficiency at Advanced Level

For students who wish to go beyond the level of language learning just described, 'the immediate goal of communication' is still important; yet at A-level other elements of communicative competence are brought more clearly into play. Referring again to the situation of England and Wales, some indication of the desired aims of A-level appear in *Guidelines for Written French at A Level* (1986), with contributions from representatives of several of the external examining groups. Specific reference is made there to how A-level should differ from GCSE in respect of lexis and syntax; for the former, A-level should mark a progression in the 'development of vocabulary appropriate to discussion, argument, analysis and evaluation' (*Guidelines for Written French at A Level*, 1986: 3); for the latter, there should first be a greater mastery of the basic structural core assumed to be imperfectly learnt prior to A-level. As students progress through their course, they should develop in both areas a higher level of performance judged according to the following criteria:

> *range* of lexical resources
> *accuracy with which the available resources are handled*
> *variety* of syntactic structures
> *precision* of use of syntactic structures
> sensitivity of *idiom* and *style*
> *appropriateness* of language to content
> achievement of *communication*.
> (*Guidelines for Written French at A Level*, 1986: 4, emphasis in the original)

Above all, however, the *Guidelines* seek to encourage 'the current shift towards the practical and communicative use of language, without jeopardising that intellectual exploration which is the aim of the A level French examination as a whole' (*Guidelines*, 1986: 4).

These principles are upheld and expanded upon in the later subject core for A-level foreign languages in England and Wales, published by the School Curriculum and Assessment Authority. There, tasks are advocated which are based on authentic texts and which give students greater insight into the culture of the target language community. In addition, they are to extend students' 'knowledge of and ability to exploit a range of linguistic structures and communication strategies', and allow them to show the capacity to 'manipulate the target language with confidence and to extend their powers of personal expression' (School Curriculum and Assessment Authority, 1993: 2).

These recommendations, in themselves evidence of the influence of the communicative view of proficiency, are reflected in A-level syllabuses where effective communication in the spoken and written language is an important assessment objective. In many respects A-level's assessment of proficiency is very much in line with the theoretical notions of communicative ability discussed in the previous section. Bachman's (1990) organisational and pragmatic competences are called upon in papers that test grammatical and textual proficiency (e.g. essay writing), or illocutionary and sociolinguistic skills (interpreting language in listening or reading comprehensions for example). A high degree of strategic competence is also required as students assess, plan and evaluate how they implement their knowledge in a variety of tasks ranging from role-plays to composition in the foreign language.

Nevertheless, the emphasis is firmly on *effective* communication in the sense that meaning should be expressed in a very clear and persuasive manner. In this respect, more value is placed on accuracy and formal mastery than at lower levels of language learning, as well as a far deeper and more explicit knowledge of the linguistic code. Assessment objectives include the manipulation of the target language 'accurately in spoken and written forms', showing the ability to 'choose appropriate examples of lexis and structures and to transfer meaning from and into the target language' (School Curriculum and Assessment Authority, 1993: 3). Candidates are required to present their ideas and opinions in a precise and logical manner in the target language, dealing with topics from a wide range of contemporary issues from international affairs to environmental issues. Having reached A-level, learners are asked to respond to a greater variety of texts, frequently of a discursive, imaginative, philosophical or socioeconomic nature and of extended length.

At A-level, therefore, grammatical accuracy is viewed as inextricably bound up with *effective* communication, in which meaning is unambiguously and fully expressed. Nevertheless, the tasks at this level are such that many of them cannot be completed successfully without the precise and accurate use of linguistic forms, as is not always the case at GCSE level. Reviewing the type of tasks presented and assessment procedures used in German A-level examination papers, Rock (1990: 21) comments on the marking of re-translation questions set at that time by some examining groups. To score highly, candidates must take care with 'spelling, cases, adjective endings, verb agreement and word order'.

Moreover, GCSE and A-level seem to differ not merely in their emphasis on linguistic accuracy. Considering the notion of proficiency from a somewhat different angle from that taken by other writers, Cummins (1979, 1980, 1984) suggests that there are two basic types of ability that can be assessed. In one formulation of this view of proficiency he discusses the concepts of 'Basic Interpersonal and Communicative Skills' (BICS) and 'Cognitive/Academic Language Proficiency' (CALP). BICS constitute 'the manifestation of language proficiency in everyday communicative contexts', CALP 'the manipulation of language in decontextualised academic situations' (Cummins, 1984: 137). While neither type of proficiency is held to be superior to the other, CALP tends to take longer to develop. Time and maturity are crucial factors — considerations that are not always taken fully into account in syllabus design.

Elsewhere, Cummins presents a slightly different view of how different types of language tasks can be categorised, although the basic underlying principle remains the same. Language tasks can be characterised by the degree to which they are cognitively demanding/undemanding and context-embedded/context-reduced (Cummins & Swain, 1986: 153). The cognitive demands a task makes on learners depend largely on how much information it requires them to cope with at once; the extent to which it is context-embedded or reduced determines how much learners must rely on 'extra-lingual' clues or on their linguistic competence, to process the language with which they are confronted. This seems to tie up with the notion of BICS and CALP, in so far as BICS are called upon largely in cognitively undemanding, context-embedded tasks, CALP in cognitively demanding, context-reduced ones. As far as GCSE and A-level language learning are concerned, while the former seems to develop BICS to a large degree, with its emphasis on functional, transactional, context-embedded language, A-level requires a high level of CALP as well (see Johnstone (1989) for a further discussion of BICS and CALP). For example, questions on civilisation topics to be answered in the foreign language are very cognitively demanding, as the candidate has to concentrate on linguistic accuracy and fluency at the same time as coping with the high-level mental concepts involved. Oral examinations test the ability to negotiate, or to express opinions on current affairs, as well as what Johnstone (1989: 96) calls 'conversational management'; they thus seem to call on both BICS and CALP at once. Skutnabb-Kangas (1984: 111–12) suggests that BICS and CALP are not necessarily related nor developed simultaneously, and that an individual's ability to use language fluently in concrete, everyday situations 'says nothing about her [sic] ability to use language as a cognitive instrument in cognitively demanding situations where contextual clues are not of much help'.

It has been argued that, within England and Wales at least, there is too little continuity between the proficiency developed at GCSE level and that tested at A-level. Chambers (1989) comes to a similar conclusion in a review of the various syllabuses available for students, underlining the need for A-level to change, while Walmsley (1990: 10) approaches the question from the other end, claiming that GCSE 'is not an adequate preparation for higher-level language work'. Others have underlined in particular the decline in written accuracy of students entering A-level programmes from GCSE, which they in part attribute to the greater emphasis placed on the area of oral fluency at this earlier level (Metcalfe *et al.*, 1995).

This is a contentious issue, but writing from a more international perspective, Skutnabb-Kangas (1984: 112) suggests that it takes a long time to develop a high level of CALP in a foreign language. Indeed, there is the suggestion that academic language skills take between five and eight years longer to develop than ordinary communicative skills (Cummins, 1981). This has implications for language learning in contexts wider than the UK. While other countries may not offer an exact parallel with the UK's GCSE/A-level split, largely because differences in education systems mean that students pass between levels of language learning at different ages, there is some evidence of similarly difficult stages of transition in various parts of the world. Schultz (1991), for example, reports on the situation at the University of California at Berkeley. There, students experience difficulties in moving from intermediate language courses, where they develop a basic awareness of French grammar and can write on a personal topic in simple language, to higher level courses, which require the ability to write discursive essays on complex themes.

In countries where learners of English as a Second Language (ESL) study other subjects within the mainstream classroom, similar difficulties may be faced. These students may have developed social communicative skills, either in class or through living in the English-speaking community, but can experience problems in using English in a more academic context in other areas of the curriculum as they move through the educational system (O'Malley & Chamot, 1990).

Finally, returning for a moment to the specific situation within the UK, it may be that for some students the two years of an A-level course is too short a time to foster this ability if insufficient ground work has been done in previous years of study.

Key Findings

Learners' views on becoming an advanced language learner: new challenges

How far are these hypotheses about the gap between GCSE and A-level language learning borne out by the reactions of students themselves? The research project outlined in Chapter 1 sought answers to this question in two areas. On the one hand, semi-structured interviews with 24 students (12 male, 12 female) in seven schools and colleges in England were designed to pursue the subject from a qualitative standpoint. Details of these students are given in Appendix D, Table D7. On the other hand, quantitative data indicating the extent of learner difficulties was gathered by means of a questionnaire distributed to 49 schools in England and Wales.

Comments from the interview with students provide an introduction to the question of learners' difficulties, reflecting their perceptions about the new demands made upon them in a general sense. Students were interviewed several weeks into the first term of their A-level course. In the following discussion, figures given in brackets refer to the number of students making particular comments. Where quotations from students are given, these are followed by (F) or (M) to denote the gender of the speaker.

Although not asked directly whether A-level work was easier or harder than they had expected, several students volunteered information on this subject. It became apparent that some teachers had forewarned students of a gap between GCSE and A-level work with the result that certain students (five males, three females) claimed that the course was easier than they had expected or not very different from earlier language study. A further explanation for this phenomenon was sought in an examination of the type of work they had been involved in up to the time of the interview (as ascertained from the teacher questionnaire and interview), as it was possible that those who had started A-level topic work proper might experience greater difficulties than those who had revised previously studied themes and structures first. Evidence for this was, however, somewhat inconclusive, in so far as the group was divided equally between students who had experienced the former and those who had experienced the latter type of instruction. On the other hand, all of the four students who felt A-level was harder than they had expected had commenced topic work at the time of the interview.

Further insights were provided by comments regarding the perceived differences between GCSE and A-level work. Students from different schools (three males, three females) emphasised the change in working habits demanded by A-level, in so far as they felt that while to succeed at GCSE 'you didn't have to do much' (M), A-level 'starts to actually challenge you' (M). Furthermore, the need for systematic learning and assimilation of material at advanced level was contrasted with the more *ad hoc* approach associated with the topic work met at GCSE. One girl claimed that prior to A-level

> you know you're just going to spend one term talking about, you know, holidays, and it's only at the final oral that you just have to make sure you remember everything. (F)

Regarding the content of the course, interesting comments were made by some students (three males, five females) concerning the different approach they were now required to adopt towards grammar. Particularly in the case of students of German the view was expressed that grammatical accuracy had not seemed to matter in their previous language classes, that 'you just write anything' (F), 'it didn't really matter whether you got the genders or whatever a bit wrong, you'd still get marks for the sense of the thing, but now you'd lose marks if they're wrong' (M). One student added that it was only now that she was beginning to realise that she was writing inaccurately. Another gave the impression that where grammatical explanations were desired by students these were not always encouraged by teachers preparing students for the final examination at GCSE level:

> toward the end it was a rush to get . . . to get everything ready for the exam, and things like if we didn't understand why a certain ending was there, it was, 'Oh, it doesn't matter for the exam'. (M)

Others (two females, three males) felt that they would have preferred to have had more grammatical awareness before embarking on A-level work.

Although the majority of students indicated that their enjoyment of language work prior to A-level had contributed to their decision to pursue it further, a third of the sample expressed either some reservations regarding the adequacy of their earlier studies as a preparation for the advanced course, or a preference for the type of work they were now engaged in. One criticism was that the gulf between the largely transactional language taught at GCSE and the language of opinions and discussions required at A-level was too great. Furthermore, the suggestion was that the approach adopted at A-level was ironically more 'communicative' and 'authentic', 'much more realistic to real life' in the words of one male student, in the sense that it gave them the skills needed for *talking* to native speakers rather than just interacting with them to obtain goods and services. The views of students in this respect are worth citing at length:

[At GCSE] it's just a case of it's something so that you can speak French enough to go to a foreign country and speak and ask for food and to ask for services and where petrol stations are, you can't necessarily talk to French people, cos when I went on the French exchange, I couldn't hold a conversation with my penfriend. (F)

The subjects [at A-level] are much more deep, I mean, more meaningful, I mean they are more meaningful and all you do at GCSE is just talk about holidays and all that. I mean, they are good when you go away on holiday, but, I don't know, if you want to have a discussion with a French person, they don't really help. (M)

In spite of the aims of communicative language syllabuses to promote communicative skills, these students did not feel that this had been achieved by teaching them how to 'survive' in the sense of obtaining goods and services. For them, language for expressing their thoughts and feelings was considered to be more in line with their communicative needs. In addition, it might well respond more closely to their conceptual needs; while overly complex or abstract topics can be demotivating to students (see later), there is the danger that in comparison with other areas of the curriculum, such as history, foreign language learning might appear to deal with trivialities such as 'buying a train ticket' if the emphasis is firmly placed on acquiring transactional language. Grenfell (1991: 6) similarly argues that in such cases the language syllabus is a 'transactional wolf in a communicative sheep's clothing', that does not fulfill the desire of students to express themselves in the foreign language.

Language learning difficulties: a more detailed discussion

The questionnaire completed by students of French and German half-way through the first term of their A-level course provided more detailed information regarding the aspects of their language learning that students had either coped well with or found difficult. From 600 questionnaires sent out, 384 students (165 male, 219 female) returned completed copies, giving 284 French (162 female, 122 male) and 146 German (87 female, 59 male) responses, some students answering for both languages. Information regarding the background of respondents is presented in Appendix D, Tables D1–D4.

The students were first asked to write brief statements about the aspects of their language course which they were finding easy or difficult, or where they felt they had strengths or weaknesses (Sections A/B of the questionnaire). Similar questions were posed regarding how they felt their language learning would develop, a theme not examined in this book but discussed in detail elsewhere (Graham, 1994). Turning to more specific problems, students were then asked to show to what extent they felt that various statements about the potential difficulties involved in A-level work applied to them (Sections C/D). This set of statements was derived from other students during the pilot stage of the project. The questionnaire as a whole appears in Appendix B1.

Comments made in response to Sections A/B fell into a number of categories, indicating what students saw as their strengths and weaknesses. Appendix E1 presents in graphical form where students' concerns chiefly lay, with numbers referring to the percentage of comments each area attracted. The most important of these areas are discussed later.

At first sight, the figures in Appendix E1 offer some surprises, in view of the fairly large percentage of students indicating *grammar work* of some kind as a strength. Indeed, for French 'tenses' forms the single largest category in this area, even though it was more often cited as a weakness than a strength. These findings may be explained in part by a more detailed examination of students' comments, and in some cases by reference to the teacher questionnaire (see also Chapter 5). First, there is clear indication that the type of language work many students experienced during the first weeks of the A-level course was largely grammar-based, explaining the large number of references to structure, both positive and negative. Second, it emerged that certain aspects of grammatical work were felt to be easy, particularly when compared with other areas of the course. Many students commented that it was the revision of grammar in general and tenses in particular that they had found easy, several schools clearly emphasising basic structures before embarking on A-level work proper. Some evidently welcomed this new focus on structure, as the following observation shows:

I have found that a full explanation of grammar points (e.g. cases) has made almost everything to do with the language easier. I have discovered that German really *is* quite logical, after all. (M)

Yet a larger group highlighted problems with the learning of grammar, the greater emphasis placed on it at A-level compared with earlier study and the number of conjugations and declensions to cover.

Third, there is the likely possibility that students in different educational establishments were faced with different forms of work on tenses. While some, as indicated, began their course with a revision of key structures, other students of French had already been introduced to the subjunctive, the pluperfect and past historic — and found the experience a difficult one. Furthermore, those struggling with tense work most frequently did so when it came to actually using tenses, rather than coping with their more 'mechanical' aspects such as their construction and endings. There seemed also to be some variation in the degree to which students had been asked to familiarise themselves with grammatical terminology (e.g. pronoun, subject/object), with some teachers, particularly those of German, evidently adopting a very form-focused approach in the early stages of the course. Several students appeared to have found these terms difficult to master, as comments referring to the 'nomalitive' or 'monative' [sic] suggest!

The situation regarding *oral work* is similarly complex. For both languages this appears as the language skill with which students felt most confident. The timing of the questionnaire may have contributed to this outcome; personal experience suggests that many teachers concentrate on oral skills rather than written work in the early stages of A-level and students are therefore more likely to comment on it. This may also explain the relatively low number of comments referring to writing either as a strength or as a weakness. Alternatively, other aspects of the course may have appeared to be so greatly different from earlier work that speaking was seen as one area where students could be at ease. The large number of students who felt that nothing had been easy in the course would seem to partially support this latter interpretation.

Nevertheless, the result is a plausible one in its own right and is indeed largely unsurprising. The promotion of oral proficiency is generally felt to be the main goal of the communicative approach. Yet like tenses it is an area mentioned as a weakness and as a strength in almost equal measure — again perhaps an indication of the different demands that are made on students in different classrooms. Oral work was described as easy mainly by students who had encountered tasks involving BICS (Basic Interpersonal and Communicative Skills). These included conversational language use and role-plays. For those citing oral work as an area of weakness or difficulty, the expression of ideas and opinions formed the largest sub-category, one student regretting 'being unable to speak and express myself in decent German'.

Further support is given to the argument that at A-level, oral work is potentially a source of anxiety and difficulty for students in the results of Section C/D of the questionnaire (Appendix E3). There, students were asked to tick various statements if they felt they had difficulties in the area of language learning described. Two were concerned particularly with aspects of fluency and the expressions of opinions in oral work. Among students of French, 63% felt they had difficulty in 'Expressing [my] ideas in spoken French' and 43% in 'Answering quickly in oral work'. For

German, the corresponding figures were 56% and 41%. The following comments, written by students beside these statements, suggest that a lack of vocabulary, confidence and familiarity with discussion work were at the root of many students' concerns:

> I don't like to express myself in class, as I always feel that I'm going to say something wrong. (F)
>
> Didn't do enough oral GCSE work, so it's difficult now. (F)
>
> Word order and vocabulary don't always flow into my mind. (M)
>
> I need a bit of time to translate into English then back into German. (M)

Students were also very ready to express their feelings about *listening comprehension*, especially in the case of French. In the figures presented in Appendix E1, listening has a surprisingly low position in the hierarchy of perceived strengths. As the obvious partner of oral work within the communicative framework, aural competence is recognised as a vital component in language proficiency. Moreover, it is frequently (and perhaps almost dismissively) paired with reading as a 'passive' skill, with the implication that it is more straightforward than those such as writing which require a more 'active' response from the learner. One would therefore expect it to have been cited more frequently as a strength than is the case here. Instead, it comes behind 'Reading' and 'Vocabulary' and only slightly ahead of 'Writing'. Furthermore, it emerges as the most frequently cited difficulty after tenses, with more than twice as many comments referring to it as a weakness than as strength. For students of German it does not appear as an out and out strength.

Where listening was cited as a difficulty, many respondents highlighted their comments with exclamation marks or underlining, suggesting that the task was more than just a challenge. Several referred to problems in coping with authentic listening rather than the more scripted kind met at GCSE. This was particularly true for French listening tasks, where for some students 'the speaking is too fast to be able to understand it' (F). Other problems mentioned arose from the sudden jump in the level of difficulty of vocabulary and grammatical structures.

Not all comments referred to pre-recorded material. Several students had problems in understanding classmates or their teacher, with one respondent lamenting that his teacher addressed the class 'as if we were fluent A-levellers' (M).

Some teachers had similarly high expectations of their students in the field of *reading comprehension*, as suggested by the following:

> I have found vocabulary, mainly in the set books (Balzac) to be very difficult, and this makes them a long-winded task. (M)

This student's frustration is perhaps unsurprising, given the early stage at which he was being asked to embark on such a task. In general, however, most students seemed to find reading relatively easy, with more than twice as many students of French citing it as a strength rather than as a weakness in Section A/B of the questionnaire. Yet the picture is rendered rather more complex by the reservations several students expressed about this skill, even if they had felt it was one of their strengths. Those learning German were particularly ambivalent towards reading, claiming that only 'some' comprehension tasks had been easy or that they were manageable in certain circumstances, for example 'as long as they have no slang and I am given time and a dictionary' (M). Indeed, it is possible that those who felt that reading was relatively easy did so because of the assistance they could find in the dictionary, relieving some of the pressure experienced in other activities such as listening where more immediate comprehension is required. This is supported by responses to Section C/D of the questionnaire, where Item 11 referred to difficulties in 'Reading a text without a dictionary': 67% of students of French and 72% of students of German felt that this statement applied to them. The phrasing of the item was deliberately chosen to try to capture what was hypothesised to be the main coping strategy of learners in text processing. It appears that many students are lacking in effective strategies for dealing with unknown words within a written text. This is hinted at by some of the comments made against Item 11, with one female French student showing perceptive insight into the matter:

> I think I rely on my dictionary too much and not my own judgement.

Elsewhere, the dictionary was described as a 'lifeline'.

These findings confirm in some respects those reported by Rees (1995). In her investigation of the reading difficulties of students of French at the GCSE/A-level transition stage (in 1990), she observes that many learners had problems coping with longer written texts, containing more complex vocabulary and structures. However, in the present study, difficulties with reading comprehension seemed to be more acute for students of German, for whom learning and understanding new *vocabulary* was also more problematic. In Section C/D of the questionnaire, Item 1 referred to 'Coping with the new vocabulary I have to learn'. This was ticked by 49% of German students, compared with 35% of French students. A similar picture emerges from responses to Section A/B of the questionnaire. There, students of German highlighted vocabulary learning as one of their major preoccupations, together with the case system and word order. The difficulties experienced with vocabulary in German may be attributable to a shift from practical to more abstract language. Whereas students of French are probably helped to make such a progression by the fact that numerous cognates with English abstract terms exist, this is not the case for German, where students are likely to be faced with seemingly unrelated, lengthy and impenetrable items of lexis.

Problems arising from teachers' expectations were once again apparent from comments made by students. Several referred specifically to the 'vast' or 'huge' amount of new lexis they were required to absorb, or 'cram in', as one boy put it. The use of such terms gives the impression of certain students feeling overwhelmed by the learning task and teachers' demands, inability to cope with 'the amount of vocabulary and the pace we are expected to learn it!' (F), in the words of one student of German.

While the number of students in Section A/B who cited *writing* as a weakness was not large, interesting comments were made by those who did see it as a problem. Furthermore, these and Section C/D, which focused on particular aspects of the skill, suggested that the situation was in some ways similar to that of oral work. It was apparent that in several schools teachers were approaching the question of writing by exploiting the strengths and skills students already possessed, rather than demanding more advanced work from the start. Respondents mentioned that they had coped well with tasks of a structured, factual nature, ones that seemed to require proficiency in the area of BICS referred to earlier. These included descriptions and letter writing. On the other hand, a large number of students mentioned difficulties in essay writing, singling out the expression of ideas, limited vocabulary, the length and structure of their compositions as specific problems. Above all, however, accuracy was described as a major stumbling block in all sections of the questionnaire. In Section C/D, Item 6, 'Writing accurately in French/German' was ticked by 59% of French students and 67% of German students. Comments made underline the high expectations held by some teachers in the early stages of advanced work, and the gulf perceived by some students between the demands of GCSE and A-level language learning. One female student of French lamented that

> Accuracy is marked at a much higher standard despite we haven't yet learnt a higher degree of this.

As with oral work, writing is a skill where the leap from BICS to CALP can be only too evident if students are required to go beyond simply communicating meaning and to combine it with clarity and accuracy of expression as well. How the gulf may be made more manageable will be discussed later in the chapter.

With regard to the different topics studied at A-level, relatively few students referred specifically to difficulties in adjusting to more abstract themes of discussion in any section of the questionnaire. This is surprising, given what was said earlier in the chapter concerning differences in GCSE and A-level language learning, and in view of the comments made by students regarding particular skills such as writing. It may be that these specific comments absorbed some of the more general concerns regarding the GCSE/A-level gap. On the other hand, many students reported that they had been looking at topics with which they were already familiar and so viewed this area of their language learning as a strength. What was felt to be more problematic was discussing these topics on a different level:

> A-level enables you to express your views/opinions on a particular topic. This is a new concept, and hard to apply what I have learnt at GCSE to A-level. (F)

It was also evident, however, that some students welcomed the fact that topics studied at A-level were 'controversial, unlike topics studied at GCSE. They are interesting and appealing' (F). This is a theme that will be returned to in a subsequent paragraph, where students' approaches to the challenges of advanced language learning are discussed.

Gender Differences (Appendices E2 and E4)

The question of gender will be considered fully in Chapter 4. Here, however, it is worth considering briefly some of the differences in the perceived strengths and weaknesses of male and female students as an introduction to the theme. From a consideration of Appendix E2, where girls' and boys' responses to Section A/B of the questionnaire are presented in terms of percentages (very small categories are omitted), certain gender differences emerge. Perhaps most notable for both languages is the larger percentage of girls who felt that nothing in their course had been easy. Male students of German appear to be less comfortable with reading than their female counterparts but more comfortable with oral work and general grammar (that more girls than boys referred to cases as a strength may suggest that the former chose to be more precise in their comments on grammatical areas).

An examination of students' perceived weaknesses gives a different perspective. In this instance, differences between the two sexes are less pronounced. The most apparent ones seem to be a greater reference to difficulties in grammar, oral work and writing by French girls, and to listening, tenses and translation by French boys. In German, girls seemed to have perceived greater problems with cases.

In general, gender differences for students of German are less obvious. Why this should be so is not readily apparent; it may be, as suggested in earlier paragraphs, that the gap between GCSE and A-level work in French in certain tasks is more marked. Combined with an apparent greater tendency for girls to comment on their difficulties, and boys to suppress them (see later), this may account for the more pronounced gender differences in that language.

This review seems to produce contradictory findings but there are certain elements which are more or less constant across the two questions, in French at least: greater worries about oral work, writing and grammatical/tense work on the part of girls, and about listening on the part of boys. The last of these may have something in common with the findings of Rees and Batters (1988) regarding boys' dislike of tasks perceived as 'passive' ones.

If one turns to Section C/D (Appendix E4) where a more clear-cut comparison between the sexes is possible, confirmation of some of these tentative conclusions is to be found. Again, very few differences emerge when German is considered on its own, with only use of the case system showing a significant difference between boys and girls. For French, however, one is struck once more and perhaps more forcefully this time by the divergence between male and female perceptions of oral work, (Items 3, 12 and 16), dealing with verbs/tenses (Items 4 and 5) and affective concerns (Items 27, 28, 29). The application of vocabulary (Item 2), expressing one's ideas in writing (Item 10) and applying work learnt at GCSE to A-level (Item 7) also show a difference between the sexes.

If figures for both sexes are combined (Appendix E4, Table E4.3), excluding Item 24, which is not common to both languages) these differences still apply. It is possible that there is a connection between the two main areas figuring here, namely oral work and affective concerns. The latter will be discussed more fully in Chapter 4, but here it is worth considering briefly their relationship with oral work. This skill is arguably the domain in which students are most likely to feel 'on trial' and to sense most keenly the gap between their desire to express themselves fully and their more limited linguistic capabilities. A vicious circle can be created, with anxiety about oral performance and negative self-comparison against others further inhibiting spontaneity of expression. Difficulties perceived in written and grammatical work may similarly intertwine with general anxieties about one's performance and ability.

Boys thus emerge as less prone to what has been called 'communication apprehension' (Horwitz *et al.*, 1986), discussed fully in Chapter 4. Indeed, it is worth noting that the mean average number of difficulties in Section C/D ticked by boys is lower than for girls (female French, 10.4; male French, 8; female German, 11.7; male German, 9.5). Similarly, when asked at the beginning of the questionnaire how difficult they felt it had been for them to achieve the grade they did at GCSE, more boys than girls felt their grades were 'very easy' to obtain. The differing figures for males and females may be an indication that the former genuinely experienced fewer difficulties and that the small number studying a language to A-level represent the more proficient linguists out of the male population. Alternatively, they may have been less prepared to admit to others, or to themselves, that they were experiencing problems — a conclusion supported both by past research and the information obtained in talking to students (see Chapter 4).

Implications for the Classroom

Students' transition solutions

How then are we to tackle the difficulties of adjustment faced by A-level students? Having outlined so clearly their perceptions of the main problems arising, they are perhaps the best ones to approach in the first instance for suggestions regarding solutions to the issue.

Within the framework of the interview, learners were asked to suggest ways in which the transition to A-level language work could be made easier or, where few problems had been experienced anyway, explanations for their successful move from one level to another. Students in the latter group (one male, two females) felt that they had been helped by the delaying of topic work until basic grammatical structures had been revised. Such an approach seemed to be more common for German (perhaps because of the shorter length of time for which most students had been studying it). As will be discussed in subsequent chapters, however, this method may bring with it problems of its own, for example in terms of possible demotivation where students feel they are covering familiar ground, or where conversely the new emphasis on grammatical explanations may confuse rather than reassure.

Another student (female), by contrast, felt that it was more beneficial to have been faced with 'real' A-level work from the start, in that it had made her realise at an early stage what was expected of her and had prevented complacency. Along with two other students (one male, one female) she also suggested that it was very much up to individual students to come to terms with the transition themselves, warning that 'if you sit there and feel sorry for yourself you'll never get there'.

Her attitude is indicative of a large degree of self-direction, as discussed in later sections. Of course, not all learners have such a naturally developed level of autonomy and it was more frequent for students to suggest alterations in course design or teaching methods when asked for possible ways of making the transition less abrupt. In terms of the arrangement of the school year certain students (two males, four females) felt that the period between the date of their GCSE examinations and the start of the A-level course was too long, resulting in a loss of fluency and familiarity with the language. It was suggested by some that schools and colleges should encourage students to spend this period preparing for the new academic year, and perhaps devise special bridging courses for them. In line with the earlier comments concerning the 'easiness' of GCSE work and its lack of harmony with A-level work, other students (two males, two females) suggested that the former should be made more testing. The alternative of making A-level easier was further mooted by two of the students within this sub-group. More extensive reading (including literary texts) at GCSE level, it was suggested, would have helped students adapt more easily to A-level work, as would greater emphasis on and explanation of grammatical structures. One male student of German was particularly eager to emphasise that he felt he had emerged from GCSE level with no insight into grammar at all, something which he regretted:

> I thought when I was doing GCSE that it was a bit of a cruise, you know, I did it and I got an 'A' and I had no idea about grammar, I still don't . . . if you could try and convince them [students] during GCSE to learn grammar and how useful it would be, by taking some longer texts with them, I'm sure that would have an effect. (M)

Similar views were voiced by a further student, again of German, who referred to a desire to be able to rely on his own judgement when deciding on which grammatical form to use, without having to rely on indications from his teacher:

> Mr X, he sort of says something, he witters on about it's going to be in the dative, and I think, 'Well how do you know that? I don't know that . . . the only reason I know that is because you tell me and I take your word for it.' . . . And I'd really like to sort of be able to be sort of more on my own two feet with the language, and I'd think, 'Wait a minute, this is this, and this is that, and I don't need anyone to tell me about it. (M)

It may be argued that the autonomy referred to in this quotation is related to an awareness of effective learning strategies, which might help mitigate the sense of helplessness experienced by some students in the face of work of a more difficult nature. The idea of a form of strategy training was put to students as a way of easing the transition. Interestingly, six of the seven students who were not in favour of this were male. Within this group several boys gave the impression that their rejection of the idea was attributable to a strong 'personal agenda' which might be disrupted if they were asked to reconsider their learning methods. Most of this small group insisted that they had their own ways of learning and were happy with them, and that other people's suggestions for methods might not suit them. Such a reaction underlines the need for learning strategies to be introduced in a diplomatic, non-insistent manner; at the same time, it also indicates perhaps a degree of inflexibility on the part of these male students. In this regard, it is perhaps worth noting that two of the six were classed by their teachers as less effective students, leading one to wonder whether they might not benefit from reconsidering their learning methods.

Where students reacted positively to the suggestion of learning strategy training, comments regarding which language learning activities should be emphasised formed five groups. The first of these included guidance of a very general nature regarding how to work effectively at A-level and was mentioned by three female students. They further suggested that they would have appreciated more information from their teachers concerning what was expected of them during the course before it began. In the area of learning strategies proper, the comments of two female informants are particularly enlightening, underpinning the observations made in previous sections regarding vocabulary learning. They felt that techniques for learning vocabulary would be helpful as, in the words of one student, 'nobody ever tells you how to learn vocab., so I don't know how to do it' (F). Likewise, others (one male, two females) suggested that strategies for remembering and handling grammatical rules, tense formation and usage would be beneficial.

Finally, guidance in tackling listening comprehension (one male, two females) and reading comprehension (two females) would have been appreciated by another group of students.

New approaches

Building upon some of the questions raised by students themselves, it seems clear that we need to reassess the way in which we present new language and tasks to learners at this level.

Referring back to Cummins' (1979, 1980, 1984) terminology, students seem to come to A-level relatively strong in BICS, and then suddenly (almost overnight, as it appears to some!) are asked to develop a level of CALP high enough to discuss such matters as 'pollution and deforestation', to quote one student. A similar leap from BICS to CALP is required in written work, if students are asked to go beyond simply communicating meaning and to combine it with clarity and accuracy of expression. Students' comments regarding worries in both skill areas suggest that many had been placed in situations where there was a mismatch between the sophisticated concepts they needed and wanted to discuss and the rather less sophisticated linguistic means at their disposal. Indeed, the interview revealed that some topics broached were so cognitively demanding that students felt they would not have been able to deal with them in their own language. These included Maastricht and European unity, French history, German fairy tales and the influence of television on children. Care should be taken not to overestimate the sophistication of learners who, after all, in most instances have not reached adulthood and often do not share teachers' interest in or familiarity with such topics.

While one can understand the sense of urgency with which certain teachers embark on their A-level syllabus, some the demands made upon learners may result in low morale and demotivation, as will be illustrated in Chapter 4. Furthermore, students' familiarity with oral work from earlier language study should not lead us to be over-ambitious in what we expect from them. Building upon strengths with activities such as role-play, within familiar topics like 'The family' or 'Leisure' needs to precede whole-class debate.

Similar points can be made in relation to writing. Confidence with new vocabulary and structures needs to be established within the familiar framework of such tasks as writing letters, composing short paragraphs or diary entries, before full-scale essays are demanded. The skill of writing these needs in turn to be *taught*, rather than assumed to have been developed in other areas of the curriculum. Schultz (1991) argues that we should not underestimate the difficulties students experience in producing argumentative essays. While the ability to write a descriptive or narrative composition in the mother tongue develops in children at an early age, skills of argumentation appear much later. It is therefore not surprising that discursive writing in the foreign language presents such a challenge to learners.

In listening and reading the progression students are required to make is of a slightly different kind, but no less problematic, involving the ability to cope with a wide range of unfamiliar lexical items and, in the case of listening, speed of delivery as well. Here again, a gradual approach would seem to be preferable, with a progression from short to lengthy texts, from the simple to the more complex, being advisable. Indeed, Chapter 5 indicates that many teachers are already adopting this approach with some success.

It may be, however, that it is not enough to tackle the question of learners' difficulties as they move to more advanced language work merely from the point of view of what language we present them with or what demands we make of them. The solutions suggested by students themselves indicate that more work needs to be done in teaching learners *how* to carry out the skills we expect of them, rather than just assuming that they have acquired them in earlier years. This appears to be particularly true of listening and reading, and also of vocabulary learning. As with oral work, vocabulary expansion appears to be an area where sudden transformations were anticipated, often to the frustration of the students involved. It seems that it is too readily assumed that students have already developed efficient strategies for coping with the task. As mentioned in the previous section, some students suggest that in fact more guidance from teachers in this area would be welcomed.

It is arguable that vocabulary learning is a skill that needs to be taught and nurtured like any other. While some students are evidently able to find their own solutions to the problem of committing large numbers of lexical items to memory, others may need more assistance in discovering the best method for them.

These observations can be applied equally to the learning of new grammatical structures. If students are to be asked to learn such items as conjugation and declension tables, as data from the student questionnaire and interview suggest is so, then they should be assisted in developing effective strategies for the task.

At the same time, however, while it is recognised that many teachers feel the need to establish a firm grammatical base at the beginning of the A-level programme, it is possible that the methods outlined in the previous paragraph are not the most effective for all students. Earlier in this chapter it was suggested that students divide into two categories: those for whom the more form-focused approach of A-level means greater clarification and those who are confused by it. In turn this may indicate that learners have to reach a certain stage in their language learning before they can progress from absorbing language mainly as prefabricated structures to a more analytical and generative use (cf. Bialystok, 1988). Forcing them to go beyond the particular stage they have reached is likely to be at best fruitless, at worst liable to lead to viewing grammar as some obstruse topic totally separate from communication. The latter was found to occur in some students who had received very form-focused instruction that did not suit their particular learning style (see Chapter 3). This is not to say that structure should be allowed to simply emerge from texts studied; as Thorogood & King (1991) argue, this leaves too much to chance and leaves some students feeling insecure about their progress in terms of grammatical understanding. Rather methods of presentation need to be devised which constantly underline the function (in terms of meaning) performed by structural forms. These might include exercises such as those proposed by Clark (1993), where, for example, learners write an 'autobiography' to underline the meaning and use of different tenses. Such teaching strategies, should, however, take into account the fact that individual students vary in their ability or readiness to analyse grammatical structure. It is likely that teachers may have to present a grammatical point in a number of different ways to their students. Peck (1988) suggests that many teachers tend to use a small number of techniques for presenting grammar and similarly argues for greater experimentation and variety in this area.

Whether A-level is the best time for students to be faced with the task of absorbing large amounts of grammar is another question. In later chapters it will be argued that one possible reason for the proficiency of more effective language learners involved in the project was their mastery of basic structures in earlier years; these learners then seemed able to devote more processing space to the acquisition of vocabulary and the development of oral and written fluency. Echoing the views of such writers as Ellis (1990), Sharwood-Smith (1981), and, with reference in particular to British language learners, Heafford (1993) and Hooper (1989), it is suggested that form-focused instruction has a place in communicative teaching even for beginning language learners. This is not to advocate a return to the grammar-translation method, but rather to hypothesise that by drawing students' attention to grammatical features and patterns in the early stages of language learning, one can help them, in the words of Heafford (1993: 57), 'extract meaning more rapidly from the large quantity of language material to which they should be introduced'. This approach, to which one might apply the term 'consciousness-raising' (Sharwood-Smith, 1981), does not require learners necessarily to produce forms correctly from the start (a skill which seems subject to the developmental restraints discussed earlier), but rather emphasises the part played by 'cognitive understanding' (Fotos & Ellis, 1991: 609).

These observations evidently have implications for how foreign languages are taught at earlier levels, and it will be interesting to see, in England and Wales, what impact the National Curriculum's greater emphasis on pattern recognition will have on students' handling of structure at A-level.

These, then, are some of the initial implications for teaching strategies to ease the transition to A-level language learning. The question will be revisited and expanded upon in each of the subsequent chapters. The methods employed by learners themselves, however, in adapting to change, will be the focus of the next chapter.

3 Learning Strategies: Processing Language and Managing Change

Introduction

In the last chapter it was suggested that one of the major factors influencing the successful transition (or otherwise) to A-level work was the learning strategies that students had either developed or been taught. Several attempts have been made in the past to identify the range and nature of the techniques used by students. Some of these studies have highlighted important issues regarding what makes a good language learner and these are discussed later. Yet less attention has been paid to the way in which advanced learners learn and to how we can encourage them to use effective strategies. This chapter seeks to address both of these issues, by focusing on what we can learn from the learners themselves.

It is useful to make a distinction between learning strategies and study skills, which are often held to be one and the same thing. Writing about learning strategies in the field of education in general, Nisbet & Shucksmith (1986: vii) place strategies at a higher level than skills, the former acting as 'executive processes' that coordinate and apply skills. Thus learning strategies tend to be unobservable mental processes, while study skills are more overt techniques, such as keeping one's class notes in a logical order. Referring specifically to language learning, Ellis & Sinclair (1989) suggest that study skills are product oriented, learning strategies process oriented; study skills are often taught specifically to help students pass external examinations, while the aim of learning strategies is fundamentally one of self-examination and insight into and control over one's learning.

The Good Language Learner Revisited: Beginnings

The title to this section incorporates the name of a study by Naiman *et al.*, (1978), perhaps the best known investigation into the notion that successful language learners can be differentiated from less successful ones by the strategies they employ in approaching the task. This idea has occupied a number of researchers over the past 25 years or so, and indeed several attempts have been made to classify these strategies. One of the authors of *The Good Language Learner*, Stern, was among the first to produce some sort of classification (Stern, 1975). The list of learning strategies he drew up is based on his own experience as a learner and teacher and the background literature on language learning. This list or taxonomy includes such features as tolerance of uncertainty, readiness to practise and use the language and a generally active approach to language learning. Some strategies might be thought to be applicable mainly to language learning where emphasis is placed on formal correctness, for instance those relating to rational understanding of the language as a system. In addition, the list is speculative, as Stern recognised, and is without firm foundations in empirical research.

Nevertheless it is useful in providing an initial framework for further investigations into learning strategies. The same is true of the early work of Rubin (1975). She draws upon more concrete evidence in outlining various strategies, having observed and talked to good language learners and their teachers. In her taxonomy the strategies emphasised include a willingness to guess, to appear foolish, to practise and to monitor.

Both Stern's and Rubin's classifications are limited in the sense that they emphasise ways in which learners maximise the amount of time spent on learning, in itself a likely component of success, without identifying specific strategies that lead to more efficient learning. That is, they have outlined the general *approach* of the successful language learner. Furthermore, no consideration is given to whether such approaches are unique to the good language learner; it may be argued that unsuccessful learners adopt similar strategies, e.g. practising. What is surely important is why such strategies seem to work for some students and not for others.

The later study by Naiman *et al.* (1978; reprinted 1996) placed more emphasis on the relationship between the general psychological make-up of language learners and their behaviour in the classroom, between

> (1) the strategies and techniques the learner consciously develops and employs, and (2) certain learner characteristics, in particular personality and cognitive styles factors, which are likely to influence the use of strategies and techniques and thereby outcome. (Naiman *et al.*, 1978: 44)

The study was conducted in two parts. First, 32 successful and two unsuccessful adult language learners were interviewed about their language learning experiences. Three case studies were subsequently compiled from these interviews. Second, a main classroom study was carried out involving grade 8, 10 and 12 learners of French in Toronto, who were tested for certain personality traits, such as tolerance of ambiguity, introversion or extroversion and empathy. Classroom observation was carried out in the hope that some of the observable learning behaviours of successful and unsuccessful learners could be correlated with these affective and cognitive factors.

The interviews with the adult subjects produced several pertinent insights into the language learning process. Most thought they had a good memory (50%) and were interested in analysing languages (66%); 47% thought motivation was important; 82% favoured actively producing the language from the start of learning. Interestingly, 94% saw learning as a largely *conscious* process, whereas the unsuccessful learners felt it was something one effortlessly acquires; 78% thought it was a help to have learned more than one language; 85% had felt some discouragement, frustration, impatience or confusion during learning. About half had felt inhibited or embarrassed. Many emphasised the importance of action in learning, seeking out speaking situations to overcome shyness.

Naiman *et al.* went on to classify such observations into strategy types, which may be summarised as follows: *an active task approach,* active involvement in the learning process, seeking out learning opportunities; *realisation of language as a system,* e.g. analysing the L2 and making inferences; *realisation of language as a means of communication and interaction,* e.g. looking for situations involving communication, emphasising fluency rather than accuracy in the initial stages of language learning; *management of affective demands,* e.g. learning to laugh at oneself; *monitoring of L2 performance,* e.g. asking native speakers for corrections (Naiman *et al.*, 1978: 13–15). The authors also identified what they refer to as specific techniques, such as imitation of teachers/native speakers to aid sound acquisition.

In Naiman *et al'*s. main classroom study the initial aim of observing learning strategies was abandoned in favour of using interviews and correlational analysis to concentrate on the importance of cognitive and affective variables in foreign language learning. This was largely because the researchers were unable to identify more than a few specific strategies and techniques in the classroom observation sessions. Consequently, no relationships were identified between the use of learner strategies and learner variables, which is disappointing in view of the original goal of the study.

Recent Developments in Learning Strategy Research

Learning strategies and the secondary school classroom

Later studies have looked further at the interaction between strategy use and certain learner variables, for example, age. Pursuing further work by Chesterfield and Chesterfield (1985), who suggest that there is a natural developmental sequence to the emergence of certain learning strategies, Grenfell and Harris (1993, 1994) considered the learning strategy use of 100 pupils in six London schools, in Years 7 and 9 (the first and third years of secondary schooling). The investigation was carried out within the framework of the Flexible Learning Project, established by teachers and novice teachers at Goldsmiths College, London, whose aim was to help teachers and students work towards greater pupil autonomy and away from the traditional teacher-centred classroom. This included the use of group work and a carousel of activities, in which pupils rotate through a number of different language tasks (Harris & Frith, 1990). In the second year of the Flexible Learning Project, pupils were asked to indicate on a checklist (based on the strategy taxonomies of Stern (1975) and Rubin (1981)) which strategies they used in their language learning. At the end of the project, pupils recorded areas of strategy use in which they felt they had made the most, and the least progress.

Both Year 7 and Year 9 pupils reported making progress in using common sense to work out the meaning of words, and in strategies involving social interaction, for example asking each other for help. Looking up words in the dictionary remained a difficulty for the two groups of pupils, something which more advanced learners also find problematic as later sections in this chapter make clear. Most interesting, however, are the differences in strategy use reported by the two year groups. While the younger pupils felt they did not use the strategy of looking for cognates to aid comprehension, Year 9 pupils cited this as an area of progress. Grenfell and Harris (1994) interpret this as evidence that in the early stages of language learning, pupils assume that the L1 and L2 are entirely different from each other. An awareness of the similarities takes time to develop, although the authors go on to question whether this 'developmental' sequence might not be alterable with more explicit teaching about learning strategies.

Furthermore, in other areas there was a 'regression' in strategy use. Year 9 pupils became less confident in using some strategies associated with speaking skills, perhaps because of the pupils' age (14–15 years) and the heightened self-consciousness that often emerges at that time. While Year 7 pupils reported making progress in reading through work to spot mistakes, Year 9 pupils indicated that this was an area where they had made the least progress. Grenfell and Harris give two possible explanations for this: it may be attributable to the older pupils' greater use of the type of set phrases frequently taught for GCSE, which might have led them to be less 'analytical' in their approach to their work; or to motivational factors relating to the age of the pupils.

The study highlights the difficulty in tracing a clear-cut development in learning strategy use related to the age of learners. As Grenfell and Harris (1994: 9) emphasise, 'any developmental sequence in learner strategies has to take account of pupils' social and emotional stage of development'. These 'emotional' factors continue to influence the language learning behaviour of older learners, as Chapter Four indicates.

Learning strategies and gender

The relationship between gender and strategy use has received the greatest attention in the work of Rebecca Oxford. Most of her investigations have employed a questionnaire, where strategies are divided into two types: direct or primary strategies, and indirect or support strategies. The former includes such sub-categories as formal practice (i.e. grammatically based) and functional practice (i.e. communication oriented), the latter general study strategies and affective strategies.

Examining the learning strategies of 1200 university students of French, Spanish, Italian, German and Russian, Oxford and her colleagues found that gender had a 'profound effect on strategy choice' (Oxford & Nyikos, 1989: 294). Females showed greater strategy use than males for general study strategies, formal-rule related practice and conversational/input elicitation strategies, while males showed no greater strategy use than females on any factor.

These findings were replicated in a study involving 78 adults, including language students, language instructors and professional language trainers at the US Foreign Service Institute (Ehrman & Oxford, 1988). The languages being studied included Indonesian, Thai, Japanese, Turkish, Italian, Hungarian and Arabic. In addition to completing a questionnaire on the strategies they used, the language learners were also tested using the Myers–Briggs Type Indicator (MBTI), a measure of personality type and general learning style. As in the previous study, gender differences in strategy use were marked. Gender differences were strongest in the use of strategies for general study strategies, authentic language use, searching for and communicating meaning and self-management strategies. These differences were also related to psychological type as identified by the

MBTI; women appeared to favour intuition, and feeling over thinking, whereas the reverse was generally true for the men.

These findings have been intepreted as indications of more general sex-related differences. Oxford *et al.* (1988) claim that women's greater use of social interaction and conversational/input elicitation strategies in language learning can be explained by reference to research that has pointed to females' greater social orientation (Maccoby & Jacklin, 1974). Similarly, the work of Tannen (1987) suggests that compared with males women are more likely to try to reach agreement through negotiation; likewise, Coates (1986) reports that women seem to ask more questions than men. Oxford *et al.* (1988) also comment on the implications of the university-based study. The language course being followed by students was of the traditional, analytic rather than communicative kind, with great emphasis on the attainment of good grades. It is argued by Oxford *et al.* that the female students' greater use of general study strategies and formal rule-related practice strategies can be associated with a desire for social approval and a tendency to conform in an academic setting, traits which are sometimes attributed to females.

Metacognitive, cognitive and social/affective strategies

Oxford's grouping of learning strategies into those that are applied directly to the storage, retrieval and manipulation of language and those which have a more indirect effect is an important one and has been taken further in the work of O'Malley and Chamot. They emphasise the difference between *metacognitive* and *cognitive* strategies. Metacognitive strategies refer to 'higher order executive skills that may entail planning for, monitoring, or evaluating the success of a learning activity' (O'Malley & Chamot, 1990: 44).

Cognitive strategies, on the other hand, 'operate directly on incoming information, manipulating it in ways that enhance learning' (O'Malley and Chamot, 1990: 44). This might include such activities as grouping items to be learned into categories or using a dictionary to find out the meaning of a word. A third category of strategies is also defined — *social/affective strategies*, which cover 'either interaction with another person' or exercising control over emotional or affective responses to learning (O'Malley & Chamot, 1990: 45). Such strategies could involve asking questions for clarification or discussing one's worries about language learning with another person.

These distinctions are important partly because they give some indication of which strategies are the most crucial in determining the effectiveness of learning. It seems that metacognitive strategies, that allow students to plan, control and evaluate their learning, have the most central role to play in this respect, rather than those that merely maximise interaction and input. Investigating in a related study the learning strategies of effective and ineffective learners, Chamot and Küpper (1989) found that more successful students used learning strategies more often, 'more appropriately, with greater variety, and in ways that helped them complete the task successfully' (Chamot & Küpper, 1989: 17). The *effective* use of strategies is highlighted as a key issue. Ineffective students used fewer strategies and often used strategies 'that were inappropriate to the task' (Chamot and Küpper, 1989: 17). Thus the ability to choose and evaluate one's strategies is of central importance.

Investigating Learning Strategies: Methods and Approaches

Many writers (e.g. Cohen, 1984) have commented on the limitations of more traditional research techniques like classroom observation in the investigation of how learning strategies are employed by students. Such techniques are inadequate because they 'cannot capture what [students] are thinking about, how they are thinking, or how they feel' (Cohen, 1984: 101). The same conclusion was reached by Naiman *et al.* (1978) and Rubin (1981). In my own investigations of advanced learners, efforts to gain information on learners' strategies through observation proved so unfruitful that the technique was reserved for gathering background details on the type of instruction students were receiving. Instead, information regarding learners' strategies was gathered through a semi-structured, so-called 'retrospective' interview and a 'think-aloud' interview.

A distinction is sometimes drawn between *thinking aloud, introspection* and *retrospection*, although the first two categories may at first sight appear almost identical. On the one hand, thinking aloud 'involves externalising the contents of our minds — what we are currently aware of — as we engage in a particular activity, *without in any way inferring the mental processes or strategies involved*' (Mann, 1982: 87, emphasis added). Introspection, however, has the added dimension of requiring subjects to analyse the mental processes they are performing during the completion of a task.

The difficulty with all of these various categories is their tendency to overlap. Indeed, students' think-aloud comments reported later in the chapter suggest that they might be engaged in different types of self-report while completing one task; they might begin by simply externalising thoughts going through their head, then make inferences about the processes involved and finally make an observation which would suggest an element of looking back on what they had done. The comments were thus probably an amalgam of thinking aloud, introspection proper and retrospection after a few seconds. Therefore two categories only were chosen for the means of gathering information: thinking aloud which refers to comments made by students while performing a language task, and retrospection, where they were asked to report on what they usually did when involved in a language learning activity.

Thinking aloud — a theoretical framework

But how are students able to report on their learning behaviour while performing a task? The framework of thinking aloud assumes that any information we process passes initially into our short-term memory before some of it is transferred to our long-term memory. It is during this first stage that the information is thought to be accessible for verbal report. But in tasks which we have learnt to perform automatically, the short-term memory stage will be bypassed and so the mental processes involved will usually be inaccessible to verbal report.

Although thinking aloud seems to offer almost direct access to learners' thought processes, its reliability and validity have been called into question by some writers (e.g. Seliger, 1983). Such objections revolve around four main issues:

(1) Thought processes are not really accessible for verbalisation as they occur in the main at an unconscious level. Thus in verbal reports on second/foreign language learning subjects are most probably commenting on what they have learned (products) rather than how they learned it (processes).

(2) Hence critics of the method would assert that verbal reports are essentially incomplete and therefore of limited value.

(3) We cannot be sure that respondents are reporting truthfully on their thoughts; it is possible that an element of guesswork or inferencing is involved.

(4) The act of reporting on one's thoughts during a task may influence and change the performance of the task.

In response to the first argument it is of course true that some processes are automatic and therefore occur at a subconscious level. One would not expect these to be accessible, as explained earlier. Verbal reports do not (or should not) claim to reflect information that is not processed by the short-term memory. Indeed, Ericsson and Simon (1980) point out that subjects are most likely to 'pad out' their reports with guesswork when they are forced to introspect on processes which they do not normally pay attention to. Certain thought processes, however, do occur at a more conscious level, such as trying to work out the meaning of an unfamiliar word. They may then be accessible to introspection. Furthermore, it is possible that we can get some insight into processes that are normally automatic and therefore not reportable in certain circumstances. As several authors (e.g. Smith & Miller, 1978) point out, if tasks are presented in a novel and challenging way to respondents then the normally automatic processes will be rendered non-automatic and therefore accessible to introspection.

If we accept the limitations of verbal reports outlined earlier then the question of their 'completeness' in the sense of the second argument becomes essentially a non-issue. They do not pretend to be a total reflection of what is going on during the execution of a task. We can, however, talk about their completeness in respect of how far they reflect the information that is processed in short-term memory during the normal performance of a task. Steps can be taken to increase the likelihood that all such information is verbalised by subjects; tasks should be straightforward and not call upon excessive powers of concentration (cf. White, 1980: 109), enabling subjects to devote sufficient energies to the task of reporting. Pre-training is also important to ensure that subjects are aware of what is required of them, and during the reporting they may need prompting or reminding about what they should be commenting on. However, such prompts must be carefully worded and be of a general nature in order to avoid influencing subjects' responses.

Regarding the claim sometimes made that the task of verbalising one's thoughts may alter the nature of the mental processes involved or the way in which the task is completed, Ericsson and Simon (1980) point out that in tasks already based on language (such as comprehending a text), putting one's thoughts into words does not put any extra demands on the short-term memory. Hence they conclude that thinking aloud 'will not change the structure and course of the task processed, although it may slightly decrease the speed of task performance' (Ericsson & Simon, 1980: 226).

Retrospective interviews

These are less controversial in nature, generally taking the form of semi-structured interviews enquiring about students' usual learning behaviour. While think-aloud interviews tend to focus on the particular, retrospective interviews allow access to a much wider range of strategy use. It is of course possible that students may forget to mention some of the strategies they generally employ. It is possible to minimise this risk of forgetting by providing subjects with an outline of the areas they are to be asked about prior to the interview. This outline must be very general, in order to lessen the risk of the 'Hawthorne effect', where students who are too aware of the interviewer's interests try to give the answers which they believe are required (Cohen & Manion, 1989: 202).

By using *both* forms of interview it was hoped to maximise the advantages and minimise the disadvantages that each brings. Hence the investigation into A-level students' learning strategies began with a retrospective interview to gather general information as to how they learned a language and in particular how they tried to overcome the difficulties they had mentioned in their questionnaire. Then, at the start of the second term, a sharper perspective was sought by means of a think-aloud interview, which probed more deeply into students' strategy use and also helped to corroborate points made in the first interview. The areas covered were reading and listening comprehension, grammatical manipulation and writing. The materials and language tasks chosen were selected on the basis that they were demanding enough to elicit conscious strategy use, while not requiring excessive concentration. They were also judged to be typical of the tasks students are asked to perform in internal and external assessment at this level, following discussions with the students' teachers, a review of A-level course books and external examination material. The cloze passages were of the 'rational' cloze type referred to by Black (1993) in which target words are selectively deleted. These included grammatical areas which the questionnaire had shown to be problematic for students — tenses, and verb, case and adjectival endings. All language activities were based on one theme for each language (holidays for the students of French, leisure for students of German). The tasks are reproduced in Appendix C.

Learner diaries

These were used to give an extra insight into the strategies of advanced learners and also to probe any affective concerns they might have about their language learning. The use of diaries to analyse the experience of language learning is a fairly recent phenomenon in second language acquisition research and few studies of learners' strategies have employed them as a data-gathering tool.

As with most forms of self-report data diary studies can be criticised for their apparent lack of objectivity, which may threaten the validity of the information contained in them. Their subjectivity stems from two possible sources; first, from the diarist — how can we be sure that the learner is being completely honest, not writing to please the person who set the task of diary-keeping or to create the right impression ('self-flattery', in Oller & Perkins' (1978) terms); and second, from the reader of the diary, whose interpretation of the information may involve a further element of bias. The second point may not necessarily be a problem if we recognise the nature of the investigation being undertaken. Bailey and Ochsner (1983: 188) go so far as to claim that foreign language diary studies are essentially 'creative research' (emphasis in the original), interpreted by a reader in the same manner as a literary critic interprets 'an art genre', with which they may be compared.

Similar comments may be made regarding how far the conclusions drawn from the diaries of individuals can be generalised to give insights into language learning as a whole. Bailey (1983: 95), in her review of several diaries, emphasises that generalisation is inappropriate in this case, in so far as diary studies reflect the individuality and diversity of learners and that 'in the complex, real-life world of the language classroom . . . every student can be viewed as functioning in a unique learning environment'. She does point out, however, that findings can be compared if not generalised.

Returning to the question of the 'truthfulness' of learners' diary entries, this too may be less of a problem than some critics suggest. Bailey and Ochsner (1983) claim that in using diaries we are less interested in the veracity of the events that are reported than in the diarist's interpretation of and reaction to them. This may be so, but it is still possible, and advisable, to encourage subjects to express themselves honestly and unreservedly. Bonodana (1990) suggests that students' honesty largely depends on the relationship they form with whoever has asked them to keep the diary and on their understanding of what will happen to the information they provide. It is possible that with learners in the 16–19 age range such a relationship is easier to establish than with an older or younger group, in that students are mature enough to appreciate the seriousness of the project but young enough not to have yet developed the sophistication needed for deception! Evidently, however, it is important to establish an element of trust in students.

Bearing these points in mind, students were asked to comment on three or more language learning activities a week, over two 4-week periods. They noted what in the task they had found easy or difficult, then what they felt they had learned or achieved. This last point was intended to give students a sense that completing the diary could help them to monitor their progress and take steps to improve it. It also provided information about students' ability to analyse their language development and to propose ways of directing their learning in the future.

Key Findings

Coping with learning and learning strategies

Verbatim written transcriptions were made of each think-aloud and retrospective interview, which were then scrutinised and instances of strategic behaviour highlighted. The learner diaries were similarly examined for further evidence of the themes identified in the interview. It was more difficult, however, to draw firm conclusions from the diaries regarding strategy use, as different students completed a different number of diaries and not all chose to comment on all language learning tasks. One student completed the retrospective interview only, withdrawing from the project before the think-aloud interviews and diary study began.

In order to categorise the learning strategies these students reported using, two pre-established classification lists were taken as a starting point and added to when the strategies they included seemed inadequate as descriptions for A-level students' learning processes. The taxonomies thus used were adapted from O'Malley and Chamot (1990: 137–9), and Oxford (1985, 1986). This working framework appears in Appendix A2. Strategies mentioned by students which were not felt to be included in the original categories are indicated in this appendix by an asterisk.

The strategies highlighted in each transcript and diary were then coded using this list and in the case of the interviews simple frequencies calculated for each student. Each language learning activity was taken in turn to assess those strategies most frequently used by the students as a whole. For the think-aloud data only, the mean average occurrence of each strategy on each task was calculated per male, female, effective and less effective student, with particular attention paid to strategies where there was a difference of 30% or more between the groups of students. Student effectiveness was established according to comments made by the students' teachers together with my own observations of their performance during the think-aloud tasks.

While such a quantitative approach was deemed desirable in order to give a broad picture of the learning strategies used by advanced language learners, it was felt essential to go beyond this. Insights were sought into the differences between students which might well be masked by strategy categorisation and enumeration. We need to examine not only the frequency of learning strategies but also the appropriateness of their use. Indeed, in almost all of the skill areas investigated, contrary to expectations there was no firm evidence of effective students using a greater number of strategies; it was how these strategies were employed that was the crucial factor. Each transcript was therefore re-read to assess the general approach of the student, to note any interesting idiosyncrasies or recurrent features. Qualitative comparisons were then made between male and female students and between efficient and less efficient learners (see Appendix D, Table D7, for details of each student).

In the following discussion, definitions and examples of the categories of strategies mentioned can be found in Appendix A.2. Where appropriate, quotations from the retrospective interview are marked (I), with the gender of the student shown as (M) or (F).

Listening

Strategies associated with this skill can be divided into two groups: first, those used by students to try and improve their performance in this area, and second those employed during the process of comprehending a passage.

In the first group, three main strategies were noted during the retrospective interview. Two may be referred to as *creating practice opportunities* and *naturalistic practice*. This ranged from students who took part in exchanges or who spoke to penfriends on the telephone (seven males, eight females), through those who claimed to listen regularly to the L2 on the radio or television (three females), to those (three males) who were rather more half-hearted in their approach. The nonchalant approach to listening practice of the third group can be summed up by a quotation from a student of German:

Sometimes if there's nothing on TV I watch German programmes on that, but that's about all. (I, M)

It was not, however, possible to draw any distinction between the strategy use of effective and less effective students in this area.

The third strategy involved a degree of *self-management/philosophising*. During the retrospective interview, five students, all effective learners, made comments which indicated that they had thought about the listening process and what it involved. These included the dangers of concentrating too narrowly on individual words at the expense of one's understanding of the whole, or of being distracted by 'false friends', dealing with redundant items in the text and the difference between one's active and passive vocabulary knowledge.

In terms of how students actually listened, key strategies to emerge included several metacognitive strategies, for example attentional strategies such as *selective* and *directed attention*. These involve students deciding prior to hearing the passage that they will (i) listen out for specific details and (ii) concentrate on the task in hand and not be distracted. These strategies are held to be particularly important as support strategies for monitoring, itself considered to be a key differentiating factor between effective and ineffective learners (O'Malley *et al.*, 1989: 422). On the other hand, some forms of attention were misapplied by a group of students, who by focusing excessively on particular words they deemed to be important (the strategy referred to as *narrow focus*) actually lost concentration and impaired their understanding of the text.

Other strategies observed were *advance organisation*, the process whereby students preview aspects of a forthcoming language task. A concrete example of this might involve students preparing for a listening task by thinking about what they knew about the topic concerned, in terms of general knowledge and any L2 vocabulary related to it. *Comprehension monitoring*, where students check that they have understood correctly, vital for effective listening, was used, but not greatly. By contrast, *inferencing from context*, where clues given by the context of the passage are used to work out the meaning of unknown items, was widely used and with varying effectiveness. This included the rather negative strategy for which the name *'hearing in' from context* was chosen, whereby students are so influenced by the general context of the passage that they claim to hear items that are in fact absent and use this to make sense of the passage as a whole.

There were differences in the type of strategies used by different kinds of students, with more effective learners employing more often *selective attention, problem identification* (e.g. identifying words in the passage that hold the key to its comprehension), *inferencing meaning from the tone of the speakers' voice* and using *cohesion markers* or *emphasis markers* such as 'it's important that . . . ' to identify the key sections of the text. Nevertheless, it was *how* strategies were implemented that was the most important factor. This was the case with selective attention. In the majority of retrospective interviews students claimed to listen out for the 'key' words in a passage, i.e. to attend selectively. Yet on a second reading the impression was gained that the word 'key' was being used in two different ways. In some cases (six males, three females) it referred to the words in the passage that students were able to recognise or understand immediately; in others (three males, two females) to the words that were judged to be important in grasping the meaning of the passage, such as the main verb of a sentence. While the former strategy can be beneficial and is perhaps more natural for students whose decoding skills and vocabulary may be limited, it is arguable that the latter is a more efficient strategy in text comprehension. Words that are instantly 'recognisable' may be irrelevant to the overall meaning of the text, may distract students from the central meaning of the text and lead to erroneous conclusions being drawn. This became clear from the think-aloud data.

Where less effective students used selective attention in that interview, it appeared that when they *could* correctly identify and decode key words or phrases within a passage, they were often unable to interpret what they had discovered and to extract its full meaning, partly because of a failure to recognise the relationship of the items in question to the surrounding text. In turn, strategies such as *inferencing from context* were then misapplied to 'pad out' the key item. Unsurprisingly, weaker students further appeared to be handicapped by their slowness in recognising key items, whereas better students not only identified them more quickly, but in greater number, resulting in fewer 'gaps' to be filled in by inferencing and elaboration. Rather than identifying just one key word in a phrase, they often highlighted ones which were interconnected and were able to see the relationship between them; for example, while most students were able to identify and decode the noun 'Streß' ('stress') in the German passage, weaker students tended not to notice the framework in which this was embedded, that it was important for the speaker that his leisure did not in itself become stressful — 'daß sie halt nicht in Streß ausartet'. Instead they tended to assume that the speaker looked to his leisure time for relief from stress experienced at work. Often the words recognised by better students carried more weight as far as the meaning of the phrase in question was concerned and they frequently highlighted verbs and nouns. Similarly, key words were often filtered through the strategies of comprehension monitoring, problem identification, and in the case of a few very good students, double-check monitoring (e.g. checking one's initial interpretation of a word in the light of its use later in the passage). This allowed them to correct any hypotheses that had been erroneously formed around the key words identified.

Weaker students were further hampered in the fact that they frequently misheard words or syllables which better students recognised automatically, and they sometimes tried to transcribe what they believed they had heard, thus becoming distracted from the sentence as a whole. Thus Student G interpreted a section in the following way (NB the comprehension text appears in italic print next to the student's comments on it; the symbol + indicates that the student was being asked what she/he was thinking, while an asterisk is used to indicate language reproduced with error, as in the transcripts):

> *Mir persönlich ist eigentlich wichtig, daß ich teils eine sinnvolle Freizeit-gestaltung habe und anderseits aber nicht zu sehr ausgefüllt bin mit Freizeit* . . . . .
>
> *(For me personally it's important that on the one hand my leisure has a meaningful structure and on the other that I'm not too overwhelmed with leisure pursuits . . .)*

> (During listening 'transcribes' '*sind volls freind') . . . she said some-thing like, um, 'persönlich',um, and then she goes '*mit meiner Freizeit', then something I didn't understand, which was something like 'sind', which I wrote down as '*sind volls freind' . . . something, and 'voll' is full, so I think, I think what she was saying was, 'I've got quite a full social life'.

Unable to see any connection between the isolated, misheard items he collected, the student then seemed forced to expand upon this by means of inferencing and elaboration.

This extract is a prime example of how weaker students, rather than using context and prior knowledge less often than their more effective peers as some have claimed to be the case (e.g. O'Malley *et al.*, 1989) were obliged to employ such strategies when their word recognition skills and unaware-ness of syntactic relationships left them unable to make sense of what they heard. Thus *'top–down' processing strategies* predominated over *'bottom–up'* ones. In the former, background experience or prior knowledge of the text's context guide one's understanding; in bottom–up processing, individual items in a sentence are decoded until a meaning is perceived. Many writers have referred to the superiority of top–down over bottom–up processing (e.g. Hosenfeld, 1984) in both reading and listening comprehension. On the other hand, there is a body of writing (relating chiefly to reading but arguably just as applicable to listening comprehension) which suggests that the recent tendency to emphasise top–down processing is not without dangers, in that in some cases the role of bottom–up, decoding strategies is ignored altogether (Eskey, 1988). An 'interactive' approach is advocated by such authors, where equal value is attached to both forms of processing. Listeners and readers must be both good interpreters (top–down) and good decoders of texts (bottom–up) (Eskey, 1988).

The weaker A-level students interviewed not only depended heavily on context, but were also less adept at using it than more successful students. Taken together, the strategies of inferencing from context and 'hearing in' from context were ineffective in completing the task on 72% of occasions when used by weaker students, compared with 58% for stronger students. Taken separately, however, inferencing from context was unsuccessful for both groups to an equal degree (63% of occasions).

Indeed, both groups were distracted by context on a number of occasions, and it was perhaps an added impediment, rather than an aid to comprehension, that the theme of both the texts was so close to the students' own experiences. This was particular true of the German text, where the first speaker was not only the same age as the listeners, but was also studying for 18+ examinations. Students seemed to identify with the speaker, with the result that when only a few words in a passage were understood, they expanded upon them in a manner which may have reflected their own concerns. For example, on hearing that the first speaker was studying for her 'Abitur', Student W ventured that she probably felt her school work was more important than her leisure.

Even though effective students were thus not immune to the possible distractions of inference, 'hearing in' and *world elaboration* (where meaning is worked out by using knowledge gained from general, prior experience), they were less reliant on them and seemed better able to combine them with other strategies. These were sometimes bottom–up strategies, as when Student B effectively used *transfer* (or knowledge of cognates) in conjunction with inferencing from context to work out that young people on activity holidays camping near a mountain, hill or rock, might try out climbing (*'S'ils s'arrêtent près d'une montagne, une colline, un rocher, ils peuvent s'initier à l'escalade'*). He commented that the final noun 'could possibly mean climbing', pointing to the similarity between 'escalade, escalation'.

In general, inferencing and world elaboration within the listening comprehension exercise seemed to be less beneficial for students of all types than was the case for reading. Fewer items of vocabulary were recognised automatically by students, with many misanalysing words in the way previously described above, forcing them to turn to the passage's context for interpretations. It is worth noting in this respect that the four students who were judged to have given the best performance on this exercise used inferencing and world elaboration the least.

Reading

In terms of strategies aimed at improving reading skills, students adopted a similar approach to that used for listening comprehension. The chief strategies in the retrospective interview were again creating practice opportunities and naturalistic practice. As in listening, students varied in the type of activity they engaged in and in the energy they devoted to practising reading outside of class. One group (four males, five females) reported reading on their own initiative L2 magazines or literary texts. Yet few of these appeared to do so on a regular basis or for any great length of time. One, for example, mentioned occasionally reading 'a few lines of a German magazine' (I, F). Pickard (1995: 37) describes a similar lack of enthusiasm for what he calls 'out-of-class strategies' among British language students at Humberside University, especially when compared to the approach of students from other countries. Some effective students (one male, three females) did, however, appear to create reading practice opportunities on a regular basis and with specific goals in mind, such as gaining greater fluency in reading and writing.

Regarding strategies employed during the reading process, it is perhaps significant that in this sample of students the overall incidence of monitoring was relatively low in both interviews, except for comprehension monitoring in the think-aloud interview. This last strategy has been identified in several studies (summarised in Block, 1986) as a key strategy for successful reading comprehension, as has flexibility, embodied in the strategy of substitution. Key metacognitive strategies such as double-check monitoring and problem identification were employed relatively infrequently by students.

The main strategies which appear to have been used more frequently by effective students include double-check monitoring, comprehension monitoring, problem identification, substitution (trying alternative solutions), resourcing (looking up a word), interpretation (trying to avoid a verbatim, unstylish translation) and reading the passage aloud in the L2 to help comprehension. Metacognitive strategies in general were more widely used by stronger students. Weaker students made greater use of selective attention, strategy monitoring, translation, transfer, word analysis (looking for a word's meaning by breaking it down into parts), narrow focus, sentence analysis (breaking sentences down into grammatical units to aid comprehension) and omission (skipping over unknown items).

There are, however, a number of problems with this comparison between the two groups; for example, resourcing might be associated with an inability to decode rapidly and so one might expect it to be used more frequently by weaker students. The key to this seemingly paradoxical state of affairs lies as before in *how* learners employ different strategies and *in what combinations*. This becomes clear if we look at some key strategies in more detail.

The first of these is comprehension monitoring. More effective students were not content with a simple, cursory verification that they had interpreted a word or phrase correctly, but double-checked to see whether their interpretation fitted in with the sentence, or indeed the text, as a whole — generally, that it made sense. Sometimes this was quite a straightforward process, involving a simple re-reading of the text. In other instances, students took more complicated steps to ensure that their interpretation was the correct one, testing and either accepting or rejecting various alternatives or hypotheses. This is illustrated by the following, an interpretation of Lines 14–20 of the German reading text. The text as a whole reports the findings of a survey showing that some young people experience stress because they have too many leisure pursuits to fit into their spare time:

> *Das entnimmt der Wissenschaftler einer Repräsentativuntersuchung des [ ] BAT-Freizeit-Forschungs- [ ] instituts, in der 2000 Jugendliche ab 14 Jahren befragt wurden. (The educationalist concludes this from a representative survey carried out by the BAT Institute for Leisure Research, in which 2000 young people from the age of 14 were questioned.)* [The square brackets indicate the line breaks in the original.]

> I think it's saying that that was . . . it could either be saying that the people, *'Wissenschaftler'*, are representatives of this institute, or it could . . . but 'institute' has got a small 'i', perhaps meaning it's not a noun, or it could be saying that the people asked were representatives of the main group of 14 to 19 year olds . . . + . . . because the *'des'* is genitive, so it's got to be 'of' something and also it says . . . at the end it's got the sentence tagged . . . this phrase tagged on, which if it had the meaning, they were . . . the people in the know were representatives of the thing, it wouldn't really make sense, cos that doesn't seem to tally with the rest of the sentence. (Student A)

Such students as these displayed a willingness and an ability to rectify any breakdowns in comprehension. It is perhaps noteworthy that Student A's reading of the German passage was one of the best in the group.

Weaker students, by contrast, where they did realise that their comprehension was faulty, were often unable to follow up this realisation by any remedial action (this was true also of *strategy monitoring*, where students often realised they were tackling the task in an inappropriate manner but were able to find a suitable alternative approach). Sometimes they 'checked' their original faulty interpretation without really asking themselves whether it was indeed plausible, as in another student's reading of the same part in the previous German text:

> Something . . . free time institutes, um, *'Jugendliche'*, *'2000'* . . . something about after 14 years there, so, going back, *'entnimmt'*, *'nimmt'*, to take, *'nehmen'* is take, isn't it, or . . . so *'entnimmt'* might be undertake, possibly, the undertaking of . . . not too sure about that, actually, that

might be . . . but maybe that would be *'unternimmt'*, but if we say it's undertaking, possibly, the under taking of the teaching, or the . . . yeah, the teaching of a . . . with a representative. (Student I)

Although expressing doubt about his interpretation of *'entnimmt'*, this student, as he sought to verify whether his understanding was indeed correct, was unable to see that it fitted neither the context nor the syntactic structure of the passage. This echoes the processing mode of Hosenfeld's (1979: 62) 'Cindy', who contrasts her reading strategies with those of a more proficient student:

After he guesses a word, he stops to see if it fits into the sentence; I don't stop to see if it makes sense.

Perhaps Student I would have benefited from a similar comparison between his mode of comprehension monitoring and that of Student A.

Yet Student I did at least make some attempt to verify his original interpretation; other weak students did not go even as far as this, merely registering that a breakdown in understanding had occurred and that they realised their reading of the text was unlikely to be appropriate. They often skipped over items crucial to the understanding of the passage. Similarly, several students exhibited in the think-aloud interview elements of what Kimmel and MacGinitie (1984: 164) call a 'perseverative text processing strategy', whereby they form an initial hypothesis regarding the text's meaning, 'then hold on to that interpretation rigidly in spite of disconfirming information in the later text'.

As occurred in the listening passage, this initial interpretation was frequently based on inferencing from what was taken to be the passage's context or on students' general knowledge gained from experience (world elaboration). In the case of Student H, such a reliance on these strategies was necessitated by a very poor knowledge of lexis or of syntax. The failure to decode certain key words meant that he was unable to establish accurately the overall theme of the German passage given in the opening lines, which in turn made inferencing less successful than it might otherwise have been. Instead he latched on to certain words from which he inferred his own context; for example, at the start of the text he extracted *'Freizeit'* ('leisure, free time'), *'Hamburg'* and *'Schlaf'* ('sleep') and expanded on these by means of background knowledge to give the following interpretation:

Hamburg — Eine neue Art von Anstrengungen raubt jungen Leuten den Schlaf: Der Freizeitstreß. (In Hamburg, a new kind of pressure is robbing young people of their sleep: leisure-related stress.)

Hamburg . . . um, a new place I think from . . . a new place, um, I'll miss that out cos I don't know what it is at the moment (+ '*Anstrengung*'?) Yeah, and '*raubt*'. Um, young people . . . '*schlafen's*' to sleep, oh, young people come when they're free from stress . . . I guess it's an area that's been designed where young people can come where they don't have to do anything connected with school. (Student H)

Top–down processing involves making predictions about a text's meaning based on 'prior experience or background knowledge' (Carrell, 1988: 101). Crucially, however, readers should continue 'checking the text for confirmation or refutation of those predictions' (Carrell, 1988). There was no evidence of such checking in Student H's use of inferencing and he appeared to be wholly distracted by the idea of 'free time' as a general concept. No awareness was shown that his interpretation was in conflict with the lexis and syntax of the sentence. Throughout, the 'theme' of free time rather than stress caused by too many leisure pursuits dominated this student's thinking.

By contrast, two other poor readers were hampered by an approach which almost totally ignored context. Yet while they were less likely to be led by prior knowledge to erroneous interpretations of sections of the text, their lack of knowledge of lexis and syntax, inadequate bottom–up decoding skills, combined with a total neglect of context, meant that they extracted very little meaning from the text at all, incorrect or otherwise. Although Student L managed to ascertain that the French text was about activity or working holidays for young people, he failed to apply this knowledge to later parts of the passage. This is surprising, given that both texts were chosen for their affinity with the range of experiences of 16 to 17 year olds. The failure to take account of context, combined again with a disregard for syntax, led to interpretations such as the following:

> *Rencontres enrichissantes, confrontation avec les réalités, elle a pu se faire une vraie idée d'un pays du du tiers-monde. (Finding the encounters she made very enriching, coming face to face with reality, she was able to form a true impression of what a third world country is really like.)*

> OK, '*rencontres enrichantes*' . . . um, to meet rich people . . . + . . . um, well, cos it's got rich in it, I don't actually know what the word is, but it looks like that, um . . . to meet rich people, maybe it's some sort of work for rich people. (Student L)

In all of the above examples, there is evidence of a failure to draw on both linguistic and contextual knowledge when tackling unknown words or phrases. While more effective students were not immune to the distractions of context/world elaboration, they seemed better able to temper their initial predictions by making use of their knowledge of syntax, or bottom–up decoding strategies such as resourcing. Even when more successful learners misinterpreted elements of the text by inferring meaning from context, this was less disastrous to their overall comprehension of the passage, because they were able to recognise or decode almost automatically enough of the surrounding text to make the occasional misreading less important. As many writers have pointed out (e.g. Hosenfeld, 1979; Haynes, 1984), to be an effective contextual guesser students have, almost paradoxically, to know and recognise many items of vocabulary:

> The more words they know, the fewer they must guess, and the greater are their chances of guessing the remaining correctly because they have more contextual information. (Hosenfeld, 1979: 60)

Inferencing from context is just one of the strategies employed by effective students in interpreting texts, while for students with a weaker grasp of vocabulary and syntactic knowledge it may have to stand on its own as a (not always effective) decoding strategy. Or, alternatively, but less frequently, it may be totally by-passed. The difference in reading approach between these types of learners can be depicted diagrammatically, as shown in Figure 2.

As indicated by the question mark in Figure 2, while the unilinear approach of less effective learners may sometimes lead them to a correct understanding of the text, the risk of misinterpretation is high and certainly higher than for effective readers with their multi-pronged form of attack.

Having examined students' employment of top–down strategies such as inferencing, it seems appropriate to ask whether they made more effective use of bottom–up ones, such as resourcing. Unfortunately, both weaker and stronger students lacked skill in using a dictionary — all were given total freedom to consult one as they wished during the think-aloud tasks. Over half the attempts by students to find the meaning of a word or phrase by using this resource failed. Evidently, as Heald (1991: 30) expresses it, using a dictionary effectively is a 'small art', with many pitfalls for the unwary.

One initial problem that weaker students encountered was knowing which items to look up in the dictionary; while more effective students showed greater awareness of which words carried the most meaning in the phrase or sentence (such as the verb), less effective ones tended to be distracted by items they were unfamiliar with but which were often of little importance to the meaning of the sentence as a whole. By contrast, essential items were often ignored. For example, Student H, when reading the

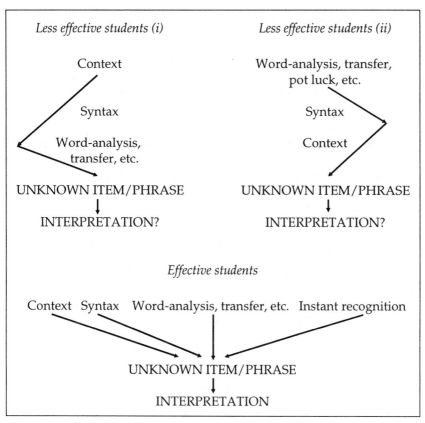

Figure 2. Differences in reading approach

German passage, tried to look up the surname of Professor Horst Opaschowski but passed over '*Anstrengung*' ('strain, pressure') and '*raubt*' ('robs') in the first sentence, which might have given him the key to the passage as a whole had he checked their meaning.

Even if appropriate items were checked, students faced further difficulties, which may be divided into two groups: the first, involving what one might call the technical aspects of looking up words. For the proficient (probably adult) reader it may seem obvious that inflected items need to be looked up under the uninflected or canonical form; some students, however, failed to observe this procedure, or if they did attempt it, were sometimes uncertain how to arrive at the canonical form:

> *Das entnimmt der Wissenschaftler einer Repräsentativuntersuchung des BAT-Freizeit-Forschungsinstituts . . . (The educationalist concludes this*

from a representative survey carried out by the BAT Institute for Leisure Research . . .)

I don't understand the second word in the sentence (looks up *'entnimmt'* in dictionary in third person form) . . . I can't find it . . . . it's probably . . . I would have thought a verb, which . . . *'*entnimmen'*? (Student H)

If students were unable to find immediately the exact equivalent of the item for which they were looking, or to make sense of the meaning they did find, then some lacked the flexibility to look elsewhere under different headings or to look under the root from which the item is derived. Student G, for example, when looking up the noun *'Erziehungswissenschaftler'* (German text, Lines 6–7), was puzzled by the definition of 'pedagogics' given for *'Erziehungswissenschaft'*, as he was unfamiliar with the English term, and it did not occur to him to look at the meanings given for *'Erziehung'* ('education'). A more successful student, by contrast, when unable to find the French term *incollable'* ('infallible', 'expert') in the dictionary, proceeded to look for 'collable'. Although this strategy did not lead to the correct interpretation of the item, it is illustrative of a more flexible approach to dictionary use which many students seem to lack.

This inflexibility was also encountered when students had to select the appropriate meaning of an item when several were given in the dictionary. They often chose automatically the first alternative given under the entry, without reading on to gain further information.

Sometimes taking the first definition given for an item did lead to the selection of the correct meaning in a literal sense, but failure to read on, or to check the local context of the passage, meant that an incorrect meaning was assigned to the item:

Zumindest behauptet derHamburger Erziehungswissenschaftler und Professor Horst Opaschowski, daß bereits 79 Prozent der 14-bis 19jährigen über zu wenig Nachtruhe klagen . . . . (The Hamburg educationalist Professor Horst Opaschowski at least claims that already 79% of 16 to 19 year olds are suffering from too little sleep.) (Student I)

[Looks up *'behaupten'* in dictionary] 'maintain', so . . . so I guess that means something to do with maintaining [. . .] so it's just sort of saying maintaining a constant sort of watching of the up . . . watching of the teaching, the way children are being taught.

Combined with a lack of attention to the syntax of the phrase, or to markers such as *'daß'*, resourcing acted here more as a hindrance than as a help.

Indeed, ignorance or unawareness of syntactic constraints contributed generally to the second group of resourcing difficulties noted, when students had to apply the meaning of a lexical item which they had found in the dictionary to the phrase or sentence as a whole. In the following example, the student correctly found the meaning of *'rencontrer'* ('to meet') and *'enrichir'* ('to enrich'). Yet because she interpreted the noun *'rencontres'* ('encounters') as a verb, and was unable to recognise *'enrichissant'* as an adjective ('enriching'), taking it firstly as the object noun of the verb and then seizing upon *'enrichissment'* in the dictionary, she was unable to gain much meaning from the phrase:

> *Rencontres enrichissantes, confrontation avec la réalité, elle a pu se faire une vraie idée d'un pays du tiers-monde (Finding the encounters she made enriching, coming face to face with reality, she was able to form a true impression of what a third world country is really like.)*

> (Looks up *'enrichir'* in dictionary) . . . so that's 'to enrich' . . . to meet . . . that doesn't make sense . . . (reads on in dictionary) . . . 'enriching' . . . to meet enriching . . . . oh (reading on again in dictionary) . . . 'enrich-ment', so that's similar to the English one, to meet enrichment. (Student Q)

More successful students, on the other hand, seemed better able to recognise and respect the syntactic role of items, and to interpret correctly what they had found in the dictionary in the light of this and of the global and local context of the passage:

> *Les gens respirent le bonheur malgré leurs problèmes . . . (The people radiate happiness in spite of their problems . . .)*

> (Looks up *'bonheur'* in dictionary) [. . .] 'happiness', OK, um, so it means happiness, um, I'll have to look up the *'malgré'* . . . (does so) . . . 'in spite of', so they breathe happiness in spite of their problems, it's like they give off happiness vibes or something. (Student N)

Moreover, unlike Student Q, Student N double-checked that her interpretation did indeed make sense. Once again, this may seem an obvious strategy to the well-practised reader, or to language teachers, but from the think-aloud data it is clear that resourcing is not a straightforward activity for a number of language students. As with many other strategies, students need careful and ongoing training in its *effective* implementation.

This is just as true of making use of cognates (the strategy know as 'transfer') and word-analysis, where an item is broken down into parts to obtain its meaning. The occurrence of each of these two strategies varied according to the language involved, with word-analysis being much more frequently used with the German text, and transfer with the French one , no doubt because of the different nature and roots of the two languages.

Regardless of language, however, the strategies seemed to pose yet more pitfalls for less effective students, with 73% of their attempts to use word analysis and 71% of their efforts to use transfer being unsuccessful (compared with 54% and 39% for more effective students). Once again, the key to success seemed to lie in part in the suitable combination of the two strategies with others, such as inferencing from context, double-check monitoring, interpretation to avoid a too literal translation, and a respect for syntax. Problems with both word-analysis and transfer arose when students ignored or misapplied one or more of these elements, as in the following example of an attempt to use transfer:

> *elle a pu se faire une vraie idée d'un pays du tiers-monde.* (. . . *she was able to form a true impression of what a third world country is really like.)*

> To do a good idea, um, in a country of . . . *'tiers-monde* . . . don't know, something world . . . um, layers of the world? (Student L)

Similarly, compare the approach of a less and a more effective student in using word-analysis:

> *'Les gens respirent le bonheur malgré leurs problèmes', dit-elle ('The people radiate happiness in spite of their problems', she said.)*

> Um, *'le bonheur',* the good hour? . . . I don't know, um, in the break or something. (Student L)

> They cope with their problems . . . *'le bonheur', 'bonheur'* . . . like they have like good humour about their problems, I think . . . + . . . well *'le bonheur'* is like . . . that means like . . . I don't know, you get *'heur-'* . . . like fortunately, don't you, and *'bon'* means good. (Student U)

Not only did Student U make good use of context, double-check monitoring and interpretation, but she was also able to identify correctly the particle *'heur',* unlike the many students who associated it with *'heure'* ('hour'). Indeed, as Haynes (1984: 171) found in her study of ESL students, problems arose for students using word analysis when 'the word they access in memory is spelled and/or pronounced differently from the word on the page'. For example, students of German misread the verb *'verpassen',* to miss, as *'verbringen',* to spend, or as *'passieren',* to happen. When students read words aloud, they frequently mispronounced them, which was perhaps a contributing factor in this respect.

Word analysis, for German at least, was further influenced by students' awareness or ignorance of the effect of prefixes and suffixes on vocabulary items. For example, the effective Student A was able to interpret successfully, if not totally accurately, *'Erziehungswissenschaftler'* as 'intelligentsia, the people who . . . who know things', not only by making use of 'wissen' ('to know') but also because, as he explained, 'it's got *'-ler'* on the end, and that means people.''

Transfer led to problems when students ignored the syntax of the sentence, as happened frequently with the German sentence (Lines 14–18) *'Das entnimmt der Wissenschaftler einer Repräsentativuntersuchung des BAT-Freizeit-Forschungsinstituts'*, where the professor was frequently taken as being a representative of the research body. Similarly, in the French text, Line 15, *'en vous attribuant une bourse'* ('by awarding you a bursary') was misinterpreted as, for example, 'you give money'.

Students with a wider knowledge of English vocabulary were, unsurprisingly, better able to make use of transfer, as in the case of Student B, who rightly assumed that *'une bourse'* was similar to the English 'bursary'. It was, however, perhaps surprising that overall little use was made of cognates in places where it might have been expected. Only two students made the connection between *'une bourse'* and 'bursary' or 'reimburse', and several vocabulary items were looked up in the dictionary which students might have been expected to know through their similarity with English. These include, in the French passage: *'enrichissantes'*, ('enriching') *'respirent'* ('breathe') *'évader'* ('to escape'), 'attribuant' ('awarding'); in the German: *'raubt'* ('robs') and *'-streß'* ('stress').

Writing

The strategies which were most frequently used by students included *planning, drafting* and *monitoring one's production*. The latter took the form of monitoring from the point of view of accuracy, the clarity or fullness of meaning expressed, the style and sophistication of language used, or whether the language being attempted was within one's capabilities (*language repertoire monitoring*). Students sometimes monitored for accuracy or style using either *auditory* or *visual monitoring* (judging whether something looked or sounded right), or *reference to rules or patterns*. Strategies for finding the words they needed to express themselves included *substitution, translation, transfer, resourcing* and *circumlocution/paraphrase*. *Production evaluation*, the checking of completed work, was also used. *Creating practice opportunities*, mainly in the form of writing to penfriends, was reasonably common, but chiefly among girls. It was also observed that between the first and the second interview, auditory and visual monitoring became less frequent, while pattern/rule application was more often employed, perhaps because pupils had been exposed to more grammar instruction by the time of the think-aloud interview.

Different types of students varied little in the number and range of strategies that they used, but it was noted that the metacognitive strategies of planning and monitoring for meaning, style and sophistication were more common among effective learners, while two cognitive strategies, transfer and translation, occurred more among less effective ones.

There is a degree of ambiguity in the literature that discusses the skill of writing, as to whether certain strategies can be characterised absolutely as 'good' or 'bad'. This is particularly true of planning, monitoring and evaluation. While a number of research reports and texts aimed at professionals (e.g. Hedge, 1988) which are concerned with the promotion of effective writing emphasise the importance of these strategies, others suggest that they may not always be conducive to good writing. Zamel (1983) argues that insisting that students make plans before writing can limit the flexibility of ideas, the interweaving between thinking, writing and re-writing which is the mark of the proficient composer. In a study of ESL writers that author found that both the best and the worst of them did not plan before composing. Similarly, Perl (1979) reports that ineffective writers devoted a great deal of effort to checking their work for surface errors such as spelling. Among the learners I interviewed, the strategies of planning, monitoring and evaluation were reported by both effective and ineffective students.

A qualitative consideration of two main strategy categories, planning and monitoring, illustrates again the importance of the manner in which students use strategies. Regarding the first strategy, the retrospective interview indicated that students divided into those who planned entirely in English (seven males, three females), those who planned entirely in the L2 (one male, one female) and those who planned first in English and then translated this into an L2 plan (six females). Students also differed as to whether planning meant thinking about the topic to be considered (four males, two females), jotting down a few ideas in paper (two males, six females) or writing a more detailed plan which took the structure of the composition into consideration (three males, three females). Stronger and weaker students were fairly evenly distributed among these groups, but with some differences between them. More effective students who planned solely in English commented that they tried to stay within the limits of the range of vocabulary and grammatical structures which they felt competent in handling; as one effective student of French explained, 'I won't think up something too difficult, that I know I won't be able to write down in French' (I, M).

In the think-aloud interview, effective students were more likely to outline in very general terms the ideas which they wanted to express, while for their less effective counterparts more detailed planning was often a prelude to an almost direct translation of an English phrase. For two students, this led them to be over-ambitious, sometimes resulting in dictionary use and ambiguous expression, as in this example from Student K. Students of German were asked to write about what leisure meant for them:

Für mich die Freizeit ist mit meinen Freunden irgend von Schule gegangen.

I'll start it *'Für mich die'* . . . I think it's *'die Freizeit'* . . . *'ist'* . . . so I'll write that (writes *'Für mich die Freizeit ist'*) . . . . . . it's . . . for me free time is . . . in English I'd probably say 'anywhere but school', or 'away from school', *'weg'* means away, but . . . you can't really say in German *'*von die Schule weg, die Schule weg'* cos it doesn't really make sense at all, does it? (addressing interviewer) . . . um, so I could always, um, *'mit'* . . . anywhere, anywhere, can I use the dictionary? . . . (looks up 'anywhere') . . . anywhere . . . *'*irgend'* . . . *'*irgend . . . von Schule gegangen'* . . . (writes *'*mit meinen Freunden irgend von Schule gegangen'*).

This contrasts with the picture of *effective writers* presented elsewhere. Chamot and Küpper (1989), for example, report that in their study eight exceptionally effective students of Spanish were characterised by the ability to direct attention to the task at hand, thinking and producing ideas in the target language while writing, remaining within known vocabularies instead of trying to translate English words or phrases, and finding alternatives for words they could not immediately recall.

As far as monitoring and evaluation are concerned, numerous studies of the composition process have suggested that effective writers focus firstly on meaning and content and then secondly on formal aspects. Indeed, in this study weaker students monitored for accuracy slightly more on average than stronger ones, yet their use of this strategy tended to be less effective. In some cases monitoring was inconsistent, for example checking adjectival endings in some instances but not in others. Frequently monitoring for accuracy was combined with *pattern/rule application* and *academic elaboration* (using knowledge gained in class), but the problem here was that often such knowledge was imperfect and inappropriate patterns applied. Writing that on an ideal holiday the weather would be hot, Student R verified her sentence *'*J'espère les vacances seraient chaud'* on the basis that 'the future tense has imperfect endings on'.

Certain students (including two of the most effective) mentioned the importance for them of maintaining concentration on what they were expressing; this was achieved by checking for errors of spelling and grammar *after* the main ideas had been formulated on paper, perhaps pencilling in or underlining items they were not sure of. As one girl explained in the retrospective interview, she did not check genders while she was writing, 'cos otherwise I sort of stop and then I lose everything'. In the think-aloud interview, when she registered that an item might not be correct, rather than pondering over it there and then, she wrote it in and went on to the next sentence. At the end of her composition she re-read the paragraph, paying particular attention to the items that were in doubt, reassessing them in the light of the passage as a whole — rather than considering them as isolated sentences, as tended to be the case with weaker students. She further seemed concerned to show to the reader that she had responded fully to the paragraph title.

For two less effective students, however, who reported worrying about 'getting it right', there was an indication (echoed in the think-aloud interview) that their concerns about formal accuracy, e.g. spelling and grammar, impeded their writing. Effective students, whose skills in these areas were probably more automatic, appeared to be more concerned about the style and sophistication of their writing, with the best of them showing an awareness of the composition's audience, in their efforts to produce compositions that went beyond the standard that they had achieved at GCSE level.

Several students spoke of assessing formal accuracy by using their awareness of how the language should look or sound. Once again, there was a qualitative difference in exactly how various students used this form of monitoring. Stronger students reported basing their judgement on such considerations as how they had seen or heard certain words or phrases used in the past or on their appreciation of what sounded like stylish or coherent French/German. Two effective female students claimed to read their essays aloud to themselves to help them concentrate, and to ensure that what they had written sounded like correct French or German in terms of how words linked together. Another effective student used judgements made on sound and appearance in conjunction with rule application.

Weaker students tended to refer to items 'just looking/sounding right' or to claim that they put things down on instinct. Another reported 'slap[ping] down what I think is correct, what sounds right' and reading his work back to himself for the meaning *he* could get from it, claiming 'it makes perfect sense to me' (I, M). The think-aloud interview and comments from his teacher, however, indicated that his judgement of what was correct or not was somewhat limited. This is similar to Perl's (1979: 326) comments on a poor L1 writer, who when editing his composition,' 'read in' the meaning he expected to be there' in parts of the composition where such errors as the omission of words occurred. It may also be the case that for less effective learners their knowledge of formal aspects of the language or contact with the L2 in terms of narrative writing is insufficient to allow them to make adequate judgements based on 'what sounds right'. Such a strategy seems to be effective in the hands of more proficient students because it is supported by a stronger underlying knowledge of language in both its structural and communicative aspects.

Weaker students were further hampered in their production monitoring by uncertainty, yet they almost never sought to double-check their hypotheses and often just passed over items that they thought were incorrect. At the same time, however, frequent pausing because of uncertainty had the effect in some cases of interfering with the flow of the student's writing. Partly as a result of this, and of the tendency to over-use translation and transfer, the compositions of such students were fragmentary and unstylish. It is perhaps worth citing Student G's thought-processes at length for the insights they give into how a lack of confidence over grammatical matters can hinder composition:

> *Für mich Freizeit ist ein Zeit wann ich kann mit meine freunden sein. Ich darf sport treiben, oder ich kann nach ein klub gehen. Mann kann mit seine freunde quatchen.*

I'm just guessing at the gender of *'Zeit'*, because I just don't know (writes *'*Für mich Freizeit ist ein Zeit'*) . . . and I'm thinking, can I put . . . I've put *'*Für mich Freizeit ist ein Zeit'*, which I'm thinking is OK, maybe apart from *'ein'*, could be *'eine'* or *'einen'*, I'm thinking, can I put *'*Wo ich kann mit mein Freunden sein'* . . . you could say it in English, it's free time is a time where I can spend . . . when, I'd have thought, I can spend time with my friends, so I can say *'*Wann ich kann'* . . . so I'm going to put that down . . . *'ich kann'* . . . (writes *'*wann ich kann mit meine freunden sein'*) and again, you see here I don't know if it's *'mein'* or *'meinen'* or whatever, because I'm just . . . I have . . . I just don't know [. . .] so I'm thinking, already I've written one sentence, and I've got the message across fine, but I haven't . . . by writing *'*ein Zeit'* and *'*meine freunden'*, I could have already made two mistakes, just because I didn't know [. . .] so I'll just carry on, because I'm not . . . by dwelling on it, I'm not going to make it any better [. . .] this is the problem, I write things down not knowing if they're right or wrong, and not ever actually getting off my backside and going and working out if it is or not.

His final comment might also be taken as a perceptive insight into an important difference between some effective and ineffective learners!

Other problems arose among less effective students, who were ready to undertake surface editing (for example, genders), yet were oblivious to more important flaws in their writing which were more detrimental to the intelligibility of their work. This is true of Student K, who checked genders but little else. Furthermore, in spite of their apparent regard for monitoring of accuracy, it sometimes seemed as if weaker students were so preoccupied by the message that they wished to convey that they were unable to see that the inaccuracies in the phrase they produced prevented this meaning from emerging for the reader. As mentioned in the discussion of the retrospective interview, there was a tendency in some to 'read in' the meaning which they believed they had imparted, suggesting an inability to place themselves in the position of the reader who would be unlikely to see it in the same way.

Generally, better students were more conscious of the need to apply vocabulary and structure carefully so as to maximise comprehension on the reader's part. Like the less effective students, they also applied rules of grammar to help monitor the accuracy of their work, but were usually more successful because they had a firmer grasp of the pattern to which they were referring. Importantly, they were better able to find an appropriate substitution when changes were necessary. These factors appeared to give them more confidence in their writing, so that the pauses necessitated by monitoring were shorter. Thus 'the rhythms generated by thinking and writing' were less likely to be disrupted by editing (Perl, 1979: 333).

Regarding evaluation of work corrected by a teacher, the retrospective interview suggested that this was not always carried out in a profitable manner. While personal experience suggests that the majority of teachers invest a great deal of time and effort in correcting students' mistakes, previous research indicates that students pay little attention to such corrections (Cohen, 1987). Furthermore, it has been argued that correcting written work does little to improve students' performance in this area (Leki, 1990). Among the students in the present project, the four least effective claimed either that corrections did not help them or that they took no notice of them. Two male students added that looking through or re-writing corrections was a mechanical process, as the words of one suggest:

Sometimes, when you just copy out the ones that he's put all these red marks on and you copy out that bit, you don't take it in, you're just copying it out [. . .] I know that I'm not learning it when I do it, but sometimes you haven't got the time to . . . you're trying to get it done. (I, M)

Likewise, both effective and ineffective students reported 'reading through' their corrected work, but amending errors by re-writing, making a mental note of them, or analysing errors (including assessing their seriousness) was more common among effective students. It is likely that the degree of mental processing involved in the exercise influences how profitable attention to corrections ultimately is.

Oral work

The principal difficulty experienced in coding strategies for oral work lay in the inevitable overlap with those used for dealing with affective concerns about speaking in front of others. It was decided for the sake of clarity to exclude from this section any strategies that were clearly being employed to overcome anxiety of this sort. Instead, these will be reported separately in Chapter 4. Oral work featured only in the retrospective interview, as too many problems were envisaged in asking students to think aloud at the same time as speaking in the target language!

Speaking, as a production skill, appears from the comments made by students to involve similar strategies to those employed in writing, including *planning* what to say, *selecting* what to say, perhaps by using *formulaic phrases*, and a degree of *translation*. In contrast with their approach to writing, however, very few students reported using strategies of *monitoring* or *evaluation*. It is probable that given the more fleeting and transitory nature of speech, there is less opportunity to employ such strategies; or, if they are used, students are less likely to be aware of them. Nevertheless, it may be that the absence of objective evaluation strategies contributes to the low opinion some students (mainly female) have of their capabilities in oral work.

The type of planning students engaged in varied according to the form of oral work, with role-plays, creating dialogues and presentations tending to involve more planning in English. Translation was then used as students converted the framework they had devised into the L2. Discussion work, however, also involved planning in the L1 in some instances, with four weaker students reporting formulating ideas in English in their head and then translating them into the L2. The time involved in such a process sometimes meant that they missed the opportunity to contribute to the conversation, which in turn caused frustration. Even students who did not directly report thinking in English mentioned difficulties attributable to their need to think carefully about how to express their ideas in the L2. It would appear that for them the higher level vocabulary of discussion was not so readily retrievable as the formulaic phrases they had learnt in earlier years; nor did all students have the ability at this stage to manipulate the language at their disposal, as in the case of the student who claimed he had to take his time while speaking:

> If you just rush headlong into it, usually you haven't got the ability to change a sentence once you've gone in completely the wrong way. (I, M)

Hence also the need for some students to *rehearse silently* before speaking, particularly those who were overly concerned with matters of accuracy and pronunciation.

Several students engaged in a degree of self-management/philosophising regarding the best way to improve oral performance. Most of these (mainly effective or very effective students) emphasised the importance of speaking as much of the L2 as possible in class. In this they resemble Seliger's (1977) 'High-Input Generators', for whom a high level of verbal interaction in the language classroom correlated positively with a high level of overall linguistic achievement. This is not to say that in the present study, all effective students contributed frequently in class or that all frequent contributors were effective students. In a number of cases the opposite was true, suggesting that the combination of a number of different strategies is needed for success at A-level. As Allwright (1988) points out, it may not be exposure to the spoken language alone that leads to success, but rather what learners do mentally with the language with which they come into contact.

Closely related to self-management or philosophising strategies are those involving *creating practice opportunities* and *naturalistic practice*, with students who emphasised the importance of class participation seeking out a number of opportunities to use the L2 orally. Again, there was a qualitative difference in the number and type of opportunities that certain students sought out. The majority of references made relate to exchange visits, but these varied in the frequency and amount of time spent in the foreign country. More effective students also created practice opportunities in this country, either in class by contributing as much as possible, or deliberately trying to re-use expressions they had just learnt (one male, one female), or outside class, by talking in the L2 to family or friends who spoke the language (three females). Some of the most effective students used a number of these strategies. Another effective (male) student had developed a friendship with a French native speaker resident in his home town and spoke French to him, while a boy who was generally less effective in his studies but highly proficient orally spoke to his penfriend in French on the telephone.

Compared with the subjects of other studies of classroom learning (e.g. Chamot & Küpper, 1989), these A-level students appear to have made wider use of affective strategies such as *cooperation* and seeking *clarification*. This is likely to be a reflection of the amount of pair and group work students engaged in within the communicative classroom.

The relatively high incidence of *risk-taking*, a strategy similar to that highlighted by Naiman *et al.* (1978) and others as beneficial to language work, suggests that these students felt less constrained by concerns about accuracy in oral work than was probably the case prior to the advent of communicative language teaching (but see later). This may also explain the low incidence of monitoring strategies. However, although many students claimed they would volunteer an answer even when they were only partly sure of being correct, further examination of the responses reveals that they varied considerably in how much of a risk they were prepared to take. One group (seven males, three females) gave the impression that they would answer in such circumstances regardless of how uncertain they were of the answer, while another (three males, eight females) expressed some reservations about always answering in such a situation. Deciding factors included *how* sure they were of the answer, whether anyone else seemed to be going to suggest an answer as well (in which case they tended to remain silent) or how confident they felt on the day. A quotation from one of the few boys to express a degree of anxiety about group oral work illustrates the variability of risk-taking and its close relationship with self-esteem:

> If I know I'm right, I'll definitely answer, but if I'm unsure, depending on how I feel that day, I'll think, 'I'll make a fool of myself getting it wrong', or if not I'll think, 'Well, never mind', you know, 'Can't be perfect all the time'. (I, M)

Grammar learning and grammatical manipulation

While the think-aloud interview probed the way in which students completed grammatical exercises, in the retrospective interview they were asked in addition to outline how they attempted to develop a mastery of grammar and its rules.

A noticeable difference between grammar and other learning situations reported so far is the higher incidence of *self-diagnosis strategies*. This is likely to be attributable to students' awareness of their shortcomings in this area, as suggested by the questionnaire. The number claiming that, where they were unsure of grammatical points, they investigated them further indicates that for some students at least a clear understanding of and certainty regarding form was welcome (cf. the questionnaire). At the same time, however, there was relatively little evidence of students actively *creating practice opportunities* by re-using new structures whenever possible, with many of them (as for vocabulary) choosing to improve their grasp of structure by rote learning of verb and declension tables.

There further appeared to be a relatively high degree of *rule search and application* among A-level students, with several claiming that when writing they consciously applied rules they had been taught. Such rules were often reinforced by reference to dictionaries or grammar books (resourcing), particularly in the case of girls. On the other hand, there emerges a fairly sizeable group of students whose method of judging grammaticality was not based on reference to rules. Several *'non-rule' strategies* were mentioned, including monitoring by how something sounds, how it appears on the page or by some internal, stylistic notion of what is grammatically acceptable. These strategies received 12 mentions (six male, six female) in total. Some learners, like the following student of German, emphasised that they would be unable, if asked, to explain why a certain utterance was correct or not:

> I couldn't . . . I couldn't say to you what . . . what the correct way of using it [the case system] is, but I write it and it's . . . it's right. (I, F)

There was no apparent relationship between this form of monitoring and the time spent abroad by the student, as might have been expected.

Instinct sometimes predominated over, and seemed separate from, rules taught formally, as when one had to decide which case to use with a preposition in German:

> We've learnt all the FUDGEBOW and all this kind of thing, but it . . . you don't think about that when you're writing it, you don't think, 'Is that . . . does one of those fit FUDGEBOW, and if so, what is FUDGEBOW?' . . . I often write things out as I believe I've heard them in the distant past, it just sounds right, like, 'This problem', I just think, 'Would it be 'dieses Problem, diesen Problem?'' . . . I just kind of try and remember the sound, but I don't usually consciously sit down and work out what what it's going to be, look up the gender. (I, M)

Related to this is the group of students for whom the assessment of grammaticality was even less of an exact science and who claimed to rely on pure *guesswork* rather than on rules, sound, appearance or style. Their comments additionally highlight an element of *passivity* regarding structure. When asked how he might go about making sure he chose the correct verb form in an exercise designed to practise tense work, one student of French remarked:

I sometimes hope, rather than looking it up [. . .], just wait and see what the teacher says. (I, M)

A student of German felt reluctant, or unable, to adopt the analytical approach to grammar taken by some other students:

I find it very difficult to try and sit down and work it out myself, because I'm not very good at, like, the studious work, especially in languages, [. . .] I just can't sit down and teach myself how to put different things in word order, it just has to come naturally. (I, M)

Though he admitted that this was in part due to laziness, his comment also reinforces the notion that in regard to formal structure there exists different learner types, which one might liken to Hatch's (1974) 'data-gatherers' and 'rule-formers'. The former group of learners tend to concentrate more on the development of fluency in language use rather than on accuracy, the latter group adopting a more analytic, rule-based approach. By looking at students' reported strategies in the area of grammar, particularly those involving self-management/philosophising which often illuminated students' attitudes to the teaching and learning of grammar, it was possible to place most learners in the data-gatherer or rule-former category. The data-gathering group contained five boys and three girls, the rule-former group four boys and seven girls. This first group included six students classed as less effective, the second group nine classed as more effective. It might be argued that communicative language teaching does not encourage an analytical approach and that it is surprising that the number of data-gatherers among A-level language learners is not higher. Nevertheless, it seems possible for some students, who at the GCSE stage of language learning have received similar grammar teaching to their data-gathering peers, to emerge as rule-formers within the A-level situation. It might also be objected that data-gatherers make up in oral and listening skills what they lack in analytical expertise; in some instances this was the case. Interestingly, however, a number of highly effective students who appeared at the interview stage as rule-formers had also developed elements of data-gathering and thus confidence in the spoken language. On the other hand, when the opposite approach is adopted, that is, trying to promote analytical tendencies in students who are primarily data-gatherers, problems can arise. This was made clear in the case of one student who was desperately trying to come to terms with German grammar, particularly the case system, and had been encouraged by his teacher to analyse sentences in order to identify the role of individual items and thence which case was applicable. The confusion that this created as expressed in his

diaries and think-aloud interview was such that the suitability of an
analytical approach for all students is questionable.

If we consider the strategy use of effective and less-effective students in
the two think-aloud tasks, then across both tasks effective students used
the following strategies more frequently: double-check monitoring, problem identification, production monitoring, translation and resourcing.
Many of these duplicate the strategies observed in the reading comprehension task. Less effective students, on the other hand, were more likely to
use the strategies of omission and word-analysis. While the first of these
may indicate a less precise deciphering of the passage, the second suggests
an over-concentration on individual items rather than with the passage as
a whole. By contrast, effective students tended to repeat sections of the text
to themselves or read it aloud in the L2, which suggests a greater concern
with sense-groupings rather than with individual items.

At first sight, it seemed that for Task A, where students had to provide
the correct form of given verbs to complete the text, there was a broadly
equal application of predominantly *form-based strategies* (e.g. pattern/rule
application, sentence analysis) and predominantly *meaning-based* ones (e.g.
translation, inferencing from context). Nevertheless, while this harmony of
form and meaning was evident in a small number of cases, the numerical
analysis concealed the fact that all too rarely were rule-based and
meaning-based strategies used in conjunction with one another.

Neither the French nor the German Text A required total comprehension
in order for students to be able to select the appropriate forms of the
bracketed items with which to fill the gaps. While many students did,
however, translate, interpret or summarise parts of the text, the meaning
they extracted was often subordinated to the rule or pattern to which they
referred, which did not always result in an appropriate form being selected.
For example, for the first two gaps of the French text, the *'vous'* pronoun
correctly signalled to students that the second person plural ending to the
verb was required, which most supplied by referring to a paradigm they
had learned. The same process, however, was then applied by all but one
student to the gaps in two later sentences: *'la cohabitation peut vous ____
(agacer)'* ('living with other people might irritate you') and *'cela ____
(pouvoir) vous coûter'* ('that might cost you dear'). Any meaning which
students had extracted from the text was overridden by the generalisation
that the presence of the *'vous'* pronoun within the phrase meant that an *'-ez'*
ending was appropriate. This over-application of rules was often at the
expense of meaning, as if in some students' minds the two were separate
entities, at least as far as 'grammar exercises' are concerned. This is in part

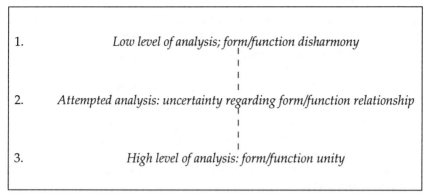

1.   *Low level of analysis; form/function disharmony*

2.   *Attempted analysis: uncertainty regarding form/function relationship*

3.   *High level of analysis: form/function unity*

Figure 3. Three different states of, or approaches to grammatical knowledge

suggested by one (less effective) male student of French, who when asked if he was thinking about the meaning of the sentence as he tried to fill in the gap, replied:

> Not really the meaning, it's just a test, if I was doing a comprehension I would, but normally I'd just look for the endings. (Student J)

The application of patterns and rules is, however, most interestingly examined for what it seems to reveal about the stages learners pass through as they strive towards proficiency. Taking as a starting point Ellis' (1992) interpretation of interlanguage theory, it is possible to identify within the present group of students three different states of, or approaches to, grammatical knowledge, as suggested by Figure 3.

Of the students interviewed, the majority could be said to fall into the middle group, although it must be emphasised that Figure 3 represents a continuum, with some students hovering between two groups. The broken line joining each stage further indicates that the movement from one stage to another is unlikely to be a direct one, with students possibly advancing at times and regressing at others. A small number of male students, three studying German, one studying French, seemed to belong predominantly to the first group, in that they displayed little awareness of the functions that grammatical forms fulfil. In many instances they proceeded by relying on 'instinct' or 'guessing'. Student G, for example, working on the German Text A, explained in a digression that as *'unser'* ('our') in its uninflected form made perfect sense to him as he read a phrase, he was unaware of any reason to change it, except for the fact that experience of such exercises in the past indicated to him that he 'ought' to. Student K, while showing an awareness that in German preceding adjectives are inflected, did not appear to have gone any further in analysing the case system, relying on 'pot luck' to select a case and ending for the same item:

> *In unserer Klasse stellten wir uns die Frage, wie Jugendliche in _____ (unser) Gemeinde ihre Freizeit _____ (verbringen).*
> *(In our class we asked each other about how young people in _____ (our) area _____ (spend) their free time.)*
>
> How, um, sort of youth or young people . . . in their . . . so it'll be *'*unsere'* . . . as in (writes *'*unsere'*) . . . I think, but I wouldn't bet money on it, cos my grammar's terrible . . . + . . . um, because I think it'll be in the . . . nominative? . . . accusative or dative, or whatever, it's one of those. (Student K)

The think-aloud transcripts from several students, whom one might allocate to the second group in the diagram, seem to provide instances of Ellis' (1992) reference to linguistic forms which have been only partially absorbed, and 'float around' within the learner's interlanguage. This is indicated in part by the many idiosyncratic rules learners (both effective and less effective) cited as explanations for their choice of grammatical form or item of lexis during the two tasks. For example, Student P claimed that in French, '-er' verbs are conjugated solely by removing the infinitive ending, without adding anything else, while Student A explained that in German, adjectives referring to singular nouns are not inflected. It should be noted, however, that despite these 'inaccuracies' in the middle group's grammatical systems, they are indicative of students' ability to discover patterns and to describe underlying rules, sometimes in their own language, sometimes in 'grammarian' terms, pointing to a progression towards the later stages of linguistic development signified by the third group in Figure 3.

A small number of very proficient students were judged to have reached the third stage of grammatical awareness, showing an appreciation of what Widdowson (1990: 89) describes as the reciprocity of lexis and grammar, two elements that 'act in concert in the discharge of their semantic duty'. Student T displayed signs of this awareness in her reference to both context and grammatical forms in the following extract from Task B, where students had to find suitable items from a given list to fill the gaps:

> *Fixez-vous de _____ objectifs personnels. Cela vous _____ du bien.*
> *(Set yourself _____ personal goals. That _____ you good.)*
>
> *'Cela vous'* . . . that'll do you good, um, *'cela vous'* . . . it could be *'fera'*, like in the future, that would do you good, I don't think anything else will fit in there, so I'll bung that in there for the minute (writes *'fera'* after *'vous'*) . . . + . . . well, like you, and *'du bien'*, you know, good and

'*cela*', that normally means that or this, like but they've just talked about '*se fixer*', so this is saying that'll do you good, if you fix your objectives, and so that's in the future. (Student T)

Vocabulary learning

The most obvious feature of vocabulary learning as described by the students (in the retrospective interview only) is the degree of uniformity in strategies employed by students, with *list-making, rote learning, masking* and *self-testing* dominating. Indeed, the way in which students described the procedure was astonishingly similar in most interviews, with a large number of subjects responding to the question, 'How would you learn a list of new vocabulary?' in words very much like the following:

> I read it through looking at it, and I usually have one side of the page in French and another in English, I look at the French and then I cover up the French side, look at the English and see if I can do the French bit and then the other way round. [It's just] Continuous looking at it. (I, F)

For some students (two males, four females), most of whom were classed as less effective, these were the only strategies used for vocabulary learning. This relatively low occurrence of *mnemonic devices* echoes Reiss' (1985) finding among American college language students. She suggests that unsuccessful rather than successful language learners rely more heavily on mnemonic devices. In the present study, however, neither group of students used them to any great degree. Yet cognitive psychology strongly indicates that the enhancement of the material to be memorised (through mnemonic devices or other forms of engagement) significantly improves its retention (see Nyikos, 1990). The suggestion made in relation to the student questionnaire, that some A-level students are not learning vocabulary in the most efficient manner, finds support in these data. Additionally, one teacher commented informally to me during the course of the project that when her students were tested on vocabulary they had supposedly learnt a few months earlier, the amount they had retained was low.

Managing change — general study habits

While students' strategies relating to particular learning tasks can tell us much about how they process language, we need to consider also their general approach to their work in order to gain some insight into how they cope with the demands made upon them by the A-level course. In many respects these appeared as new demands for the students interviewed. In contrast to the guidance given at GCSE level regarding what to learn and when, most students felt that their teachers expected them to organise their own work and spend extra time on study outside lessons in more self-directed learning. Related to the theme of self-direction is the way in which students monitor their progress and the general philosophy they adopt concerning the best way to learn a language — in short, the kind of higher, metacognitive strategies they apply to language learning as a whole. Information relating to these matters was gathered during the retrospective interview and through the learner diaries.

Students were judged to be using *organisational/scheduling strategies* if they reported one or more of the following: setting aside specific times for specific pieces of work or tasks; keeping a diary of work to be done and its completion date; deciding on an order for task completion, for example, completing shorter pieces before longer ones. The first of these strategies was the most widely used. Some students mentioned that the way work was set made it difficult to adopt any specific routine for studying or to devise schedules, in that the amount and timing of work set by their various subject teachers varied from week to week. This meant that several students (five males, six females) reported dealing with homework as and when it arose, with no particular organisational structure in mind. In addition, four students (two males, two females) admitted to being badly organised in their work, in so far as they often completed it at the last minute.

Some students mentioned the strategy of reviewing what they had done in class immediately afterwards or at the end of the day, thus monitoring and evaluating their learning. They varied, however, in which aspects of their work they reviewed and in the manner in which they went about it. Certain students (seven females) reported looking back over vocabulary noted, with four of them making a specific effort to commit it to memory. Others (three males, four females) mentioned reviewing grammatical points covered in class, with two checking that they had in fact understood as well as they thought, three following up on areas with which they had problems or were not sure about, and two simply re-reading. A third group (one male, two females) simply tidied up their notes if they were not clear, or transferred vocabulary and grammar noted to the appropriate section of their file. One female student claimed she re-read literature passages covered in class if she had had difficulties in understanding them.

Generally, the most effective students were the most active in their approach to reviewing, testing their comprehension of grammar or learning vocabulary. Perhaps significantly, one of the most effective students of the group (Student M) claimed to learn regularly vocabulary noted, which may explain her performance on the think-aloud reading task.

There was some evidence of students trying to meet the extra demands of an increased work-load by spending time outside lessons on self-directed learning, for example independently deciding to learn vocabulary or to engage in extra reading. Twelve students claimed to spend five or more hours a week on work outside lessons (although some of this time was devoted to work set by their teacher). Six of these students had been classed as more effective. Three weaker students seemed to spend longer on their work because, as one of them expressed it, 'it takes me longer to work out things than other people, like if a homework's only supposed to take half an hour, it normally takes me about an hour and a half' (I, M).

Progress monitoring was also considered to be an important aspect of reflective learning and of adapting to change. Several students reported assessing their progress in more than one way, perhaps combining self-assessment with assessment by grades. Effective students, however, seemed more willing or able to assess their own progress, with ten of them claiming to know inwardly how well they were doing, compared with three less effective students. Five of these effective students, but only one less effective one, claimed they also judged their progress by comparing themselves with others, suggesting perhaps a greater sense of competition. In addition, however, four of these five (all female) were considered to be 'anxious' students, and these are discussed in Chapter 4 from the point of view of their tendency towards negative self-comparison.

The majority of students (19) seemed to have formulated their own language philosophy and were able to comment on what they thought was the best way to learn a language. The most frequently mentioned factor was spending time in the target language country, which no doubt reflects the value learners have been encouraged to place on communicative competence. Ten students, of whom six were effective, referred to this factor. In the same vein, two of this group also mentioned the importance of listening to the L2 outside of class. One highly effective student (Student M) felt that a sound understanding of grammar was important. She also emphasised the need to have a wide vocabulary, as did another effective learner, although, unlike Student M, he admitted that he did not really put this philosophy into practice in a very systematic manner. The need to learn actively, and to involve oneself in learning about the country as a whole, was mentioned individually by two students. Some students, when asked about learning a language, interpreted this as learning vocabulary, suggesting a tendency to see language learning as merely an accumulation of lexis. The comments of three of them, that they felt continuously re-reading vocabulary lists was the most effective 'language learning' method for them, would seem to reinforce this view.

Related to the theme of adopting a specific 'language philosophy' are four central strategies: *self-management, self-diagnosis/prescription, strategy evaluation*, and *creating practice opportunities*. These were viewed as the most important indicators of the extent to which students are able to stand back from their learning and reflect on how and why they are performing as they do in language work. As suggested by McLaughlin (1990), it may be that a highly developed capacity to do this is an integral part of what is more commonly referred to as language aptitude. During the discussion of the various language skills in the retrospective interview, several students did indicate that they were able to reflect on how they were learning and how to improve on any perceived weaknesses without any apparent extra prompting from their teacher.

The number of comments made by each student during the retrospective interview that suggested this sort of reflection was calculated. If four or more comments is taken as an indication of a fairly high degree of reflection on learning, then 13 students (six males, seven females) appear as high reflectors, 11 (six males, five females) as low reflectors. Within these groups, the majority of high reflectors (10) were also more effective students, while the low reflector group contained almost equal numbers of more and less effective students. Light can be shed on this apparent anomaly if one examines from a more qualitative angle. Some of the reflective comments of less effective learners who were also high reflectors. In the case of one male student (Student K), while he did make a number of 'philosophising' comments about how to learn a language, these were mainly concerned with how he thought he should be being taught, as in the following example:

> Ideally I'd rather we sort of kind of had an entire lesson devoted to the grammar, so I could come out thinking, 'I can do this', not, 'I can do a bit of it, maybe a bit at home, and I'll get it all right.' . . . It may be boring but I think I'd learn it better that way.

Yet elsewhere he admitted to rarely investigating grammar on his own, because of a lack of interest or self-discipline, and that he frequently 'switched off' when grammatical explanations *were* given, 'out of boredom'! Thus philosophising on its own rarely led to self-corrective methods.

Another student (Student H), while keen to reflect upon weaknesses and to take measures to improve upon them, seemed from his diary less able to choose effective remedial strategies or to assess their appropriateness.

Students' diary entries as a whole further suggested that effective learners evaluated their strengths and weaknesses, together with their strategies, more frequently and in more detail. Although enumeration was again difficult as some students wrote more entries than others, three groups can be identified. Students within the first group, the largest, seemed to analyse how they had tackled language tasks moderately well. In Section 6 of the diary, headed 'What should I do now?' (following a language task), they were able to make some suggestions for improvement. Such proposals, however, tended to be of a somewhat one-dimensional nature, and were often limited to such strategies as 'Practise more'. In the second, smaller group, learners wrote little either about how they had dealt with the task, or about what they should do next. The majority of students in this group were less effective learners. Students of the third group, on the other hand, also small, were able to write in detail about what they had done, and suggested complex, multifaceted strategies for self-improvement.

Gender Differences in Strategy Use

Given the small numbers of male and female students involved in the project, it is difficult to come to any clear conclusions regarding any differences in the strategies used by the two groups. Certain patterns, however, do seem to emerge.

Across all tasks, there was an indication of a more *careful, planned approach* on the part of girls. In listening, they used the strategies of advance organisation and directed attention more frequently than boys, while in writing, oral work and the grammar tasks, planning, monitoring, evaluating and pattern/rule application were more common among girls than boys. Girls also seem more likely to try and learn grammatical items by heart. Males by contrast were more likely than girls to use sound to determine the appropriateness of their use of language. Four boys in particular emphasised that they disliked planning when writing, preferring to get 'straight down to the essay' (I, M), even if, like one boy, they admitted their teacher had advised them to plan.

This more careful approach from girls may not, however, be totally positive. In oral work, it is possible that the higher incidence of planning, rehearsal and resourcing noted among girls is indicative of a greater hesitancy to speak spontaneously, perhaps out of a fear of 'getting it wrong'. This may also account for the lower incidence of paraphrasing among girls, who might have wanted to express their ideas exactly, again, in some cases, to avoid the perceived negative judgements of others. On a more positive note, however, females would appear to engage in a greater degree of cooperation, which may be beneficial to oral proficiency. Although some boys did enjoy working with others and found it beneficial, others showed a more independent streak, sometimes maintaining that it was too distracting or that it interfered with their own methods of working (cf. Askew & Ross (1988) who claim that boys are less willing to work cooperatively with others). Thus girls seemed to possess heightened interpersonal skills, at least in pair-work or small group situations. It is possible that females who on the surface appear to be 'Low-Input Generators' (Seliger, 1977) within a whole-class situation can compensate for this to a certain degree by gaining greater exposure to the spoken L2 on a one-to-one basis.

The readiness of females to communicate in a one-to-one situation was similarly apparent in relation to the skill of writing. Here, girls were much more likely to employ the strategies of creating practice opportunities and naturalistic practice. In the majority of cases, these two strategies took the form of writing to pen-friends. Nor did male students seem to seek out other ways of practising their written skills, apparently relying on the work set by the teacher. As well as having a correspondent, in the retrospective interview a very effective female student reported making up short paragraphs, 'little descriptions of people and places', in order to develop familiarity with new words and phrases. It seems likely that this creative, holistic approach to writing and the treatment of lexis could account for much of this student's success.

Skills associated with interpersonal communication were also in evidence in the listening comprehension task. There, there was a greater use by females of cohesion markers and the speaker's tone to extract meaning. Could it be that females are more able to detect the emotions and feelings suggested by a voice and to draw appropriate meaning from this?

By contrast, in the listening and grammar tasks, males were more likely to use the strategy of problem-identification, which may suggest a more direct, almost confrontational approach. On the other hand, in the reading task, this strategy appeared as more of a female one, with boys using more frequently the strategies of strategy monitoring, translation, elaboration, omission and word analysis. This last strategy may be explained by the fact that more of the German students, among whom as a whole word analysis was more frequent, were male. It is more difficult, however, to explain why problem-identification should appear as female strategy in this skill and not in others. It is possible that in the reading comprehension passage boys were more willing than girls to pass over items they did not understand, which the latter considered to be essential to their understanding. In an exercise such as the cloze passage, however, which could be approached as a 'puzzle' to be solved, boys may have been more eager to identify key elements to tackle rather than trying to gain an understanding of the passage as a whole.

This seems to suggest an element of risk-taking and may be a reflection of a greater willingness on the part of males to take a guess without worrying about making a misinterpretation. Although all students were constantly reassured throughout the think-aloud interview that they were not being tested, one female expressed anxiety about making mistakes and quite often looked to the researcher for encouragement. It may be that in reading, as perhaps elsewhere, boys are more confident in their own abilities and are less concerned if they are unable to understand the whole passage. In this respect, however, it is also interesting to note that such an approach did not always result in an adequate understanding of the text, leading to the suggestion that over-confidence is not necessarily beneficial when it is a question of a careful analysis of language.

In all of the skill areas considered, both males and females used a mixture of strategies that can be viewed as either positive or negative; for example, girls' hesitancy in speaking seemed to be balanced by skills in cooperation and interpersonal communication. The vital question here is how we can best help them to maximise the positive and minimise the negative — an issue addressed in the following section.

Implications for the Classroom

Learning strategy instruction

The previous discussion has illustrated that while most of the A-level language learners interviewed had developed learning strategies to acquire, recall and manipulate language, they did not always use the most appropriate ones or know how to employ them in the most effective manner. It follows from this that language teachers need to address the question of *how* their students are learning, rather than merely *what* they are learning. Furthermore, it seems insufficient simply to advocate (as seems to be the growing trend) that students become more autonomous and self-directed in their learning, without giving them help and guidance in achieving that goal. Similar comments are made by Grenfell and Harris (1993) concerning the younger pupils they studied, whose learning strategies were not always sufficiently developed to cope with working independently from their teacher.

While experiments in learning strategy training in foreign languages have produced mixed results, some positive (e.g. those reported in Oxford *et al.*, 1990), some negative (Wenden, 1987), some partially successfully (O'Malley & Chamot, 1990), there are indications that steps can be taken to maximise the chances of success. One of the most vital factors is the need for strategy training to be 'informed' (Brown & Palincsar, 1982), 'integrated' (O'Malley & Chamot, 1990), and to involve a high level of 'self-control' (Brown & Palincsar, 1982). That is to say, students need to aware of the purpose and utility of strategy training, activities should be integrated into language learning tasks, and students should be encouraged to monitor, evaluate and control their use of strategies. Thus they should engage in a large degree of metacognitive reflection. Strategy training, above all the metacognitive element, should also be an on-going process, not merely occupying a few lessons at the beginning of the A-level course.

A number of strategy training programmes and materials relating to language learning have appeared in published form (e.g. Rubin & Thompson, 1982; Oxford, 1989; Ellis & Sinclair, 1989; Dickinson, 1992), and several are discussed in O'Malley and Chamot (1990). A common thread runs through most of them regarding the structure a training programme should ideally take, which may be summarised as follows:

(1) *Preparation and assessment* — the theme of learning strategies is discussed with students, and they and their teacher identify the strategies they are currently using, for example, through group discussion, diary keeping, think-aloud tasks. Students might also be invited to compare their strategies with those of other learners and to assess the relative merits of each.

(2) *Presentation/modelling* — the teacher describes and demonstrates the use of the strategy in question.

(3) *Practice* — students are given varied opportunities to practise using the strategy, initially with support from the teacher.

(4) *Evaluation* — students are encouraged to assess the efficacy of the strategies employed on a regular basis, perhaps through diary-keeping and/or group discussions of strategies employed with different tasks (see below).

Whether this instruction should be conducted in the L1 or L2 is a question difficult to answer and the literature sheds little light upon it. Suggestions drawn from O'Malley and Chamot (1990) include: using the L1 until learners' L2 skills are sufficiently developed to cope with the language of learning strategies; and teaching the language of 'metacognition' at an early stage so that instruction may proceed in the L2. Arguably, however, as learning strategies are themselves complex cognitive skills that need to be proceduralised like all others, it is asking a great deal of students of any level to perform this task at the same time as mastering new language. A compromise solution might be to carry out learning strategy instruction in the L1 and then to follow this immediately with tasks in the L2 which make direct use of the procedures imparted in the training stage.

Increasing strategic awareness — thinking aloud and learner diaries

It might be argued that teachers have insufficient time to devote to activities such as those described earlier, and that their main concern is to cover the A-level syllabus. Yet the description of learning behaviour given in this chapter has indicated that without guidance in *how* to apply learning strategies, students cannot respond adequately to, or make full and appropriate use of, the materials with which they are presented. Materials such as the learner diary and the think-aloud tasks employed in this research project can be usefully incorporated into foreign language A-level programmes, and that rather than wasting time, such activities lead to more efficient teaching and learning in the long term. Furthermore, one of the most important factors in becoming a proficient language learner appears to be the ability to stand back and reflect on one's own learning and assess which steps need to be taken to regulate it. Students need to be given as many opportunities as possible to develop this capacity and to achieve the goal of self-direction, which many teachers seem to value but few actively cultivate.

Thinking aloud offers such an opportunity, as well as acting as a diagnostic tool for the teacher who may be unaware of how students are coping with language learning activities and what their precise difficulties are. Hosenfeld (1979) outlines principles teachers should adopt when talking to students about their strategies, including the need for a preliminary practice session (with the think-aloud process ideally modelled by the teacher) and the importance of asking indirect rather than direct questions. For example, rather than asking a student whether he/she had guessed a word in a reading passage, it would be better to ask 'How did you work that out?'. Students need reassurance that the teacher is not mainly concerned that they arrive at a correct answer or interpretation, but is interested in discovering *how* that answer was reached, with a view to discussing possible alternative strategies. As discussed earlier, care should be taken when selecting tasks for thinking aloud — they should be just challenging enough to bring learning strategies into play, without placing so great a cognitive load on the learner that thinking aloud becomes impossible.

Some of the problems associated with asking students to keep a learning diary were discussed at the beginning of this chapter. One other, perhaps the most significant one, concerns the encouragement students need not only to be candid but to make regular entries. Howell-Richardson and Parkinson (1988: 79) rightly point out that many students may lack the necessary motivation for such systematic record-keeping unless they perceive that there is 'something in it for them'. This underlines the importance of a good relationship and open communication between students and teacher. Furthermore, students should be made aware from the outset of the benefits diary-keeping can bring them in terms of an understanding of how they can best learn and an evaluation of their progress. They will also be encouraged to make regular entries if certain steps are taken to make the recording process as easy and quick as possible. Both Bonodana (1990) and Lewkowicz and Moon (1985) draw attention to the demands diaries make on learners' powers of expression and their ability to analyse their learning in metalingual and metacognitive terms. While this may be underestimating the self-awareness of older learners, the task can be simplified in various ways. There is some debate concerning the language in which the diaries should be written; it may be, as Parkinson and Howell-Richardson (1989) suggest, that the use of the target language can heighten students' perception of the diaries' utility, but personal experience concerning the difficulties A-level learners have in expressing their opinions in the L2 indicates that the L1 is a more suitable medium (see also Rubin, (1981) and Murphy-O'Dwyer, (1985)). It also seems advisable to provide students with clear headings under which to make their entries and to give them precise instructions on the type of information required. This further simplifies the task when it comes to discussing learners' entries with them and reduces the likelihood of their producing vague and unfocused accounts. Rubin (1981) refers to the effectiveness of 'directed' diary reporting, whereby students are asked to comment on certain *specific* aspects of their learning.

Finally, diaries need to be collected or discussed on a regular basis, to help ensure that they are being kept in a systematic fashion.

These difficulties might suggest that diaries are a cumbersome tool with few advantages. This is far from being the case, least of all for the students involved. Several commentators on self-directed or autonomous learning advocate the use of diary-keeping for all students and not just those involved in research projects (Dickinson, 1987; Ellis & Sinclair, 1989). By monitoring and evaluating their progress students discover how to take control of their own learning, a theme that will be returned to in later chapters.

What can we learn from the learners? Recommendations regarding specific areas of language learning

These include suggestions for the type of learning strategies that students might be encouraged to employ more effectively. More precise details regarding modifications in teaching approaches are given in Chapter 5, where teachers' views of learners are discussed. Anxiety concerning oral work will be discussed in Chapter 4.

In *reading comprehension*, students should be encouraged to adopt the multi-stranded approach to reading discussed earlier in the chapter, in which both top–down and bottom–up strategies are used in harmony. In spite of the problems identified regarding the use of inferencing from context, the strategy should still be promoted but its proficient use clearly demonstrated and practised in class. Care should be taken to select reading passages whose theme lies within the students' realm of experience (this should not be overestimated!), and students invited to activate, before reading proper begins, what they already know about the topic and any L2 vocabulary associated with it. This can be done through reference to the title, accompanying pictures or to comprehension questions. The teacher can then demonstrate how the context can help in the identification of unknown items. At the same time care must be taken to emphasise how good readers use such inferencing techniques in conjunction with other strategies that can help confirm or correct the interpretation made — perhaps by explaining how they exhibit 'a critical inferring behaviour' rather than a 'wild-guessing behaviour', in the words of Hulstijn (1993: 142). It is especially important to discourage students from misusing context in allowing a theme adumbrated early in the passage to dominate their thinking, by reminding them, and showing them how to, re-evaluate their initial interpretations as they read on by employing the strategies of comprehension and double-check monitoring.

Strategies that need to be encouraged in conjunction with inferencing include transfer, word analysis and selective resourcing. Klapper (1993: 50) outlines admirably areas of word-decoding which might be taught explicitly to students, including how to exploit cognates, affixes, compound formation, morphological clues and grammatical categories to extract meaning from items. The last of these, identification of grammatical category (a skill found particularly difficult by many students in the present study) can, Klapper suggests, be facilitated by tasks which involve students in dividing sentences into clauses or sense groupings and 'boxing, bracketing or underlining the key elements (usually verb and subject)'

(Klapper, 1993: 50). Other suggestions for word-decoding activities can be found in Nuttall (1982).

Students would also benefit from more explicit instruction in using a dictionary, in particular, the need to look up items in their uninflected form, to read definitions in their entirety, to note the grammatical role of the item in the sentence and to check the meaning found against the context of the passage. Further examples of good practice in this area from teachers themselves can be found in Chapter 5.

Several of the previous suggestions apply also to *listening comprehension*, such as the use of pre-teaching strategies that invite students to activate their knowledge of the theme to be treated in the passage, and any related L2 vocabulary they know (see Glisan, (1988), and Peck, (1988) for further details). Again, students should be encouraged to make *careful* use of inferencing from context, supplementing it with bottom–up and monitoring strategies.

Other possibilities include the demonstration and practice of using tone and cohesion markers to detect meaning from listening comprehension passages, with students helped to identify words that are stressed (Eastman, 1987). This might encourage them to emphasise items which are truly 'key words' (such as verb and subject) and not just those they can immediately seize upon. Similarly, in order to discourage narrow focus, they might be shown how to listen in chunks, identifying sense groupings (Eastman, 1987).

Learning strategies relating to *writing* are similarly 'teachable'. Although this is an activity that personal experience suggests is most often carried out by students in private study, numerous researchers indicate that it is a skill that requires frequent and guided practice in class time. The results of the present study appear to vindicate this view. In particular, students require instruction in planning, drafting and revising their compositions. Group planning in the L2 might discourage the practice noted in the study of formulating ideas in the L1 and then attempting to translate them verbatim. It is also arguable that compositions of an abstract, discursive nature should be delayed even longer than seems to be the case in most schools, so that students are not tempted into this translation approach. If this is the case, then examination groups may need to revise both the number and type of topics on which they expect students to be able to write. It is possible, furthermore, that the tendency of the students interviewed to try and translate their thoughts directly from English into the L2 has its roots in the form of GCSE examination they had taken. At the time of the research project, instructions and questions in external examination papers were presented in English; from 1998, both will be in the target language. A review of the type of writing tasks set prior to that date gives the impression that many are hidden translation tasks, often involving the transfer of indirect speech into its direct form. It is hoped that the introduction of Target Language Testing may go some way to help students to develop the capacity to 'think' in the L2 (Powell *et al.*, 1996).

Other avenues to be explored in written work include encouraging students to think about the audience they are addressing in their compositions, both in terms of the style and the clarity of their meaning. This might be achieved through inviting students to assess each others' work in class according to these criteria, followed by discussion in pairs or groups of areas to be improved. Students might also benefit from discussing and practising in class some of the writing strategies used by effective students, such as pencilling in unknown items and checking them later, to prevent an interruption in the flow of writing. Information technology and word processing can be helpful in this respect, facilitating drafting and revising (see Atkinson (1992) for further ideas, particularly relating to creative writing).

Corrected written work needs to be handled with care and writing out a correct version should involve more than simply copying the teacher's corrections. Students might discuss the most helpful way of reviewing mistakes for them, for example, thinking about why errors occur; are they unsure of the rule, are they being too ambitious?

Key strategies in the area of *oral work* include those aimed at decreasing anxiety and increasing participation; these are discussed in detail in Chapter 4. In addition, students need to be reminded that to get maximum exposure to the language you need to be able to keep the conversation going. Strategy training can focus on how effective learners do this, for example, paraphrasing, using cognates (with care!), asking for help from one's classmates or teacher, using hesitation fillers. In addition, learners can be made aware of the importance of variation and register in speech. When reading or listening to the foreign language, they might notice how people's language varies according to *where, to whom* and *about what* they are speaking — these often determine how formal they are and the type of vocabulary they use. They should then try to incorporate different registers or styles appropriately into their own oral work.

Regarding *vocabulary learning*, the central issue is the need to invite students to try out and evaluate methods of vocabulary learning that go beyond the mainly rote-based techniques so many of them appear to employ — such as composing sentences that include the item to be learnt and mnemonic devices. The following are based on Oxford (1989) and Rubin and Thompson (1982).

(1) Use flashcards, writing words/phrases on small pieces of card with their meaning on the back. These can be carried and looked at in any spare moments.

(2) Group words/phrases and study them together (this is easier if they are on card). Students should be helped to organise vocabulary systematically, not just randomly on sheets of paper or in any order in a vocabulary book. Sections might include topics, or functions, e.g. phrases for agreeing/disagreeing, opening a paragraph.

(3) Say the words aloud as you study them.

(4) Record the words onto tape, then listen to the recording several times.

(5) Associate words with pictures or with similar-sounding words in English (but be careful of 'faux amis'!)

(6) Associate words/phrases with situations — e.g., problems with their solutions. Or, if words occurred on a language video, thinking back to the screen images may help their recollection.

(7) Use loci, i.e. remember words by their location on the blackboard or page.

(8) Use the keyword method — identify a known L1 word that sounds like the new word and then create an easily recalled mental image linking this with the L2 word, e.g. the French for soup, 'potage', might be linked with a large pot full of steaming soup.

(9) Use natural word associations, such as opposites. An example of this in English would be 'complicated–simple', 'acceptance–rejection', etc.

(10) Learn related words and patterns. A list of words can be organised into groups that have a common linguistic core — for example, in the French topic 'L'Environnement' some key words such as 'polluer', 'contribuer', 'diminuer' could be learnt together.

Much of this applies to the learning of *grammar*. If students are to be asked to learn such items as conjugation and declension tables, then arguably they should be helped in their search for the most effective method for them. Students need to reflect, with guidance, upon such matters as whether they remember a rule better by doing grammar exercises or by using it for communicating in speaking or writing. As before, they can be encouraged to learn from each other and invited to try their peers' strategies to see if they work for them. The following ideas are again based on Rubin and Thompson (1982).

The importance of personal organisation needs to be stressed — the way grammar is organised in the textbook may not be the easiest way for everyone to remember it. Students might reconstruct grammar charts/tables to suit their own styles of learning.

An active approach is equally important — successful learners do not always wait for the teacher to point out a rule. Students need to be encouraged and shown how to try to work it out for themselves from language encountered when reading or listening. They should then try to use the rule deduced in other combinations and contexts.

As for vocabulary, mnemonics can be helpful for learning grammar — although, as with all strategies, this technique may not suit everyone and may need personal adaptation. One example is the familiar technique of using the first letters of items and turning them into a word or phrase; for instance, in German one might remember the prepositions followed by the accusative case by thinking of the word FUDGEBOW:

Für
Um
Durch
Gegen
Entlang
Bis
Ohne
Wider

It is worth noting again, however, that care must be taken with the 'grammatical load' that we place on students in the early stages of their A-level course. For some of the students discussed in this chapter (and looked at again in Chapter 6), an approach based on the systematic learning of grammar, with all its 'technical' terms, seemed to be inappropriate and may have hindered students' progress more than it helped.

Conclusion

The development of effective learning strategies lies at the heart of promoting more successful language learning. Yet the task is not without its difficulties, as O'Malley and Chamot (1990) explain. They point to the importance of teacher interest in the process and, more importantly, to the major role played by motivation. Students who do not have the 'will' to learn may find it difficult to develop the 'skill' to learn (Paris, 1988, cited by O'Malley & Chamot, 1990: 184). Indeed, it may be argued that affective and social learning strategies should be given the same prominence as those relating to more cognitive tasks such as writing. This is the view taken and developed in the next chapter.

4 Affective Concerns and the Question of Gender

Introduction

As the previous chapter suggested, becoming an advanced language learner involves in many cases the ability to adapt to new demands and approaches. Managing this change has a cognitive component, with some students developing new learning strategies and patterns of working to help them adjust to their new situation. Yet equally important are the demands this change makes on students in the affective domain, an issue that is frequently overlooked when methods to help students 'bridge the gap' are being considered.

The term 'affective' is frequently employed in the literature of second language acquisition, yet is not without its problems as far as definitions are concerned. Gardner and MacIntyre (1993: 1) describe 'affective variables' as the 'emotionally relevant characteristics of the individual that influence how she/he will respond to any situation'. Other writers, such as Schumann (1978) and Larsen-Freeman and Long (1991) prefer to place less emphasis on learners' feelings and emotions regarding foreign language learning and in fact claim that 'social and psychological factors' give a more suitable description for how students react to the learning situation. The distinction between 'psychological' and 'emotional' is perhaps a fine one; in the following discussion the term 'affective' is taken to refer both to inborn characteristics, what Stern (1983: 385) calls 'basic *predispositions* of the learner' (Stern's italics), and to more specific attitudes and reactions to learning the foreign language. The chief focus will be on anxiety and self-esteem (including a brief consideration of the related concept of risk-taking), followed by a discussion of the role of motivation in language learning. Finally, moving outside the realm of affective factors proper, the influence of gender will be discussed.

The influence of affective factors on how well a foreign language is acquired has been discussed by a number of writers in the field. Krashen and his associates, for example, advance the notion of an 'affective filter', those 'affective factors' that screen out certain parts of learners' language environments' (Dulay et al., 1982: 46). This means that the amount of linguistic input learners receive can be reduced by such factors as low motivation, which in turn may adversely affect their acquisition of the target language. Similarly, as discussed in Chapter 3, investigations into the personality of the so-called 'good language learner' have suggested that a certain lack of inhibition, a willingness to appear foolish when communicating in the language (Rubin, 1975) are important traits for successful language learning. Later studies refined and developed these notions, examining the relationship between language proficiency and what has become known in the work of some researchers as risk-taking. The relationship is generally held to be a positive one (Beebe, 1983; Ely, 1986), particularly in the area of oral work. Beebe argues that good language learners extend their competence by taking a risk in listening to and using language which is beyond their present proficiency. High levels of self-esteem have similarly been associated positively with oral proficiency (Heyde, 1977, 1979; Heyde Parsons, 1983).

The role of anxiety, an affective response to language learning which may be seen as the opposite of high self-esteem and a willingness to take risks, is less clear. It has been considered both as an inherent trait of some learners, or as a feature that is specifically brought out by the language learning process. Studies have tended to examine the relationship between language performance and either *trait* anxiety (where anxious-ness is an inherent aspect of the personality which is exhibited in a variety of situations) and *state* anxiety (where anxiousness is a reaction to specific situations only, such as test-taking or oral work). The results of such studies are often conflicting, some for example suggesting an inverse relationship between trait anxiety and aspects of language performance (e.g. Swain & Burnaby, 1976), others no relationship (Genesee & Hamayan, 1980). Such inconsistencies can be accounted for in part by a lack of uniformity in the type of learners studied, the research methodology employed and the definition of anxiety adopted. The link, however, does seem to be stronger in the case of state anxiety (also referred to more specifically as *language anxiety*). Here, the relationship with achievement is generally an inverse one (MacIntyre & Gardner, 1989; Horwitz, 1991; Phillips, 1992), although as Phillips (1992) points out, the correlation is usually a modest though significant one. The importance of language anxiety is emphasised particularly strongly by Horwitz et al. (1986: 130), who conclude from a survey of beginning level university language students in Texas that it is ' a distinct set of beliefs, perceptions, and feelings in response to foreign language learning in the classroom and not merely a composite of other anxieties'.

Yet some writers suggest that anxiety does not necessarily have a negative effect on language learning and performance, but may be of a 'facilitating' as well as of a 'debilitating' nature:

> Facilitating anxiety motivates the learner to 'fight' the new learning task. Debilitating anxiety, in contrast, motivates the learner to 'flee' the new learning task; it stimulates the individual emotionally to adopt avoidance behaviour. (Scovel, 1978: 139)

In the work of Bailey (1983), facilitating and debilitating anxiety are closely bound up with the self-image of language learners and the characteristic termed by Bailey as 'competitiveness'. This trait leads learners to compare themselves continually with others (or with an ideal self-image) and react emotively to such comparisons, wish to out-perform other learners and place great emphasis on tests, grades and teacher approval. They may experience anxiety in regard to language lessons if their competitiveness is founded on an unsuccessful self-image. Such anxiety *may* be facilitating if it prompts the learner to devote more effort to language learning; in turn, the self-image will be enhanced as learning outcomes are enhanced. Alternatively, the anxiety may lead the learner to withdraw from the learning situation, thus having a debilitating effect, in which learning outcomes are impaired and the original negative self-image reinforced (Bailey, 1983: 96).

What is apparent from more recent studies, however, is that it seems to be the more 'interpersonal' aspects of language learning, namely speaking and listening, that are the greatest source of anxiety among students. This point is made particularly strongly by Horwitz *et al.* (1986). With regard to fears concerning speaking and listening they highlight two different but related forms of anxiety. The chief characteristic of 'communication apprehension' is the frustration and apprehension of the learner who has well-developed thoughts and opinions but a limited second language vocabulary to express them. 'Fear of negative evaluation' refers to students' sense that they are unable to make a proper social impression because they are unsure of themselves and of what they are saying. Horwitz *et al.* (1986: 127) emphasise how many students fear the continual evaluation of 'the only fluent speaker in the class, the teacher' and may be 'acutely sensitive to the evaluation — real or imagined — of their peers'.

Other research into anxiety in general suggests that girls are particularly prone to worries about peer-group evaluation, as Knapman (1982) found in a study of secondary schools in South West England. The deleterious effects of such responses on language learning are highlighted by MacIntyre and Gardner (1989), who studied the effect of anxiety on students' ability to learn and retrieve items of vocabulary in the L2. They found that 'communicative anxiety' had a negative influence on students' ability to acquire and then to retrieve information. Gardner and MacIntyre (1993) hypothesise that the effect of anxiety on language learning may result from its negative influence on motivation and learning strategy use, both recognised as vital components of successful language learning. Furthermore, as Phillips (1992: 19) points out, it is not merely weaker students who suffer from the effects of anxiety; in her study of anxiety and oral test performance she found that the student of the highest ability demonstrated 'the most dramatic example of language, if not *nervous* breakdown' during an oral examination. Such students, although achieving highly, seem to do so at the expense of their emotional well-being, a consideration that needs to be taken into account in any investigation of the effect of anxiety on language learning outcomes. It must be remembered that the latter have an affective as well as a cognitive component.

The above underlines the importance that has generally been attached in the literature to the role of anxiety and self-esteem in language learning. Yet it is an area that has been neglected as far as investigations into British students' experiences is concerned, although some research has touched upon the question of anxiety in relation to younger secondary school learners (Harris & Frith, 1990; Grenfell & Harris, 1994). Yet personal teaching experience suggests it is a topic that deserves further examination. This seems to be especially true of A-level language study. One might assume that while the arrival of the communicative approach to language learning has enhanced the status of oral participation at all levels of language study, the linguistic (and perhaps conceptual) difficulty of the material discussed at A-level can cause high levels of anxiety — as indeed was suggested by the questionnaire data discussed in Chapter 2. Frustration and apprehension are likely if students are required to express complex and mature opinions without the linguistic competence to do so. The 'shock to the system' may be particularly great for those who have had little difficulty in language learning during the pre–16 stage. This may affect levels of motivation and enjoyment of language study, factors considered by the author to be of as much importance in the move from GCSE to A-level as more cognitively-based problems such as difficulties with grammatical structures.

Attitudes and Motivation

Researchers have frequently underlined the importance of motivation in learning a foreign language. Lennon (1993: 41), in his discussion of advanced German learners of English studying at the University of Reading, England, calls it 'the most important single factor influencing continuing development in oral proficiency'. As such, it has been the subject of numerous studies. Nevertheless, the issues surrounding it and its importance for SLA theory are still the subjects of debate.

A useful starting point is offered by Gardner's (1985: 147) definition of motivation. He describes it as 'the effort, want (desire) and affect associated with learning a second language'. The 'desire' element is closely associated by Gardner with the goals learners seek to achieve through language learning, and much of his work, and indeed that of other researchers interested in motivation in foreign language learning, has concentrated on this factor, which is more usually known as the orientation of the learner's motivation. Gardner has suggested that this can take one of two forms, an integrative or an instrumental orientation. In the former, the language is learnt because of a desire to identify with and move closer to the community where the language is spoken; in the latter, the language is viewed as a means to other ends, such as career enhancement or educational goals, rather than as an end in itself. It is furthermore claimed that an integrative orientation will be more lasting and more closely linked to achievement than an instrumental one, being an internal and enduring part of the learner's personality. Instrumentally motivated learners seem to be more influenced by external factors such as rewards, which, it is supposed, are less constant.

The question is not, however, as clear-cut as might be assumed. As Au (1988) and others point out, contradictory results, ranging from positive, negative and non-existent relationships between integrative motivation and proficiency, have arisen from studies in different learning contexts. Gardner and Lambert (1972) for example did find that in Montreal (a bilingual community) an integrative orientation in learning French was a stronger predictor of success. In the Philippines, however, an instrumental orientation seemed to be more important for those learning English. This second result is not totally unexpected and one would anticipate finding similar patterns in any country where contact with English-speaking countries is an important part of the economy; indeed, a study in India (Lukmani, 1972) emphasised the importance of an instrumental orientation in the learning of English. Additionally, other researchers in different contexts have questioned the importance attached to integrative motivation; for example, Burstall *et al.* (1974) found that for secondary pupils learning a foreign language in British schools both an instrumental and integrative orientation played a part in success. The complexity of the situation is such that Gardner (1988) no longer asserts that integrative motivation is necessarily more beneficial than other forms; instead he argues more modestly that integratively motivated students are likely to be better language learners than ones without this form of motivation.

Leaving for a moment the question of motivational orientation and turning instead to another component in Gardner's (1985: 147) definition of motivation, 'affect', it seems pertinent to relate this to some of the factors considered previously: risk-taking, self-esteem and anxiety. Indeed, in the study mentioned earlier, Beebe (1983) points to a link between risk-taking and motivation. Quoting Curran's (1976) view of language learning as a five-stage growth process, he suggests that difficulties may arise as learners are asked to move to a more autonomous, less teacher-dependent use of language, as they see this as a 'high risk–low gain' situation — as their communicative needs have already been fulfilled they have little to gain but much to lose in terms of self-esteem if failure is met. Thus, according to Beebe, 'learners experience a crisis in motivation because they evaluate the situation as a bad gamble' (Beebe, 1983: 45). This may go some way to explain the lack of progression which seems to occur in some A-level learners.

Another contributing factor to levels of motivation may be the way in which learners attribute causes to their success or failure. The central aspect of Attribution Theory maintains that people tend to explain their performance either in terms of their ability, the difficulty of the task, the effort they exert, or to luck, and that they are stable in the causes they attribute. Those more likely to choose ability or task difficulty tend to have lower levels of motivation, as these factors are considered to be unalterable, beyond the control of the learner and thus effort spent trying to modify them would be wasted. On the other hand, attributing success or failure to effort may lead to greater motivation, as it is within the powers of individuals to control their level of exertion. Again, this issue will feature in the discussion of anxiety and motivation among advanced language learners.

Yet the whole question of the relationship between success and failure on the one hand and motivation on the other is a controversial one. Which causes which? Numerous researchers have documented the strong positive correlation between motivation and achievement. For example, Gardner (1985) claims that together motivation and aptitude account for a large part of the variance of achievement in language learning.

On the other hand, evidence suggesting that, in fact, success fosters motivation, has been equally convincing. Studying British learners of French in the early years of secondary school Burstall *et al.* (1974) found higher correlation figures between the achievement of first-year pupils and their motivation levels in the second than between first-year motivation and second-year achievement, leading to the conclusion that achievement heightens motivation.

It may be argued that the lack of clarity surrounding the issue of motivation in foreign language learning research stems in part from notions of motivation that are questionable 'in terms of their distance from everyday, nontechnical concepts of what it means to be motivated', to borrow the words of Crookes and Schmidt (1991: 480). They suggest that foreign language research can gain much by drawing on definitions and discussions of motivation from the wider fields of education and psychology, rather than seeking to establish a form somehow unique to foreign language learners. Indeed, some writers in the foreign language field have gone some way in this direction. Moving away from the integrative/instrumental dichotomy, Dickinson (1987) refers to 'extrinsic' and 'intrinsic' motivation', which he sees as directly related to the degree of autonomy and self-direction which students may exercise in the learning situation. Similarly, a poor understanding of the objectives involved in the learning process may reduce the will to succeed (Dickinson, 1987). This may also be true if learners' objectives seem to be in conflict with the teacher's; attitudes to the learning situation may be negatively influenced and motivation severely impaired if learners are not able to pursue what Allwright (1984) calls a 'personal agenda' for language learning.

Such views are arguably closer to a more traditional educational and psychological notion of motivation than such concepts as orientation. The former is discussed in depth by Crookes and Schmidt, who cite Keller's (1983) definition of motivation:

> Motivation refers to the choices people make as to what experiences or goals they will approach or avoid, and the degree of effort they will exert in this respect. (Keller, 1983: 389, in Crookes & Schmidt, 1990: 481)

The final aspect of this seems to be of particular importance and, as Crookes and Schmidt underline, students' active (or otherwise) engagement in learning probably has greater relevance in the eyes of teachers than their reasons for studying the subject. Furthermore, Keller identifies four determinants of motivation which seem pertinent to the question of how students approach the task of making the transition from GCSE to A-level work. These are the degree of interest students have in the learning situation, the perceived relevance of the learning activities to their needs and aspirations (cf. Allwright's (1984) 'personal agenda'), expectations and attributions regarding success or failure, and outcomes, in terms of the rewards or punishments deemed to result from the learning experience.

In the present study, it was felt important to consider motivation not only from the particular perspective of second language acquisition research, but also from the more general standpoint just discussed. As such, the first student interview and learner diaries were designed to explore not only students' reasons for choosing to study a language to A-level, but also how some of the motivational factors discussed in the previous paragraphs relate to the learning of a foreign language, in terms of persistence and active involvement with the learning task.

Gender

Of all the factors held to influence outcomes in language learning, gender is the one to which the least attention has been paid. Indeed, there is so little research in this field that many of the observations made in this section will draw on learning theory in general rather than on findings made in the area of foreign language learning. Further comments on gender and learning strategies can be found in Chapter 3.

First of all, it is necessary to state what we mean by gender. Powell (1986b), following Delamont (1980), suggests using the term sex to refer to innate biological differences between males and females, reserving gender for those differences which seem to be more socially produced. This distinction seems to be warranted if one takes into consideration the opinion that gender-related differences in language learning ability are caused by social and environmental factors rather than being inborn. Such a view is of course open to question; yet a review of research into the matter suggests that innate differences are non-existent or at best insignificant (Powell, 1986b; Loulidi, 1990). The phenomenon witnessed by the majority of teachers and in part supported by empirical research (e.g. Burstall et al., 1974; Carroll, 1975, Assessment of Performance Unit, 1985), namely the higher incidence of successful linguists among girls, must therefore be attributed to such factors as socialisation, attitudes and stereotyping.

Motivation seems to be of prime importance here and, as was discussed in the last section, this is in part influenced by attitudes to the target language and its culture as well as to the learning situation in general. While there is some evidence to suggest that girls are less ethnocentric than boys and thus tend to have more positive attitudes towards foreign cultures (e.g. Burstall et al., 1974), the most important factor seems to be attitudes towards the concept of learning a foreign language. The 1985 Assessment of Performance Unit (APU) report found that 13-year old girls studying French in England were generally more positive than boys in their attitudes regarding the usefulness, enjoyment, difficulty and opportunity to make contact with native speakers associated with the subject. Byram and Esarte-Sarries (1991) likewise report that in a similar population girls expressed more enjoyment of French than boys did. It has been suggested, however, that certain attitudes are related to gender-stereotyping, with pupils conforming to the notion that some subjects are more appropriate to their sex than others (Sutherland, 1981). Certain studies such as that of Weinreich-Haste (1981) point to the distinctly feminine image associated with foreign languages, in Britain at least. Hingley (1983) suggests that there exists a myth among school children that foreign languages are easy, or soft, best left to girls, who are good at producing neat written work. Elsewhere it is argued that among British university students sciences tend to be regarded as 'hard', 'relevant' and 'useful' (Thomas, 1990) and thus more worthy of study by males than language-based subjects. There is some indication that such attitudes are less pronounced in single-sex establishments (e.g. Dale, 1974; Omerod, 1975), where there is less opportunity for gender-based judgements about school subjects to be made. In general, however, an instrumental orientation appears to be central to the motivation of boys (Thomas, 1990); in a community where such subjects as science are seen as most relevant to career prospects, it is arguable that they will be disinclined to do well in foreign languages. Carroll (1975) found that gender differences in language learning in favour of girls were most marked in English-speaking countries, suggesting that where speaking a foreign language is vital for career advancement, as is the case in such countries as Germany, its high status makes it equally, if not more, appealing to boys. More recent research, however, indicates that the situation is changing somewhat. Reporting on research conducted in secondary schools in southern England, Filmer-Sankey (1993) comments that while by the age of 13–14, girls are more positive about the usefulness and enjoyment involved in learning a foreign language and in their attitude to the foreign country, the differences between the two sexes are small. Likewise, Kenning (1992) found no differences in boys' and girls' attitudes in the secondary pupils she investigated. There may well be some truth in her suggestion that the advent of greater European unity, with the creation of a single market through the removal of trade barriers in 1993, has improved the image of foreign languages in boys' eyes, increasing their 'pay-off value' (Burstall et al., 1974).

Other factors that may possibly account for girls' apparent superiority in language learning (at some levels) are associated with the behaviour that socialisation processes or stereotyping have instilled in many females. It is frequently noted that girls are generally encouraged to be more conscientious than boys (Hingley, 1983), perhaps giving them an advantage in written work and formal language use. Oxford *et al.* (1988) associate the greater use of form-based learning strategies that they noted in females with their stronger concern for good marks and social approval. This is discussed in greater detail in Chapter 3, with supporting evidence from my own investigation regarding a more careful, planned approach to language learning on the part of females. Oral skills may be aided by females' greater interest in human contact and social interaction as outlined in such works as Maccoby and Jacklin (1974). Related to this are the findings of Gass and Varonis (1986), who examined the conversations of mixed and single-sex adult Japanese students of English. The researchers report that the greatest amount of negotiation of meaning occurred in the mixed sex pairs, with females most ready to negotiate. In three-quarters of the mixed sex pairs, males dominated in the amount of language they produced. Batters (1988) makes similar observations about male learners of French in English schools in the 13–14 years age group, reporting that they claimed to prefer learning the foreign language by speaking it, in contrast to girls, who favoured listening to it. These findings are also in line with those made in the general literature of gender differences (Berryman, 1980). One might venture to apply generally the interpretation offered by Gass and Varonis for this phenomenon, namely that males appear to progress by greater involvement in comprehensible output (i.e. practice), but females benefit from greater exposure to comprehensible input. This echoes the assessment made in Chapter 3 regarding females' interpersonal skills.

It is also possible, however, that these characteristics may give boys the advantage over girls in language learning. Holmes (1991: 215) suggests that the male desire to 'compete for the floor' in oral work can mean that girls receive 'less than their fair share of conversational encouragement'. This may be of particular importance in A-level language studies, where oral debate seems to play such a large role in class work. Similarly, where boys do decide to continue with foreign languages to an advanced level, other gender-related characteristics may make them more successful than girls, rather than less. Statistics produced by the external examining boards show that a higher proportion of male A-level candidates than females gain top grades. One characteristic might be related to the question of Attribution Theory, discussed earlier. Researchers have found that girls are more likely than boys to attribute success/failure to ability rather than to effort (e.g. Dweck & Bush, 1976; Nicholls, 1975, cited in Licht & Dweck, 1983), which may have an adverse effect on their motivation and subsequent perform-ance when the prospect of difficulty and failure is encountered, particularly in the face of new learning tasks. Ironically, highly achieving girls are the most likely to attribute their difficulties to insufficient ability, the least likely to attribute success to their own ability, instead seeing it as the result of chance (Licht & Shapiro, 1982). They tend to disregard past achievements and in general their expectation of success on new cognitive tasks is negatively related to the levels of academic achievement they have reached in the past (Stipek & Hoffman, 1980, cited in Licht and Dweck, 1983). Only fairly recent evidence of their capabilities seems able to convince them of their academic talents (Dweck *et al.*, 1980); at the beginning of a new school year, for example, they may discount their success in the term preceding the summer holidays. Perhaps this is the case for those embarking on a new A-level course, who dismiss their performance at GCSE. Licht and Dweck (1983) suggest that highly achieving girls set themselves such high standards that they rarely see themselves as successful:

> Even though they may seem highly successful by most objective standards, they may be experiencing considerable failure when they judge themselves against their own criteria. (Licht & Dweck, 1983: 92)

It is also possible that even when difficulties are experienced, boys are less willing to admit to these or to discuss them with others — as suggested at the end of Chapter 2. This element of bravado may be attributable to what MacDonald (1980: 38) calls 'notions of appropriate behaviour for each sex'.

There is the problem, however, that these views are in conflict with findings suggesting that girls employ a wider range of learning strategies than boys; learners who tend to attribute success to luck and failure to their own inadequacies should, in theory, be less inclined to believe that they can control their own performance by specific learning techniques. One explanation may lie in the greater anxiety and lower self-esteem associated in the literature with girls. Bacon's (1992) study of listening comprehension strategies indicates, for example, that males are more confident than females in their ability to tackle an aural passage. Referring to learning in general Sutherland (1983) speculates that higher anxiety levels in girls may be caused by their apparent greater need for approval. She suggests, in line with Scovel (1978), that how learners cope with anxiety determines whether it will be of the debilitating or facilitating kind. She proposes four combinations of learner and affect: high ability learners/high anxiety; low ability/high anxiety; high ability/low anxiety; low ability/low anxiety. It is possible that these categories are differentiated both by the gender of the learner and by their use of learning strategies, with a high proportion of high ability/ high anxiety learners being female, who employ a large number of learning strategies (but not always effectively) as a result of their anxiousness to do well academically. Again this is an area discussed later in the chapter.

Related to anxiety is the question of risk-taking; it has been suggested that the good language learner is prepared to take chances, to appear foolish in order to progress in language proficiency. Here again, if this is the case, then boys would appear to have an advantage over girls, in that most research points to the fact that males are more likely to take risks than females (Wallach & Kogan, 1959) and to thrive on competition (Maccoby & Jacklin, 1974). Spender (1982) suggests that the higher level of self-confidence and willingness to speak out among boys in all subject areas may be attributable in part to the greater attention they tend to receive from their teacher in class. Indeed, Chapter 3 indicated that in several areas, the male A-level students involved in this project showed more signs of risk-taking behaviour than their female classmates. The following discussion takes a closer look at the effect this degree of self-confidence (or lack of it) has on A-level students' attitudes to language learning.

Key Findings

A-level language learners: anxiety, self-esteem and the question of gender

The findings of the research project support many of the previous arguments relating to the higher level of anxiety among female A-level language learners. Evidence appeared first of all in the student question-naire, where, in Sections C/D, learners were invited to tick two statements if they felt they referred to their own difficulties:

Item 27. Keeping up with the others in the group.
Item 28. Working without worrying.

Space for students to write additional comments on these statements was also provided.

Significantly more females (23%) than males (13%) indicated that they were having difficulty in keeping up with other students in their class, suggesting low self-esteem (see Appendix E3, Tables E3.1–E3.4). The difference was still greater as far as the ability to work without worrying was concerned (female 34%, male 19%). While it may be argued that the total percentage of students experiencing elements of anxiety and poor self-esteem is relatively low, the figures for female students indicate that it is a problem that affects a sizeable proportion of this group of A-level language learners. Furthermore, comments added by some respondents indicated the anxiety that they experienced was acutely felt, particularly in the case of female students. In some there was a marked tendency to compare themselves negatively with others, as for the girl who remarked:

I feel a lot of people have a much larger understanding of the language. I don't have much confidence in mine.

Another seemed to be measuring herself against some ideal standard:

I do worry a lot that I am not good enough for A-level.

By contrast, very few male students gave further details about the form their anxiety took, merely indicating by a tick that they had problems in keeping up with others and working without worrying. This seems to suggest a degree of reticence regarding emotional concerns which was noted elsewhere in the investigation (see later and Chapter 2).

The main instrument for probing the nature and influence of anxiety and self-esteem, however, was the retrospective interview, where the 24 students were asked about any worries they had concerning their work in general, about oral participation in class and about how they dealt with such worries. Additional information came from the learner diaries, where as well as reporting on the learning strategies they had employed during various language tasks, students were asked to comment on how they felt after the activity.

The written transcriptions of each interview were scrutinised and comments relating to affective concerns noted. The number of students expressing various forms of anxiety was recorded. The learner diaries were similarly examined for further evidence of anxiety, as well as any possible change in students' affective responses over time.

The interview confirmed that high anxiety and low self-esteem were problems chiefly concerning female students. When asked about any worries they had concerning A-level language work in general, and in particular speaking out in class, only five of the twelve boys expressed any degree of anxiety. Moreover, in most cases the anxiety was felt to be no more than mild. All of the girls, however, reported worrying about some aspect of their A-level language work and in many instances the anxiety expressed appeared to be strong and deep-rooted. There was also an interesting difference in the vocabulary used by the two sexes in diary entries, when they were writing about affective concerns under the heading 'How do I feel?'. While girls freely used such terms as 'worried', 'demoralised' or 'unconfident' if they had had difficulties with their work or received a bad mark, boys were far more likely to describe themselves as 'annoyed' or 'disappointed'. This may well be an indication of stereotypical male/female attributes being enacted, with boys being unwilling to admit to anxiety, even if it is experienced, out of a concern perhaps for what this might imply about their masculinity (cf. similar comments by Kelly (1985) regarding boys' responses to difficulties in science). Thus the figures for male anxiety reported here may be underestimated.

In the following analysis, quotations have been taken verbatim from the interviews with students and from their learner diaries, denoted by (I) and (D) respectively.

The largest number of comments made referred to anxieties about oral work and in particular to whole-class oral work. This trait was exhibited by 14 out of the 24 students, but again it may be seen as a predominantly female concern. Only four boys expressed any apprehension or discomfort about speaking in front of the class, a result which challenges claims about boys' reluctance to speak out in the public arena of the classroom (Powell & Littlewood, 1982). The concerns mentioned relate closely to the 'language anxiety' (Horwitz *et al.*, 1986) discussed earlier. For most comments on group oral work, however, it is difficult to differentiate between 'communication apprehension' and 'fear of negative evaluation' (Horwitz *et al.*, 1986). The former, at least with regard to speaking in front of the class as a whole, was usually inextricably linked with a sense of being exposed to the judgement of others to a certain degree, particularly for girls. Such anxiety arose frequently in situations where students were required to answer rapidly and spontaneously. While for some, the change from a class of 30 at GCSE level to a much smaller group at A-level gave them more confidence in this respect, for others it meant increased pressure to speak and to be judged by others. Similarly, while some students were able to achieve a high level of oral proficiency despite their anxiety, for others it had very strong inhibiting effect. The unease experienced in such situations ranged from mild embarrassment and feeling slightly under pressure in the case of two boys, to a total inability to answer in the case of certain girls. The sense of panic experienced by some is well conveyed by the words of the following female student:

> It's like your turn to say something, and you don't think you know it, and you go, 'Euh' and you just . . . your mind's just like completely blank cos you're worried you're going to get it wrong and because you're worrying about that you're going to forget what the blinking words are, you just think, 'Oh, I don't know what to say at all! (I, F)

This student was an effective one, but it is arguable that for many students excessive anxiety before speaking might have a detrimental effect on performance in the long run, if it means that students come to avoid speaking out at all in such situations. Other students admitted to anxiously awaiting their turn to speak, mentally rehearsing what they were going to say. This strategy was used more frequently by girls than by boys, as was avoidance of oral participation.

Negative evaluation in oral work was anticipated from a number of directions. Three female students spoke of their fear of appearing foolish when speaking to the language assistant, where the 'inadequacies' of their linguistic performance might be all too evident in comparison with a native speaker. One student felt anxious during conversation classes because of her uncertainty as to how the native speaker would react to errors, possibly being less tolerant of them than her teacher. For two others, their fears revolved around their perceived inadequacies in the language, from the point of view of accent, grammatical accuracy, or the inability to express complex opinions in the foreign language. One of these described in an early diary entry how she felt when talking to her school's two language assistantes:

> I am still not happy with my pronunciation! In fact I am a little embarrassed of it when speaking in front of the French students. (D, F)

She later elaborated on the reasons behind her embarrassment, suggesting a concern that her oral performance might somehow reflect on how she was viewed as a person, rather than merely on her linguistic competence:

> I just can't pronounce very well and I feel strange like in front of a native speaker, I feel like really stupid sometimes. (I, F)

Anticipated negative evaluation from classmates and from the teacher was also a cause for concern, although in the case of the latter to a much lesser degree. One girl, however, suggested that the criticism of her teacher was what she feared most, even though she admitted that such a fear was largely irrational. It is perhaps worth noting that in this instance the student was of very high ability orally, with her anxieties possibly stemming from a sense that she had to live up to an ideal that she had set herself. Indeed, other examples of similar anxieties suggest that a degree of perfectionism was at the core of many students' oral apprehension, as one girl conceded:

> A lot of people have got much more confidence and they can just sort of say it and not worry if it's wrong, whereas I like to try and get everything right. (I, F)

Furthermore, as suggested in part by this quotation, oral apprehension in a number of students (one male, five females) resulted from negative self-comparison with the other members of the class, indicating low self-esteem. This was particularly acute where other members of the class were perceived to be very fluent, speaking 'really authentic French', or to have spent a large amount of time in the L2 country. Three students in particular indicated that the risk of exposing their own inferiority through oral participation was too high, and that they generally responded to negative self-comparison by remaining silent whenever possible, with one wanting just 'to sit there and shut up'. Another felt that her oral confidence had improved slightly since she had changed language groups:

> My other French class, well, they seemed to be sort of extremely fluent, well, I'm better in this class because they're not . . . they don't seem to be quite so good, because the people in my other French class had lived in France and had French families, they did all speak it as second nature. (I, F)

In reality, however, the first group had included only one bilingual speaker, yet the student's sense of her own oral inferiority was strong enough to persuade her that she was the sole member of the class not to speak with native-like fluency. Moreover, while the growth in a student's confidence is to be welcomed, it is perhaps a less healthy sign if this is achieved not through an increased sense of her own worth but through a perceived diminution in that of others.

Indeed, in several of the classes involved in the project an element of antagonism was sensed between the quieter students and those who were more confident orally. This took a variety of forms and is a rare example of the type of anxiety mentioned by a small number of boys. In two schools, students (one male, two females) suggested that they were intimidated by peers who talked 'all the time', or felt frustrated by students who 'like giving their opinions and sort of don't let you get a word in edgeways', in the words of a male student. Conversely, in another school, two students (both male) who themselves did not experience any oral apprehension, expressed disappointment and almost annoyance with others who participated infrequently in class. Both emphasised the importance of oral communication for improving their French performance generally and they felt that the silence of others inhibited this.

Furthermore, anxieties caused by perceived differences in oral ability were not restricted to those students who saw themselves as being less able. Two female subjects expressed concern about the reaction of their classmates to the fact that they *were* orally proficient and keen to participate.

For one this took the form of embarrassment at the start of the year, 'because everyone actually listens to you', 'as if they were thinking, 'Gosh, she knows so much!'' (I, F); for the other, the fear of appearing to be showing off was an inhibiting factor. These findings confirm those of Whyte (1984), investigating male and female behaviour in science lessons. There may be an element of social expectations here, in the sense of it being less desirable or acceptable for girls to be talkative (cf. Spender, 1980; LaFrance, 1991); one male teacher commented that a very able female student was 'very forthright, probably too willing to contribute her own ideas', in so far as her participation seemed to make other class members all the more aware of their comparative inferiority. On the other hand, two boys in another school had no qualms about being seen as eager to speak out in class, one summing up the feelings of both by claiming in a self-assured way that 'most of my friends just say I'm pretty over-confident anyway!' (I, M). Thus for these males loquacity was perceived rather as a positive attribute.

It is further clear that group dynamics play an important role in the development of oral proficiency and that where the aims and feelings of different sections of the class are in conflict with one another inhibitions and anxieties may arise. The key factor seems to be a fear of appearing different in some way from one's classmates, because of one's perceived weaknesses or indeed strengths in the oral domain. Moreover, this sense of 'uniqueness' in oral work can be seen as a peculiarly female characteristic, an area which will be expanded upon in the following section. Males on the other hand were more inclined to perceive that they and their classmates were faced with a similar situation, as suggested by the following:

> I think, to be honest, generally if you're speaking in front of a class someone else is doing it as well and they will have a go and I think . . . generally, you've got class support. (I, M)

It is likely that this sense of solidarity is an important factor in developing the risk-taking characteristics which in the past have been associated with the proficient linguist (e.g. Ely, 1986), at least as far as oral work is concerned.

Anxiety was not, however, limited to oral work and some students expressed concerns about their language work as a whole. A general belief in one's own abilities seems vital in language learning at this stage. It may not be possible to identify any direct correlation between low global self-esteem and the performance of A-level students, but one can surmise that greater self-confidence might make the experience of moving to A-level less traumatic. Moreover, worries concerning one's general progress in the language were chiefly expressed at the interview stage by girls

(ten), as opposed to three boys. Several aspects of Bailey's (1983) description of the competitive language learner can be seen in the responses of the
girls and one boy, including overt self-comparison with other learners, an
emphasis on or concern with tests or grades and a desire to gain the
teacher's approval. Chief among these was again the tendency towards
negative self-comparison and the most deeply felt worry was of finding
something difficult that all others appeared to tackle with ease. Once more,
this characteristic was a predominantly female one, with boys much more
likely to state that they did not worry about their work because other
students were finding it just as difficult. The girls were apparently much
less able to assess the situation objectively and indeed some of the ablest
students were the most lacking in self-confidence.

A reluctance to appreciate their achievements was voiced by those who
feared being unable to cope with the work as it got harder, even though
they might have just completed a similar task successfully. Thus one girl,
after managing to read a short story, wrote that she felt 'nervous about
future literature and that I won't be able to do it' (D, F).

In addition to judging themselves negatively against others, female
students again indicated in their comments that they were prone to
perfectionism and the setting of over-high standards (cf. Licht & Dweck,
1983), this time as regards their overall performance and not just oral
abilities. The remarks of at least four female students suggest that this was
the root of their anxiety. For three students, this applied to all aspects of
their school work, with one explaining:

It's basically worrying that it's not going to be good enough, or I'm not
going to finish it, or I'm not going to get it correct enough, I'm not going
to get a high enough answer. (I, F)

Here the repetition of 'enough' has echoes of Bailey's (1983) concept of
competitiveness with an idealised self-image.

This suggests that general anxieties, like those associated with oral work,
stem from self-esteem which is either permanently low or fragile in the face
of perceived difficulties. Indeed, the interview data lent support to the view
of Parsons et al., (1976) that in the face of new and difficult tasks girls
underrate their performance, even when they are more successful than
boys, in so far as in the present study they seemed to judge themselves
much more harshly than their male counterparts did. In several cases, the
girls had, in the words of one, a 'complex about not being good enough' to
be taking a language at A-level, as if they were discounting any past
successes (cf. Dweck et al., 1980). Not only did girls express more doubt
about their ability to cope with A-level work, they were also less likely to

give high ability or previous success in the language as a reason for continuing with the subject. While six boys referred to this factor, it was mentioned by only three girls, and in two of those cases in an indirect, diffident manner.

Coping with anxiety: students' strategies

In Chapter 3 the strategies used by effective students in processing language were reported and lessons for other students drawn from these. It was hoped that in the area of affective concerns similar observations could be made. The following paragraphs, however, illustrate how strategies by learners for dealing with their anxiety and low self-esteem were rarely of a positive nature, if they occurred at all. This underlines the need for teachers to confront the issue and to help learners take steps to counteract what research suggests can have an inhibiting influence on language learning.

The first point to be made concerns the unwillingness of the boys in the study to discuss emotional concerns during the interview or in their diary entries (cf. Tannen, 1987). As suggested throughout, this may be largely due to an overriding need to maintain a confident image in one's own eyes and in the eyes of others (cf. Deaux & Farris, 1977). It is also possible that, reiterating an earlier argument, boys were better able to conclude that they were not alone in finding certain aspects of their work problematic, and to use comparison with others as a reassurance rather than as a source of further anxiety, as was the case for several girls.

By contrast, the chief 'strategy' used by girls for coping with anxiety emerged as what was termed 'perseverance': rather than seeking to change their affective responses to problems encountered, they responded by simply trying harder.

Such perseverance appears to be related to risk-taking in oral work; whereas boys tended to refer to overcoming any apprehensions about speaking in front of others by simply putting worries out of their mind, for girls it was more of a question of *forcing* themselves to do something they disliked. For some, this involved mentally shutting out the presence of others, sometimes in a rather negative fashion which seems remote from 'communication':

> If I'm having a really bad day and no self-confidence, I just sit there and I won't say anything, but there's other days I can, when I think, 'Who cares about them? I want to learn, so, forget them!' I don't even look at them, look straight at the teacher, and think, 'Oh forget you, I was going to say it anyway.' (I, F)

This quotation highlights another strategy employed by several females (half of the sample), that of avoidance. Whereas anxieties about general language work did not usually incite students to 'flee' the source of worry, the opposite would appear to be true of oral work, possibly resulting in many missing opportunities to practise speaking the L2.

Some affective strategies were, however, of a more positive nature, particular self-encouragement/self-talk. As previously mentioned, this was especially true in the case of the learner diaries, where success was often perceived by students and confidence thus enhanced. Within the framework of the interview, however, the self-encouragement strategies reported by female students were generally more of the self-talk kind. One girl, for example, who felt nervous in tests, reported trying to 'kind of think, 'You know this, but . . . '. Yet her hesitancy suggests that such self-encouragement was somewhat short-lived, perhaps because of an underlying lack of self-esteem, fairly resistant to change. It may be that in order for affective strategies to be fully beneficial in easing anxiety, they need to be implemented in a more systematic manner, perhaps in the form suggested by the learner diaries, where learners regularly self-assess and reflect on what they have achieved (see later).

Motivation

As outlined earlier, both the goal-directed, attitudinal approach to motivation largely peculiar to second language acquisition theory, and the more educationally-oriented effort/persistence angle were adopted in the examination of the role of motivation in A-level language learning.

Reasons for studying a language at A-level

Many students cited several reasons for pursuing a language beyond the age of 16, but few were able to say which of their reasons was the most important. Thus the totals given for each reason add up to more than 24.

The chief factor cited was enjoyment (nine males, ten females), with a sub-group (five males, four females) specifically mentioning communicating in the foreign language as the aspect they enjoyed the most, which suggests elements of integrative orientation. This is true also of the students within the 19 (three males, three females) who said that their enjoyment of the subject stemmed from an interest in the culture of the L2 country or a desire to visit it. Thus there is little evidence to suggest more favourable attitudes towards the L2 community on the part of females in this study. Indeed, the 'integrative' balance was tipped very slightly in the direction of males. On the other hand, interest in the language as a language *per se* was more common among girls (although the numbers involved are small), with three girls and one boy citing this reason.

Similarly, there was little indication that boys were more instrumentally oriented, as might be supposed from a review of the literature. Indeed, girls mentioning further education and job prospects outnumbered boys by seven to four. Many comments indicated an awareness of the usefulness of language learning with regard to the European Community.

A few students (five males, two females) thought that foreign languages were particularly 'feminine' subjects, while none felt that this consideration had influenced their decision to study languages at A-level. Interestingly, these seven students all attended mixed schools, reinforcing the arguments cited earlier that certain stereotypes are more evident in co-educational establishments.

Regarding the causality factor, that is, whether achievement precedes or follows positive attitudes to language study, there is some suggestion that the former was true for this sample, in so far as a group of students (six males, three females) referred to ability in the subject as an incentive to study it further. An additional two (both female) cited the ease or familiarity of the language. One boy underlined the link between success and positive attitudes in this direction when asked what he would have done had he been unable to study languages:

> I'd have been in a bit of trouble . . . I wouldn't be happy doing anything else at A-level, because I just wouldn't be able to achieve. (I, M)

Other, less frequently mentioned reasons for studying the language included parents' ability in or experience of the language (one male, one female), and having no other choice because of how option groups were arranged (two males). It might be supposed that such reasons are rather weak incentives for language study and that this would be reflected in the degree of effort exerted by the students. If effort is viewed as the extent to which the student is 'productively engaged in learning tasks, and sustains that engagement, *without the need for continual encouragement or direction'* (Crookes & Schmidt, 1991: 480, emphasis added), then engagement manifested itself in the interview in the shape of references to learning activities undertaken off the student's own bat, over and above those prescribed by the teacher. In the case of one of the students referred to earlier, who claimed that his main reason for studying French was because his mother was 'quite good at the French language', there was no evidence of any such additional activities. Similarly, one of the students who said he had really wanted to study English rather than German expressed a disinclination towards work over and above that set, even though he acknowledged that this might be helpful to his progress.

Other interactions between reasons for studying the language and effort expended are less easily traceable. For example, a male student who expressed enjoyment of the subject and a strong desire to communicate with native speakers at the same time described himself as lazy and claimed that 'there's a couple of days in the week where I do put the extra work in and the rest I just cannot be bothered with' (I, M).

Thus it is difficult to draw any firm conclusions from the data concerning goal orientation and the effect that this might have on effort. Nor does it seem possible to trace a connection between orientation and achievement. Weak and strong students alike were evenly distributed among the different forms of goal orientation. It might be argued that such relationships are in any case difficult to determine from largely qualitative data and that it is more profitable to describe rather than to analyse. Two of the research areas suggested by Crookes and Schmidt's (1991) re-examination of the motivation 'agenda' involve the description of different kinds of motivation, in addition to the usual 'integrative/instrumental' paradigm. The patterns that emerge from the interview and diary data do allow for such descriptions, which in turn may suggest learning and teaching strategies beneficial to easing the transition to A-level language work.

Further aspects of motivation

In the light of these comments it was deemed appropriate to examine the information gathered from students first of all for evidence of motivational determinants that have been identified in education-oriented theories. As stated previously, those suggested by Keller (1983) and reported by Crookes and Schmidt (1991) were anticipated to be of particular relevance to A-level language learning. This supposition is largely borne out by the interview and diary data. *Interest* was a motivating or demotivating factor for over half the students (seven males, six females). Male students, however, were more likely than females to highlight boredom as a demotivating factor, with four (as opposed to one girl) referring either in their interview or diary to aspects of their work that they found uninteresting. These included literary work, learning vocabulary and studying grammar. This may be a reflection of boys' preference for tasks that involve their active participation rather than more contemplative ones (cf. the findings of Batters, 1988, Rees & Batters, 1988 among younger learners). One boy appeared to have a particularly low boredom threshold, mentioning his disinclination to work in such circumstances on four separate occasions during his interview. Girls, on the other hand, tended to point out the interesting aspects of their course and how this encouraged them to learn. This was particularly the case in schools where A-level topics proper had been embarked upon at the time of the interview, rather than postponing them until after a firm grammar base had been established — perhaps an indication that grammar must be carefully integrated with more stimulating work if students' motivation is to be sustained in the early months of the course.

For a group of boys and girls interest in and curiosity about a subject was sufficient motivation to spur them on to overcome difficulties they might experience with a certain task. Two students who reported difficulty in reading German texts nevertheless persevered with their literature work because of the enjoyment it gave them. Furthermore, they seem to have regarded the completion of the text as a challenge, which corresponds to Keller's (1983) *relevance* factor, as discussed in Crookes and Schmidt (1991: 488). Relevance refers not only to what students feel they need to learn, that is, 'instrumental needs', but also to 'personal-motive needs' (cited in Crookes & Schmidt, 1991), such as the need to achieve. The importance of such a factor in spurring learners on to repeat their efforts may be seen most clearly in the learner diaries, where the majority of students (20) expressed satisfaction in having accomplished something worthwhile. As Crookes and Schmidt point out, motivation is strongest when learners perceive their ability to be equal to the challenge, and both as comparatively high. This is illustrated by students who emphasised their appreciation of being 'stretched', such as the boy who noted the following in his diary concerning a listening exercise:

> I feel that as a genuine news article this was challenging and thus more enjoyable to work on and finally conquer. (D, M)

Where ability is felt to be unequal to the challenge, not only anxiety but also demotivation can result, as in the case of a male student who recorded in his diary difficulties in making notes on a literary text:

> [I feel] . . . a bit discouraged — as it takes a long time and is hard to understand — find it boring and not looking forward to next one. (D, M)

For other students, however, there appeared to be a mismatch between their perceptions of their ability and task difficulty in the opposite direction, where activities were felt to be irrelevant because they were too easy. The end result was again decreased motivation. Three students (two males, one female) expressed this form of frustration in their diary entries, one with reference to a reading comprehension, two to grammatical explanations and exercises. While it is recognised that in such instances teachers may be dealing with areas that for the majority *are* a challenge, it also seems important to incorporate a degree of differentiation into all tasks, so that all students feel that their learning needs are being satisfied.

This applies also to the other interpretation of relevance, where motivation depends on students sensing that language activities correspond to what they feel they need to learn, and to the way in which they feel they should learn. Some students (four males, one female) gave the impression of having a definite 'personal agenda' (Allwright, 1984) and of experiencing frustration and a disinclination to work to their full capacity when this agenda was felt to be in conflict with the one imposed by the teacher. During the interview one boy commented to this effect:

> If I look at a task or an exercise, and get the feeling that it's a little bit pedantic in any way, that it's driving at something that either I know already, or it's being overemphasised, I find that really difficult to motivate myself for. (I, M)

Two female students, on the other hand, seemed to be very much aware of what the teacher's agenda was and to be eager to comply with it. Indeed, one felt she had crossed the transitional point to A-level work successfully precisely because of this, claiming that 'it's just a case of just getting on with the work, and doing what the teachers expect of you' (I, F). The gender differences noted here may possibly be attributable to socialisation influences, whereby compliance is encouraged in girls, and independence in boys (cf. Oxford *et al.*, 1988). Nevertheless, where pupil/teacher conflict does exist, the problem might well be resolved by greater communication between the two parties regarding students' perceptions of their learning needs and the purpose of tasks set.

Lack of communication may further be at the root of demotivation associated with *outcomes*, or rewards and punishments. While both the interview and learner diaries indicated that for the majority of students, a low mark was an incentive to try harder, there was also the suggestion from some that this was true in some circumstances only. One determining factor appeared to be whether students understood why their mark was lower than they had expected, and whether teachers were consistent in their allocation of marks. Similarly, where increased effort was not acknowledged by the teacher, after initially trying harder to improve, students became frustrated and discouraged, as the following comment suggests:

> Everyone seems to improve, and the mark doesn't go up, and it's starting to annoy everyone . . . if it carries on much longer everyone's going to . . . like just not bother at all. (I, F)

Inevitably, teachers face the dilemma in assessing work as to whether to grade it according to the absolute standards of A-level, or relatively against students' earlier efforts. This suggests, however, that the latter can play an important role in motivating students.

At the same time, difficulties may stem from the fact that some students are too reliant on external motivations. Certain students (one male, three females) claimed that they needed the pressure of tests to motivate them to work; for two others (both male) the admonishments of teachers or parents were required. As Crookes and Schmidt (1991: 489) suggest, the effects of external evaluation tend to be short-lived and may inhibit the formation of more intrinsic goals. Control over one's own learning appears to be a vital component of motivation and has associations with Keller's third determinant of motivation, *expectancy*. This has been touched upon already in the discussion of anxiety, gender and students' attributions concerning success or failure. Where it is possible to perceive a link between the learning strategies one employs and learning outcomes, the locus of control is an internal one and motivation levels tend to be higher. This stands in contrast to one male student who could see no way of overcoming his difficulties in literary comprehension and who seemed to feel that his problems were attributable to an external cause, that is, task difficulty (at the same time as claiming not to worry about his work). Avoidance of the task, rather than perseverance, was the end result:

> I'm not really sure what to do, I'm . . . I'm probably going to ask the teacher soon, but I mean, I can't just read it, because I don't understand it, and it's pointless really . . . I've got a book to read, I can't bring myself to do it, because it'd take me ages. (I, M)

Implications for the Classroom

One of the clearest messages to emerge from the research project is the need for teachers to address the issue of students' affective difficulties, given the extent of anxiety and low self-esteem among girls and the importance of positive motivation for all learners. It could be argued that as anxiety *may* have a positive as well as a negative effect in terms of spurring some learners on to be more diligent, we need not concern ourselves overly with students' affective problems in the early stages of A-level courses. Yet it seems likely, in the more interpersonal aspects of language learning at least, that these concerns have a more detrimental influence. Furthermore, easing the transition to A-level work is not merely a question of helping students to adjust on a cognitive level, but also of encouraging growth as a person and not just as a foreign language learner.

In addition, prevention would seem to be better than cure and might reduce the number of students who never get beyond the first few weeks of A-level work because they feel unable to cope with it.

Working towards equal opportunities

These questions are of importance not least because of the extent of the problem of anxiety among female students, who, in the UK at least, make up a large proportion of advanced language learners. Furthermore many of the findings in the research project regarding gender and affective factors can be viewed as depressing. They indicate that for all the efforts made in the field of education to counteract gender-stereotyping, such stereotypes are still being re-enacted by A-level students, with females apparently characterised by nervousness, low self-esteem and excessive conscientiousness, and boys unwilling or unable to show many signs of an emotional response to the learning situation. In addition, social expectations relating to gender seem to play a part in the extent to which males and females participate in class oral work, which in turn may influence their general level of language proficiency (Ely, 1986). Earlier in the chapter reference was made to a male teacher's rather negative view of an able female student's willingness to speak out; by contrast, some male students in the study regarded their verbosity as a positive characteristic in the eyes of their peers. From this it seems evident that there is a need for teachers to be more aware of the possibility that females are being restricted in their oral participation by the fears and social expectations just mentioned, and from this awareness to ensure that equal opportunities within oral work exist for both sexes. How this might be achieved is discussed in the following sections, where possible solutions to the affective difficulties in general are presented which take account of the question of gender differences.

General anxieties: the question of control

Running through the earlier discussion of affective factors is the sense that feeling in control of one's language learning is paramount in the development of a positive image regarding one's ability to achieve proficiency. It was suggested that those who attribute their learning difficulties to low ability, rather than to lack of or inappropriate effort (mainly females), not only suffer from low self-esteem but also feel paralysed in their ability to progress in their language learning. During the course of the research project it emerged that it is possible to give students a greater sense of being in control of their learning by increasing their awareness of the effect of the learning strategies they are employing and encouraging them to be generally more reflective about their language learning. Objective self-assessment is also important. All of these things can be achieved by the use of learner diaries as in the present study, where students recorded the learning strategies they had used on various tasks, what they felt they had achieved, the steps they were going to take next, and how they felt about the learning process. Many students' entries provided enlightening insights into their growth in confidence. Several learners (one male, six females), who had initially expressed anxiety about their work, reported in their diaries feeling less worried about their ability to cope with certain exercises after they had seen that they *could* in fact complete them successfully. One female student for example in the second term wrote of her progress in reading comprehension:

> [I feel] . . . Really pleased that I coped so well and without the long time it would have taken me a few months ago. I'm proud that I've come this far from GCSE level work. (D, F)

It seems probable that the process of keeping a diary helped in this building of confidence, in that students were forced to assess what they had achieved and without necessarily referring to marks. Several who had expressed a lack of confidence in their abilities later commented that they had benefited from looking back at earlier diaries and seeing how they had progressed. Encouraging such self-assessment is particularly important at the beginning of A-level work, where, in the face of new challenges, students may lose sight of what they have already achieved in the earlier stages of their language learning.

Yet in the case of one student, interestingly a boy, such growth in self-confidence was not apparent and his diary entries show a high level of anxiety and low self-image throughout the period. Furthermore, he wrote more diary entries than almost any other student and reported to have found them useful in assessing his progress. He also gave the impression of being very conscientious and hard-working. Yet, as if unable to assess objectively or appreciate any achievements that might have resulted from his increased efforts, this student may have created a vicious circle for himself, which might be depicted as shown in Figure 4.

Several factors seem to be involved in this particular instance. The student in question had the lowest GCSE grade of all the subjects involved in the project and it may be that he was genuinely unable to overcome difficulties that had faced him from the start of the course. Yet this would be to take an unduly pessimistic view of the capacity of any student to make progress. The answer seems to lie rather in the learning strategies adopted, which were highly labour-intensive and involved him spending long

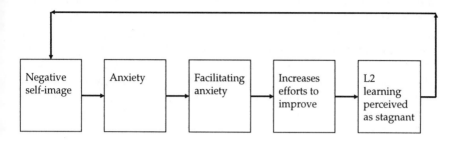

Figure 4 Anxiety and inappropriate learning strategies: a possible pattern

periods of time on his work — a trend that was also noted among several girls in the study, who similarly reinforced their efforts and turned to such strategies as rote learning when they received low marks for their work. These may well have been inappropriate to the task at hand, so that fewer advances were made than might have been expected. In the case of the male student, this kind of increased effort did not lead to corresponding progress, perhaps reinforcing his self-image as an unsuccessful learner. His general approach to learning is the subject of a case study in Chapter 6.

The vital element here seems to be the ability to evaluate the learning strategies one has used and, if necessary, to adopt different ones which may be more appropriate and effective. In this way, success and failure become associated with the learning techniques employed, which are controllable, rather than with ability, which is less so. In turn, anxiety regarding one's achievements may decrease. In the diaries of many of the other anxious students direct links *were* highlighted between strategies and the achievements in which they resulted. For example, one girl who earlier had felt very nervous in oral work commented that her confidence was growing because she could see a relationship between input and outcome:

> Having prepared it I can understand what we're talking about in the lesson, I can participate without feeling that I'm going to make mistakes. (D, F)

Such introspection does not, however, come easily to many students and is likely to need cultivation by the teacher. This can be incorporated into the learning strategy instruction discussed in Chapter 3. After keeping a diary for a week or so, students can be encouraged to share their observations in small group discussion regarding both effective modes of learning and their feelings in relation to their language study, including their assessment of their achievements and the goals they have set for further study. Teachers can assist in the development of goals that are realistic and appropriate, so that students experience success at regular stages. In addition, such discussion sessions could provide the opportunity for the explicit teaching of affective strategies to help students deal more effectively with anxiety than appears to be the case for many at present. A starting point for this might be the encouragement of greater openness within the group regarding students' difficulties, so that they are more aware of their commonality. In this way, the tendency towards negative self-comparison highlighted in the study might be reduced. Suggestions for activities that can be used in this area are to be found in some of the literature of instructed language learning (e.g. Crookall & Oxford, 1992; Foss & Reitzel, 1988). Foss and Reitzel, for instance, expand on the problem-sharing technique mentioned earlier; after noting in a diary the anxieties they have experienced in their language learning, students then pool these and they are written on the board. Not only does the simple act of showing learners that they are not alone in feeling as they do go some way in diminishing these anxieties, it also provides the opportunity for students to realise in many instances that their fears are not rational or productive. For example, in the research project one female student reported worrying about communicating with native speakers for fear that she might make errors and be judged foolish. It would be useful here for the teacher to point out and perhaps illustrate through recordings that native speakers themselves are not always totally accurate or fluent in their speech, and yet are rarely thought less of as people because of it. Thus students begin to realise that many of their fears are unfounded and so of less concern. As Foss and Reitzel (1988: 447) point out, discussing such anxieties in this way, in small groups, students can gain support from their classmates and form more realistic expectations about their own performance.

Oral work and anxiety

This last point reminds us how closely anxiety is bound up with oral work and many of the comments made in the last few pages are applicable to coping with fears about speaking in the target language. The development of healthy group dynamics, in which students feel a sense of group solidarity, seems to be of particular importance in encouraging learners that their participation in oral work is not going to make them stand out from their peers as inadequate or different in any way.

In addition, however, it is suggested that more extensive use of pair and small group work before embarking on whole-class discussion seems likely to increase students' self-confidence. Additionally, this teaching strategy addresses the issue raised earlier of ensuring equal opportunities in class oral work, in that it limits the danger of more confident students dominating oral work and increases the opportunity of all students to communicate. This is especially important for females who may avoid participation in more open discussion work and who appear to favour tasks involving cooperation and negotiation of meaning rather than more formal debate. At the same time, more confident students are given the space to follow more closely their own 'personal agenda' within the general framework of the programme of study to be followed

As many of the concerns expressed by learners regarding oral work appeared to be linked with their difficulties in expressing opinions on quite complex and mature topics, but with a limited linguistic range, it seems advisable to build up to this gradually — perhaps even more gradually than many teachers report doing at present (see Chapter 5). In Chapter 3 it was noted that many students approach oral work by thinking through their ideas in the L1 and then trying to translate literally into the L2; by postponing more advanced topics until learners have a wider range of suitable vocabulary, such a practice might be discouraged. Similarly, it may be worth considering whether a language assistant is best used at the start of advanced work in leading group discussions, given the anxieties some students reported in expressing their opinions in front of native speakers. A better strategy might be to use him or her initially in supervising or guiding pair work, so that a more relaxed relationship between students and assistant can be established.

Motivation

Many of the recommendations made regarding student anxiety apply equally to motivation, particularly those that advocate the promotion of greater self-analysis in order to establish a link between learning strategies and learning outcomes. Self-directed learning and active engagement in one's studies can be taken as key components of motivation; without the opportunity or capacity to reflect on one's own learning and to see how learning outcomes might be improved, the move towards self-direction is a difficult one.

The motivational difficulties of one particular subject in the research project are worth considering in this respect. He had problems in talking or writing about his learning strategies, either actual or proposed. Comments relating to Section 6 of the diary, 'What should I do now?' included 'Hand it [the work] in to the teacher', 'Nothing — in class', and the space was frequently left blank. In Chapter 3 it was suggested that language ability might be linked with the capacity to stand back and appraise one's own learning methods, and the same seems to apply to motivation. The process of identifying causal connections between strategies adopted and learning outcomes plays an essential role in helping students to persevere in the face of difficulties. In the present study, the least self-directed students were those who seemed to have great difficulty in thinking, talking or writing about how they learned. In such circumstances, control of one's own learning is rendered more problematic, and, it is hypothesised, the motivation to improve is inhibited.

Once again, learner diaries can contribute to the development of greater reflection about learning, as can learning strategy instruction sessions as described in Chapter 3. Furthermore, these activities are likely to foster greater communication between students and teachers. This in itself can help in maximising motivation by allowing for the exchange of information regarding the purpose of class activities on the one hand, and the personal agenda of students on the other. For example, it may not always be clear to students why grammatical accuracy, which may well have been downplayed in earlier stages of their language learning, matters at A-level for the sake of clarity and maturity of expression. Without such an explanation, learners may well lack the motivation to devote the necessary effort to work on acquiring grammatical structures.

Similarly, it is suggested that motivation can be enhanced if teachers are more sensitive to students' learning needs in terms of setting tasks which are neither beyond nor inferior to their capabilities, both of which can be demotivating. Differentiation of tasks is an issue frequently raised in connection with younger learners, but it is equally relevant here. Many of these arguments seem to apply in particular to work on grammar, and in schools or colleges where A-level groups consist of students who studied to GCSE level in different establishments. Again, the question of grammar teaching arises here. While it is understandable that many teachers may wish to revise basic structures at the beginning of the course, this should be carefully integrated into the study of newer, more stimulating topics, so that certain students do not feel that they are marking time.

Conclusion

In spite of their differences in approach, what many students seem to be striving for in their language learning is an element of control. The way in which this manifests itself appears to differ for girls and boys: for the latter, a key factor is learning what they feel they need to know, and in a way that they perceive as appropriate to them; for girls, control is often pursued by seeking to learn everything as thoroughly as possible. Both of these approaches have their disadvantages. How can we provide students with opportunities to exercise such control in positive ways? One way of doing this may be to look at how the classroom is organised. Activities such as group work may allow male students to pursue more closely their own agenda, while female students might feel more in command of the situation with the removal of the pressure to 'perform' to a large audience. Even more important, perhaps, are the types of learning activities that are presented to students. It is possible that activities which encourage pupils to engage in self-directed learning, in the sense of examining their strengths and weaknesses and, independent of external pressures, identifying and implementing the necessary solutions, are of great value here. If pupils are helped to notice a link between the strategies they have employed and the resulting outcomes, their sense of control over their own learning could be enhanced and a powerful source of motivation harnessed. At the same time, levels of anxiety are likely to be lowered.

In addition, the measures outlined here are relevant to all subject areas, not just to the foreign language classroom. There is a case for their implementation throughout the curriculum, with schools and colleges developing a policy for addressing the issue of anxiety for all of their students, possibly within an action research framework. In order for such measures to be successful, they need to be taken on a regular basis, and not limited to the one-off icebreaking sessions that seem to take place in some classrooms. Above all, time spent on the reduction of anxiety should not be regarded as wasted time. It is hoped that this discussion has given some indication as to how confident A-level learners are likely to emerge not only as more proficient in their subject area but also as more fulfilled in terms of their personal development.

5 The Role of the Teacher: Teaching Language or Teaching Learning?

Introduction

The previous four chapters have looked at language learning largely from the point of view of students, particularly in respect of their perceptions of their learning difficulties and the methods they use in trying to manage these. While this focus has been deliberate and adopted in order to open up a different perspective on the language classroom, we still need to consider the position of teachers in learners' development. In even the most student-centred classroom, where perhaps learning is based on self-access to materials, the support and guidance of teachers is still likely to be needed. This is especially true as far as the development of effective learning strategies in students is concerned.

But before we consider how teachers can best help their students to become more proficient advanced language learners, we need to look at the extent to which teachers are aware of their students' difficulties, anxieties and present learning habits. It might seem obvious that such an awareness is fundamental to the teacher/learner relationship if teaching methods are going to correspond to learning needs; yet whether all teachers are so well attuned to their students is another matter.

To investigate this question, the research project sought information from the teachers of those students whose learning difficulties were discussed in Chapter 2. They too completed a questionnaire, based very closely on the one sent to students, which asked them to list their students' present and predicted future strengths and weaknesses. They were also presented with the same statements regarding possible learning problems and were asked to tick those which they thought applied to most of their students. Finally, as the first stage of an investigation into how (if at all) teachers try to ease the transition from GCSE to A-level language learning, questions were posed regarding the teaching strategies they adopted in this area. The questionnaire as a whole is reproduced in Appendix B.2.

One hundred questionnaires were sent to 49 schools and colleges in England and Wales. In total 70 teachers completed and returned questionnaires, giving 43 French and 30 German responses (with three respondents teaching both languages). Further details of respondents can be found in Appendix D2 (Tables D5 and D6). Responses for all questions were analysed and sorted in the same manner as the student questionnaire. Where possible, comparisons were made with the responses made in this first questionnaire. In view of the smaller number of teachers involved, however, this was not always possible and the following points of comparison are made cautiously. For similar reasons, the results from the teacher questionnaire have not been reproduced in graphical form.

From the student questionnaire it was apparent that the attitude of learners to oral work was somewhat ambivalent, in that while many cited it as a strength, many others saw it as a weakness. This was especially true for students of French, with the two viewpoints represented by almost equal percentages of respondents. By contrast, teachers were much more positive about their students' speaking skills, with over a quarter of respondents in both languages seeing it as the aspect of their work with which learners had coped best. Few teachers made reference to specific aspects of grammar, such as tenses (on which students commented frequently and on which they were fairly equally divided over ease or difficulty), or the case system in German (which was seen as a major difficulty by learners). Teachers chose instead to refer to grammar in general, with German instructors seeing this as far more of a weakness than a strength and their French colleagues being fairly evenly divided between the two viewpoints. This lack of precision may merely be a sign that teachers did not feel the need or inclination to give more detail on the questionnaire; on the other hand, it may be an indication that their perceptions of learners' difficulties were less precise than those of the learners themselves.

If we turn to the skill of listening, which for students of French was seen as quite a major difficulty and for students of German not the out and out strength one might expect it to be, then teachers' responses are again a little surprising. Teachers of French thought it was as much a strength as a weakness, while twice as many teachers of German thought their students had coped well with it as those who saw it as a difficulty. French teachers seemed to be much more concerned with writing as a difficulty, with nearly a quarter citing it as weakness and only 5% seeing it as a strength.

With regard to German, there was a large disparity between teachers' and students' perceptions of vocabulary learning and understanding. While these skills emerged as major cause for concern for students, their teachers seem to place less emphasis on them as difficulties.

Looking to the future, although writing was the second most frequently mentioned future strength in both languages, this was overshadowed by the number of teachers who felt it would become more of a difficulty as the course went on. It is also interesting to note that while students of both languages placed oral and listening work above grammar as areas where they might have problems in the future, teachers anticipated that the structure of the language would pose as many (or more) difficulties as communicative skills. Of course, teachers were able to draw upon their experience of past years in their assumption that listening and speaking would generally be areas of strength rather than of weakness. Yet it is perhaps also true to say, and particularly so for listening, that as in Questions 1 and 2 of the questionnaire they were underestimating the difficulties experienced by students and their concerns for future performance in these areas.

Experience of past language groups may also account for the greater reference by teachers to difficulties in the area of 'study skills'. In addition, several teachers felt that their students might have problems caused by a lack of general knowledge or limited opinions, or a poor command of English.

While space does not permit a more detailed examination of teachers' responses, it is worth mentioning certain factors which either support the comments made regarding the students' responses or additional ones that did not emerge from their questionnaire. The observations made in Chapter 2 concerning students' ease with work of a guided, structured nature, involving 'Basic Interpersonal and Communicative Skills' (BICS, Cummins, 1984), are upheld by teachers' comments. Similarly, difficulties in discussing or writing about advanced ideas with a limited vocabulary and grammatical range were reiterated by teachers. In addition, some teachers highlighted students' inability to comprehend more than the gist of passages set for aural or reading comprehension.

Where teachers were asked to tick statements they thought applied to their learners, further disparities emerged between the two groups' perceptions of students' difficulties. In both languages, teachers appear to have seen more problems than their students in a number of areas, including written accuracy (French), constructing sentences (German) and study skills (both languages), where there was a difference of 20% or between the two groups of respondents. On the other hand, although the differences are not so great, teachers appear to have underestimated the problems involved in concentrating on listening comprehension for both languages, and for French only, expressing ideas orally, reading a text without a dictionary, following class discussions and answering quickly in oral work.

These differences might be viewed as unsurprising, given that difficulties associated with such areas as written accuracy are more visible and thus more obvious to teachers than those which are more hidden like concentration problems. Nevertheless, it is noticeable that it is mainly in the areas usually associated with 'communicative competence' or 'passive' skills that teachers have underestimated their students' lack of confidence. This is particularly true as far as French is concerned.

Key Findings: Easing the Transition

The questionnaire thus indicated that not all teachers are fully aware of the language learning issues that concern their A-level students. On the other hand, there was evidence of a number of instructors who were taking steps to ease students into A-level. These efforts further clarify certain elements concerning students' strengths and weaknesses reported in Chapter 2.

Earlier it was suggested that students felt relatively confident when dealing with tasks of a structured nature within familiar and concrete topics. The central teaching strategy that emerged from the questionnaire completed by instructors involved using familiar topics and moving gradually from short, simple tasks and texts, with structure and support provided, to longer, more complex ones (mentioned by 29 French and 29 German teachers, where figures refer to numbers of teachers rather than to percentages).

Similarly, it was hypothesised earlier that many A-level students experience a very form-focused approach to language learning in the initial weeks of their course, in contrast to the methodology generally adopted at earlier stages of language learning. The teacher questionnaire indicated that at that stage of the A-level course a number of teachers (18 French, 25 German) were mainly concerned with the teaching of grammar, often in the form of what they saw as general revision of key structures. Others referred to intensive work on structure, frequently within separate grammar lessons. As mentioned before, however, such strategies may be less successful with some students than with others.

The number of teachers seeking to ease problems in the affective domain is encouraging (17 French, 13 German), with reference made to activities designed to promote students' self-confidence and healthy group dynamics. Whether these activities were continued throughout the course or were limited to initial lessons is not clear; the teacher interview reported below suggests that the latter is true, which is less encouraging.

In view of the relatively large number of comments made concerning students' present and future weaknesses in study skills, however, it is perhaps surprising that comparatively few teachers took steps to resolve their problems (ten French, no German). Specific areas referred to by small numbers of teachers include dictionary use, organisation, note taking and general learning habits such as checking one's work thoroughly.

It thus seems from the questionnaire that while there is some awareness among teachers of the difficulties new A-level students face, this does not always match students' perceptions of the situation. Furthermore, and perhaps more importantly, there is the indication that measures adopted to ease these difficulties are restricted in the main to the presentation of language, rather than addressing the issue of seeking to improve students' learning behaviour at a more fundamental level.

Whether this is in fact the case was the focus of the teacher interview, which sought more detailed insights into the approach of teachers to learning strategies. Nine teachers from seven schools and colleges were interviewed in the third term of the A-level course. The chief emphasis of the interview was whether teachers encouraged the development of effective learning strategies in their pupils and if so, how. Additionally, during the interview teachers frequently expressed views on the reasons behind students' strengths and weaknesses. Although they were not asked directly to make such comments, they offer an interesting perspective on how teachers see the learning process and thus are worthy of consideration.

One of the most notable aspects to emerge from the interviews was the difficulty teachers seemed to have in talking about passing on advice to students about effective language learning strategies. Similarly, Mitchell and Hooper (1990) found that the foreign languages teachers they interviewed were unable to comment on any explicit advice they might give to pupils in this area. These authors comment that a possible explanation for this may be that teachers 'have not yet fully theorised these key aspects of their work' or do not have the technical language needed to discuss language learning strategies (Mitchell & Hooper, 1990: 25). In the present study, when teachers were asked to discuss any steps they took to develop effective learning strategies in A-level students, it was common for them to reply by describing their own *teaching strategies*, rather than methods of learning which they passed on to students. This tallies very much with the findings reported in Chamot (1987), where ESL teachers were asked to comment on the learning strategies they thought their pupils used, but frequently referred to teaching strategies they employed themselves instead. While the line between the two approaches is arguably a fine one, it is still significant. Indeed, comments on teaching strategies are interesting in their own right and as such are reported here. However, efforts have been made in the following summary to separate out interviewees' *teaching* strategies and the *learning* strategies they taught in several key areas.

The 'sophistication' transition

This refers to the move from employing simple, often transactional language in everyday situations to using more complex, abstract language in the consideration of more testing issues. As discussed earlier, the questionnaire had indicated that many teachers began the A-level course by working on topics with which students were familiar from earlier study, such as the family and young people. Most of those interviewed then went on to more 'adult' topics such as crime, the press, women in society, by the end of the first term. From this the question arose concerning how teachers encouraged students to deal with the familiar topics in a more sophisticated, abstract manner, rather than merely reproducing the same language and ideas they had expressed at intermediate level. All of the comments made referred principally to teaching strategies. It was common for teachers to state that this occurred through the drawing out and manipulation of language contained within the texts with which they presented students, although more precise details about how this was actually carried out tended to be lacking. Two teachers indicated that students' motivation to discuss themes like the generation gap pushed them to express opinions on such matters and to re-use the language picked out from materials. Another felt that by encouraging students of different abilities to work together, weaker students were helped to move one step beyond their present level of competence.

Similarly, a comment was made by one interviewee regarding the advisability of employing materials which were just beyond students' present language level, using a resource which she described as likely to 'just stretch them only a bit, rather than throw them into a myriad of vocabulary that they don't understand'. This bears a resemblance to Krashen's (1985) 'input hypothesis', which suggests that learners advance to the next stage of their development when presented with 'comprehensible input', language they can understand with the help of its context but which contains elements just beyond their current level of acquisition. Another teacher, however, was more critical of what he called this 'weaning' approach, commenting instead that the move to A-level work was, of necessity, 'a little bit like walking into a cold shower'. He elaborated on this:

> I think really if you're going to make strides you have to present them with more sophisticated material and say, 'Well, look, this is', in a sense, 'this is real German and you have to come to terms with it and battle away.' That's the strategy.

Interestingly, however, the same teacher spent six weeks revising grammar before embarking on topic work proper and reserved topics which he felt would be outside students' experience, such as pollution, until the second year of the A-level course.

Oral and written work

In addition to the comments just reported regarding the motivational force of such topics as family life, a few other teaching strategies were mentioned, designed to encourage students to give their views in oral and written discussions. This most commonly consisted of the teaching of set phrases for expressing opinions. One teacher used this in the form of drills, with each student giving an opinion beginning with a certain introductory phrase. In the same school, another teacher reported devoting half a lesson each week to discussing current news events; as the nature of the topic meant that certain key words and phrases recurred, it was felt that this helped students become familiar with and re-use vocabulary of a more discursive type.

Other questions were put to teachers which were directed more specifically towards any *advice* teachers gave to pupils concerning oral work, for example, how to deal with the problem of unknown items in a role-play, or ways of generally improving their oral use of the language. Again, some teachers interpreted this as referring to the teaching strategies they used in class, mentioning for example constantly using the target language and expecting pupils to do the same, or using reading aloud to help pronunciation. Others, however, did refer to the more explicit transmission of effective strategies to their pupils. The most common was the explanation and demonstration of circumlocution and paraphrase, particularly in role-plays, with one teacher commenting that this expanded on advice that had been given in earlier years of language study. A variation on circumlocution was the advice given by another teacher to 'simplify the thought processes . . . , get a complicated idea across in a series of simple sentences'. This also involved a degree of what Chapter 3 called 'language repertoire monitoring', with the suggestion given that 'if they can say something that they know is right they are far better off doing that than launching out into the unknown'.

A further strategy discussed by one teacher with her pupils was the advisability of learning set phrases for such circumstances as arguing a point of view in a role-play.

Regarding written work as a whole, further questions were asked where the emphasis was once again on if and how teachers encouraged students to adopt effective strategic behaviour, in terms of generally improving their written work and in producing essays. Comments relating to the former were all of the teaching strategy kind, principally concerning the importance of individual counselling and correction of work. This, however, was only deemed possible by those teachers whose language classes were relatively small, generally under ten pupils. Two teachers from separate schools referred to methods that involved providing students with a structure for their writing, but in different forms: on the one hand, by using pictorial oral narration tasks often used in GCSE external examinations, described as 'a vehicle for putting in the better vocab. and the better structures that they're using, that they're learning, into a format that they're happier with'; on the other, by asking pupils to write notes on the literary text being studied, first in English and then later in German. The latter strategy may in part explain the tendency of some students to formulate their ideas in the mother tongue prior to writing.

The same comment may be made regarding essay planning, where teachers were better able to comment on help they gave students in approaching the task. Although some planning was reportedly done in the L2, the impression was gained that a fair amount of the L1 was used as well, perhaps, as one teacher claimed, 'to make absolutely certain that they'd all got the idea of what was required'.

One teacher only paid a great deal of attention to helping students gain the necessary techniques for essay writing, sensing herself that she was alone in imparting such skills:

> No one else seems to do it . . . Does anybody teach anybody how to write an essay in any other language, or in any other subject?

She thus saw the need to discuss the meaning and role of such items as the introduction and conclusion of an essay, how a structure might be developed. Students were also helped in class to produce essay plans, which were then assessed and re-drafted before the essay was written. Even at this final stage, students were reassured that they were being assessed principally on the structure of the essay, rather than on such factors as accuracy.

Although most of the other teachers interviewed did help their students with planning to a certain degree, their approach appeared to be much less systematic. In some instances essays were planned in class by the group as a whole, or advice was given by the teacher on what was required in an essay. These sessions appeared to be 'one-off' occasions, either early in the course or much later when students' earlier work had indicated that some guidance was necessary. As Chamot and Küpper (1989: 19) point out, however, new strategies take time to acquire and a single session may be insufficient. The impression was gained that most teachers assumed that students understood and were familiar with the techniques of essay writing from work in other subjects earlier in their education — although at the same time their comments on the weakness of students' performance in this area suggested otherwise. One teacher noted that a member of her second year language group, shortly before taking her final external A-level examination, had reported that she had always thought that the structuring of an essay was an idea peculiar to this one teacher, just her particular 'quirky idea'.

Vocabulary and grammar learning

Similar assumptions were in evidence concerning students' ability to learn vocabulary, supporting the suggestion made in Chapter 2 and elsewhere that pupils are often left to their own devices in this area of language learning. An indication of this came from the number of teachers whose initial response, when asked if they helped students develop effective vocabulary learning strategies, was to outline teaching strategies. Some replied that they tested students regularly, or that there existed in their class a rule that everything that was noted on the board had to be copied and learnt. Two teachers from different schools pointed out that they favoured the approach of vocabulary acquisition through use, and therefore did not actually require their students to learn lists of items — although the interviews with their students indicated that the latter nevertheless did try to learn vocabulary systematically, and often through 'rote' methods.

When pressed further, two teachers, again from separate schools, stated that they had discussed with their class alternative methods of learning vocabulary, with one firstly presenting the method she herself used and then inviting other suggestions. Students were subsequently advised to try and find the method that worked best for them. Another used the more implicit technique of turning vocabulary tests into the form of a game, for example, asking students to state how many verbs or nouns a list of items had contained, in order to encourage them to use grouping and a more active form of learning in their own methods employed at home. Two other teachers had made various suggestions to their pupils, such as not leaving all the learning to the last minute, self-testing, or grouping of words into topics, but they admitted that such advice was sporadic and that their general approach was to leave the matter to students themselves.

As far as the acquisition of rules of grammar was concerned, teachers were asked more directly to comment both on how they *taught* grammar and on any learning strategies they pointed out to students to help them in the mental ordering and recall of items of structure. Regarding the first point, all teachers reported teaching grammar systematically and explicitly to a certain degree, rather than relying totally on the approach of letting it emerge naturally from materials dealt with in class. The explicit approach was especially common for areas such as tenses and in the first few weeks of term, confirming the findings of the questionnaires. Two schools felt that the approach became less systematic as time went on.

When grammar was taught systematically and explicitly, this was largely done in what might be viewed as quite a traditional manner. Methods used included presenting structures as formulae (e.g. auxiliary verb + past participle = perfect tense), dictating notes, working through grammar exercises in class and as homework, presenting conjugation and declension tables to learn. One teacher explicitly stated that in her school students were expected to understand grammatical terminology (e.g. subject, object), and most others implied this by their responses. In another school, students were given a booklet on language awareness which explained such terms.

The testing of areas of grammar was also quite widespread, but as for vocabulary learning, and perhaps to an even greater extent, students were largely expected to find their own methods of learning structural points. In two schools, however, some guidance was given. A teacher in one encouraged a degree of self-diagnosis/prescription, advising students to deal with problematic points of grammar by using a resource item containing grammatical exercises for which the solutions were provided in the back. In the second school, students were introduced to a chanting method which encouraged them to use a rhythm when learning German adjectival endings.

Reading and listening

Although some teachers did begin by identifying teaching, rather than learning strategies in the area of *reading* (such as reading a literary text word-for-word with the class, giving them vocabulary sheets in advance of actual reading, guiding their reading with comprehension questions), their comments revealed that their understanding of the significance of effective learning strategies was greater in this language skill than it had been in other areas. This is not to say, however, that such learning strategies were systematically or universally imparted. One of the strategies most commonly discussed with students included resisting the temptation to try to decipher every word, concentrating instead on 'key' words, a form of selective attention. One teacher admitted, however, that she went no further than imparting such advice, astutely observing that teachers tended to assume that students instinctively knew which words were the most important ones in a text. By contrast, one teacher did report demonstrating the technique of effectively reading for gist, by showing how she, a native French speaker, did not need to know the meaning of a Provençal term to understand a sentence in a novel. Similarly, students in another school had spent time discussing in practical terms the difference between reading for gist and for detail.

The 'key' word approach overlapped in some respects with the strategy of inferencing from context, mentioned by three teachers, and with advance organisation, referred to by two, where students were encouraged on the one hand to predict what might occur in a passage, on the other to pre-read comprehension questions to familiarise them with its context. There was little indication, however, that students were given on-going and guided practice in these strategies, or advised to use them in conjunction with other strategies (cf. comments made in Chapter 3 on students' difficulties in using inferencing in the think-aloud interview).

'Bottom–up' strategies, that involve decoding individual items in a text, appeared to be less frequently dealt with by teachers. One only suggested to students that they should think about whether the answers to comprehension questions required them to identify, say, verbs or nouns, which might be classified as the strategy of sentence analysis. Two teachers commented on the difficulties they had experienced in encouraging students to make use of cognates and word analysis to understand unknown items. As far as the former is concerned, the teacher in question (a native French speaker) felt that students' knowledge of English was too limited to allow them to use the strategy effectively, while the second teacher claimed that while students were usually able to see that a German item contained elements with which they were familiar once she had pointed them out, they were unable to identify them on their own. It might be argued that this second example underlines yet again the need for students to be given guided practice in learning strategies.

Regarding resourcing, teachers differed in how much they encouraged dictionary use for reading. While most discouraged students from using it if they could find out the meaning of an item by using a different strategy, two teachers from the same school saw it as a more positive aid. They differed, however, in the manner in which they conveyed this to students, with one adopting a perhaps less advisable approach. This teacher emphasised that she told students always to look up words they did not know — something which seems likely to promote over-dependence on the resource and to hinder the development of other decoding strategies. Her colleague, by contrast, encouraged students to use resourcing by consulting from time to time a dictionary constantly kept by her side during lessons, even though she was a native French speaker. She commented that this seemed to surprise students, and that they themselves were unsure of using the dictionary, taking a long time to find items and often misusing the resource. Like the majority of the other teachers interviewed, however, she appeared to give no explicit guidance or practice in dictionary use, merely warning them of the possible pitfalls involved. Other examples of 'dictionary instruction' mentioned included an explanation of the various symbols commonly used in definitions, usually done once at the start of the course. Two teachers, however, in two other schools, did set students the task of reading a passage at home and preparing a vocabulary list of the key items, with the aim of promoting effective dictionary use as well as vocabulary acquisition.

As had been expected, effective listening was a skill that most teachers found very difficult to impart, and in all schools except one quite a large degree of practice was acquired by pupils outside class with tapes provided by their teachers. A further teaching strategy employed by two schools involved providing students with transcripts after a first listening.

While quite a range of strategies suggested by teachers to their students were mentioned, only one (advance organisation by skim listening on the first hearing) was reported by more than one interviewee, again underlining teachers' uncertainty regarding how to train learners in this skill. An unexpected finding was that one teacher only referred to the use of context. Sometimes strategies suggested appeared to contradict each other; for example, while one teacher reported advising students to concentrate on words they knew (although as in the student interview, no suggestion was made that these should also be the important items), another suggested listening out for items not understood, which should then be transcribed as far as possible and then checked in the dictionary. There was also the impression that quantity rather than quality was being emphasised. One teacher did claim to involve students in word-recognition practice (unfortunately no further details were forthcoming about this), but the strategy of repetition was more commonly advocated, either in the form of listening to an item over and over again when working at home, doing as much listening practice as possible, or by repeating the unknown phrase in one's mind. While such strategies may be beneficial to a certain extent, it is arguable whether they should become the sole substitute for effective and more automatic word-recognition strategies.

Study habits

Of all the areas dealt with in the interview, this was the one where the least learning strategy instruction appeared to take place. Three teachers from three schools gave fairly explicit advice on how students should tackle the 'physical' organisation of their work, for example, recording vocabulary, but none referred to the other, arguably more important, form of organisation, that is, of one's time. Nor were teachers able to report that such matters were definitely treated outside the language classroom; in schools where 'study skills' were part of the tutorial programme, their inclusion was optional, and the impression was gained that they were usually omitted. One teacher remarked that the item had been included in previous years, but that it had been dropped as students had not reacted favourably to it. Interestingly, she hypothesised that this was because the item occurred too early in the A-level programme, when the amount and type of work set did not require a great deal of organisation, so that students were unable to see how it related to the work with which they were involved.

Affective concerns

The questionnaire had indicated that quite a number of teachers were aware of the need to boost students' confidence, both in terms of oral participation and confidence in their general linguistic abilities. It was therefore anticipated that several teaching and learning strategies would be reported. In reality, the number was fairly small, and teaching strategies mentioned (no specific learning strategies were reported) were sometimes vague; for example, two teachers spoke of the need to win students' confidence and build up a friendly atmosphere within the class without being able to say how this was achieved. In two cases, boosting confidence took the form of encouraging quiet students to speak more frequently, either by asking them directly, or by devising interactive activities where each class member was obliged to contribute something. This might be likened to the 'desensitising' techniques sometimes used in psychotherapy (see Foss & Reitzel (1988) for a critique of such an approach). At the same time, however, by pointing out the need to temper the contributions of the more vociferous members of the language group, both teachers seemed to recognise that confidence is more than just the ability to perform, and that it may be affected by factors such as negative self-comparison. This impression was also gained from a teacher in another school, in a slightly different form; as well as encouraging students to work with different class members in pair-work, she further recognised the need to allow students a certain degree of space to develop and did not force them to participate if they did not wish to.

Teachers were further asked about how they helped students to monitor their own progress. In some respects, the methods employed by certain teachers in this area could be viewed as part of the confidence-building process. This seemed to be particularly true where students were involved in a process of self-assessment, carried out in conjunction with a discussion with their teacher. It is thus rather regrettable that such progress monitoring occurred in two schools only. However, in two other schools students' progress was discussed with them individually after each assignment. Three teachers from one school reported talking to pupils individually after examinations held twice yearly, but it was generally felt by them that language groups were too large for this to happen more frequently. One also commented that she tended to concentrate her efforts on those learners who were struggling and that she found it difficult to advise pupils on such occasions how they might improve their performance. This was partly because 'you don't know whether it's because they can't do it or whether they aren't putting in enough effort . . . , sometimes I feel that it's because they're not putting in enough effort'.

Teachers' Views of Learning and Learners

Echoing the sentiment expressed in the preceding paragraph, several teachers seemed to believe that many students' ability, or willingness, to work in a self-directed manner outside of class was limited and that this hampered them in several areas — in particular, vocabulary acquisition and recall, and reading competence. Teachers thus seemed to recognise the importance of learner autonomy, even though their comments reported in previous sections might suggest that they are not conscious of the need to *help* students to develop such self-sufficiency.

A lack of independent work, in the sense of reading around the subject, was also held to be a problem as far as assignments involving the expressing of opinions was concerned. This matter attracted the greatest number of general comments from teachers, with four lamenting students' apparent lack of general knowledge and opinions on wider issues, narrow interests and an unwillingness to look beyond what one described as 'school, family, social life'. Another teacher identified a good knowledge of and interest in current affairs as an important contributing factor to the success of two of her more effective learners (cf. the finding of Gillette, 1987).

Furthermore, certain teachers expressed views concerning the requirement from examining bodies that students should be able to express complex opinions on a number of issues, and the difficulty of combining this with the acquisition of greater formal control (a theme that also emerged from the questionnaire). There was a sense that students, above all those of limited opinions, were overburdened by the need to produce utterances sophisticated in both content and form. As one teacher suggested when discussing students' poor command of adjectival endings in German, 'when they're actually trying to express ideas, I think that it's just one thing too many to think about'.

Indeed, another teacher went on to question the wisdom of trying to cover a wide range of topics as required by the examination group used by her school. Her comments are worth citing at length, for the issues they raise regarding teaching strategies and syllabus design:

> X and I have been looking, thinking about what we've done and what we haven't achieved with the Upper Sixth,[1] and whether, you know, working so much in the language and trying to cover these topics and all the rest of it, we need to to do more on just trying to do something on the basic linguistic skills.

She felt that in particular students needed more help in understanding grammar as far as reading was concerned, in order to encourage more detailed comprehension, because, she explained, 'at GCSE they did stroll through it, saying, "Oh, this is vaguely about, so a sort of vaguely about answer will do", but of course it doesn't at A-level'. Such remarks reflect in many ways the findings of the think-aloud interview in relation to both reading and listening, where too much reliance on context and too little on word-recognition and syntactic constraints often hampered students' comprehension. There was thus an awareness among this group of teachers that students do not always use the most appropriate learning strategies; it is also clear, however, that the teaching of such skills is far from widespread and that its importance may indeed be only partially under-stood by those working with A-level language learners.

Implications for the Classroom

Making room for dialogue

It is not a new observation that to meet the learning needs of our students, we have first to find out what these are. Yet the disparity between teachers' and students' perceptions of learning difficulties in some skills suggests that communication between the two groups is not always as open as it might be. In many ways this is understandable; the teachers who completed the questionnaire had been working with their classes for only a couple of months at the most and in some cases they may not have taught many of the group in earlier years of language study. Thus relationships had not had time to develop fully. At the beginning of a new course, students may well be reticent about any difficulties they are having, particularly if it is a new experience for them to find language learning problematic. Nevertheless, it seems vitally important, from an early stage, to encourage the evaluation of how well students are coping with various aspects of the course. Not only can this help in allaying anxieties, as Chapter 4 argued, but it is also obviously central to the selection and development of strategies to overcome those difficulties. In addition to using diaries as already suggested, teachers might find it helpful to present students with a list of 'commonly experienced difficulties' similar to those given in the student questionnaire (Appendix B1) and to ask them to tick those they felt applied to them. In this way, students are made aware that they are not unique in their problems and are further helped to put their difficulties into words. A more open-ended section, like those in Sections A and B of the questionnaire, could also be provided, tailored to fit the needs of the group, to allow for any concerns not already covered. Alternatively, students can be encouraged to be even more open about their concerns if enquiries are put in an indirect manner; for example, they might be asked to write down points of advice for other learners considering studying a language at A-level — what should they expect to find challenging, what easy; what is enjoyable about the course? It is important to include these positive questions in order to avoid over-emphasising the negative!

Preventative measures

Some respondents to the teacher questionnaire raised the issue of tackling the lack of continuity between GCSE and A-level language learning from the other end. That is, they suggested that students should be better prepared for advanced work *before* the course began. Comments included those advocating that greater demands should be made of students at GCSE level (suggested by eight teachers of French and nine of German), either in the form of a more testing examination or of additional, more advanced work given to students likely to progress to A-level. Similar observations are made by Schultz (1991) in his discussion of methods to help undergraduate language students at the University of California at Berkeley. They are required to make the transition from intermediate language courses, which stress basic communication, to more advanced ones where they need to develop such skills as reading and discussing literary texts. In view of the problems experienced by students in the past in making this transition, the foundations for these skills have since been built gradually into the intermediate course, using simple texts, so that the transition to a more advanced level is less abrupt. This is an issue that needs to be looked at carefully in all contexts where the lack of continuity between different levels of learning is a cause for concern. If we are to narrow the divide between GCSE and A-level learning, then moving one of the sides nearer arguably addresses only half of the problem. There is the difficulty, however, of providing instruction to meet the needs of *all* learners at GCSE level, not just those who wish to continue their studies.

As an alternative or additional measure, the gap might similarly be lessened by examining how prospective advanced learners prepare themselves for the transition. Given the long time span that often exists between the final GCSE examination and the start of the A-level course, with students possibly out of contact with the foreign language for two months or more over the summer break, three French teachers suggested that preparatory language work might be set for the holiday period preceding the higher level course.

The likely effectiveness of this last suggestion, however, is difficult to gauge and depends largely on the type of work set. Unless students have already developed skills of independent learning, they may feel unable to work on their own on tasks such as grammar revision or wider reading. Possibly this is the time when more general tasks might be set where students are asked to think and perhaps write a little about *how* they have learned a language up until now, with respect to familiar skills such as vocabulary learning. A simple questionnaire, based on concrete examples, could be given.

Lessons from the teachers

While the information gained from the teacher interview was disappointing in that very few examples of strategy training emerged, several examples of good practice can be drawn from it. It is important, however, to look at ways in which the emphasis of some of these teaching strategies can be shifted, in order to build into them an element of learning strategy training and so increase the likelihood of their effectiveness.

The first example concerns the familiar theme of choosing topics that are accessible and well-known to students. Using materials with a well known context allows for the gradual introduction of more cognitively demanding and abstract tasks, providing the necessary support for students to develop the Cognitive/Academic Language Proficiency (Cummins, 1984) discussed in Chapter 2. Teachers' comments underlined the effectiveness of this measure, but further point to the need to add an element of novelty to the theme studied. While familiarity can promote reassurance, it can also lead to boredom and lack of motivation. As one teacher remarked, an element of controversy and personal relevance is needed to provoke a reaction in students, pushing them to express their views and to rework language presented in texts.

This notion of 'pushing' seems in fact to be a central one, involving finding the right balance between challenge and support, and is advocated by a number of writers (Johnstone, 1989; Grenfell & Harris, 1993). The concept of 'comprehensible input', where language is *just* beyond learners' knowledge but can be inferred from context and other clues, sums up this balance and seems more likely to encourage learners to make the new language their own than the 'cold shower' approach referred to earlier. Of course, the strategies of inferencing and making use of knowledge already gained (elaboration) will need to be discussed, modelled and practised in the manner described in Chapter 3 if the method is to be successful.

It is not always easy, however, to find material that is suitable for this approach. Several teachers responding to the questionnaire (eight French, six German) emphasised the need for textbooks to begin at students' current level of competence. There is some evidence that even when students have developed good strategies for reading in their own language, these are 'short-circuited' in foreign language reading tasks if the material is too difficult (Clarke, 1980, cited in Schulz, 1981). This is particularly true if the context of the text, or the concepts it contains, are outside students' realm of experience. Schulz suggests that many teachers underestimate the difficulty texts present to students. While my own findings suggest that many teachers do try to select short, more accessible texts at the start of the A-level course, there are many others who, perhaps embarking on literary texts at the outset, seem less aware of the demotivating effect lengthy and sometimes abstract texts can have on learners. In choosing suitable texts, teachers need to look for four aspects (Langer *et al.*, 1974, summarised in Schulz, 1981): text simplicity, with short, simple sentences, employing common words; text structure, where there is a clear and logical structure and sequence to the text; length and conciseness of essential information; and the inclusion of special 'interest-stimulators' such as direct speech or exclamations (Schulz, 1981: 45). This test is likely to give a more reliable indication of text suitability than if teachers merely read it for 'comprehensibility', as they may well be influenced by their own ability to understand the text — it is very difficult to put one's self in the shoes of a less proficient language speaker/reader in this way.

In the process referred to earlier of gaining ownership of language, reviewing and reworking a fairly limited range of vocabulary (at least in the early days) is essential. The technique suggested by one group of teachers of discussing each week what has happened in the news may well offer the chance to use a familiar framework for each discussion while allowing for an element of variety. Students could further be encouraged to take set phrases extracted from a text and to expand upon them with elements of their own language and opinions. An important learning strategy to emphasise at this point is that of language repertoire monitoring, which Chapter 3 attributed to more effective students when speaking or writing the foreign language. This involved staying within the limits of their foreign language vocabulary, making good use of what they knew they could say with confidence and endeavouring to think in the foreign language rather than trying to translate their thoughts directly. Personal contacts with teachers suggests that some regard the reworking of phrases from texts almost as 'cheating', and that students should create their own from scratch. But the evidence from the learners we have looked at suggests that we need to avoid the dangers of producing language that is a stilted word-for-word translation of the mother tongue. By combining known structures with different vocabulary, students can gain support at the same time as thinking more creatively. They should further be encouraged to do this as a form of vocabulary learning, where the item to be learnt is made into a sentence.

In order to make full use of what they know, however, students need to be made familiar with communication strategies that allow them to get round any gaps in their vocabulary or knowledge of structure. The teacher interview suggests that the importance of circumlocution and paraphrase in oral work is emphasised by some instructors. This is something that needs to be built in to all language classrooms. Nor is it sufficient merely to tell students that they should try to 'think of another way' of saying something; demonstration and practice are also required. Useful examples of activities in this area can be found in Dörnyei & Thurrell (1991). These include listening to texts where hesitation fillers are used, asking students to note how and where they are employed and then encouraging them to use them in oral work to keep the conversation going. Paraphrase and circumlocution can be practised through games involving making up definitions for unfamiliar vocabulary (Dörnyei & Thurrell, 1991: 21).

Such strategies are similarly important in developing effective writing skills, yet few if any of the teachers interviewed seemed to pay them much attention. However, teachers appeared to be more attuned to their students' needs concerning the importance of moving gradually from shorter to longer, from simple to complex written tasks — e.g. from sentences (perhaps in posters or 'diary entries'), to paragraphs and then slowly to essays. Within this approach there is room for the teaching of strategies such as language repertoire monitoring and paraphrasing, which are likely to reinforce the effect of building students' confidence, the aim of the initial teaching strategy.

Increased confidence may similarly result from a more strategy-oriented approach to the teaching of essay writing skills. Rather than simply presenting in one session the usual format of an essay or essay plan, teachers need also to work through with learners on several occasions how an essay is built up. Strategies of drafting, monitoring, evaluation and cooperation come into play here; as outlined in Chapter 3, group or pair discussions can be useful in developing these skills. Schultz (1991) suggests how students can gain more insight into the effectiveness of their own writing by reviewing each others' draft compositions. This is done according to the criteria used by the teacher for grading written work. Students review with their teacher models of both good and poor writing. Importantly, and echoing the strategy adopted by one A-level teacher interviewed, Schultz reports that in the programme he outlines, students are told to concentrate on content and organisation rather than on accuracy, having been taught in brief weekly lessons how the former function within a composition. It is dangerous to assume that at the beginning of an advanced language course students know how or why an argumentative essay is constructed as it is. They need to be encouraged to reflect upon the purpose of such elements as introductions, conclusions, paragraphing and transitions, monitoring and evaluating their writing in terms of its clarity and effectiveness from the point of view of the *reader*.

This is an approach that might be adopted also for the acquisition of grammar. From both the teacher questionnaire and interview it is apparent that many teachers at A-level place quite an emphasis on explicit grammar instruction and on the correction of grammatical errors. For students used to a more communicative approach, where they gain the impression that the transmission of a message is the most important factor and not the accuracy of the utterance, this change in emphasis may be hard to comprehend and adapt to. Strategies of evaluation and monitoring can again be demonstrated and practised in class to aid in the transfer of rules in the abstract to their effective use in actual language production. Rather than responding to teachers' corrections of errors by, for example, rewriting a corrected version, learners should be encouraged (in class) to adopt the strategy of asking themselves why their mistake matters — not because it 'offends' rules of grammar but because of the effect it might have on a reader, in terms of the clarity of expression.

All of these strategies need to be practised repeatedly. This is especially true in the case of reading and listening comprehension. Several of the teachers interviewed were already helping their students in developing effective reading strategies, such as predicting the likely content of a passage by pre-reading accompanying comprehension questions, or look-ing at the text as a whole rather than at every word. This 'strategy training' tended, however, to be sporadic or one-off and was even more so with regard to listening, where students were usually left to develop their own strategies. Ideally with each comprehension passage students should be reminded of important comprehension strategies they might employ (such as inferencing, using prior knowledge to work out meanings [elaboration], focusing on verbs and other words rich in meaning, e.g. emphasised words), and of how they could be used with sections of the text. They should then put them into immediate practice. In this respect, O'Malley and Chamot (1990) refer to what they call reciprocal teaching (developed by Palincsar & Brown, 1984). This involves the teacher initially modelling the strategies to be used; students then work in groups and take it in turns to play the part of the 'teacher', going through the strategies again and helping the group as a whole to arrive at the comprehension of the text.

As students become more proficient in using strategies, they will need less teacher support. It is hoped that at the same time they will become more self-directed, assessing how they might best approach a learning task. As Chapter 4 argued, this is likely to increase confidence and reduce anxiety.

The same is true of time-management. Much of the anxiety noted in talking to students seemed to arise from a feeling of being overwhelmed by the amount of work to get through. Yet none of the teachers interviewed reported working with their learners in order to show them how to organise their time. Once again, this is a skill that needs to be learnt, within the framework of the language classroom. More general 'study skills' programmes, meant to apply to all areas of the curriculum, seem to be less successful, as learners cannot always see how strategies apply to their situation. In class, they need to be asked to review how much time they have available, how much work they typically have in a week and which aspects of their language learning they feel they need to improve the most. From this (possibly working in pairs and with teacher guidance), they should develop some kind of structure to their working week. Periodic reviews of this, to check that the schedule is appropriate and being kept to, are advisable.

Teaching the teachers

On first reading, the steps outlined here for becoming a 'strategic' teacher may seem daunting. Indeed, it has often been observed that the greatest obstacle to developing effective learning strategies in students lies with their teachers. Lack of time, insufficient training in teaching strategies and low motivation to implement them may be some of the reasons behind this. One might also add that some teachers may be concerned about the change in their role alluded to in the title of this chapter: from the exclusive teaching of language to becoming a teacher of learning as well. Furthermore, one of the central principles of learning strategy training is that students will become more autonomous, which has obvious implications for the traditional role of the teacher.

Ideally, if some of these concerns are to be overcome, then adopting a strategic teaching approach needs to be implemented across a language department as a whole. In this way, the question of insufficient time and training can be more easily tackled, if in-service training funding can be allocated to it. To be most effective, such training needs to make teachers aware of the benefits that can be gained by learners though the adoption of more effective learning strategies. For this to happen, there has to be some discussion of more theoretical issues regarding how learners learn, for example, why reflective learners are more effective learners. In this respect, it might be useful for teachers to consider how they themselves learnt a language. Similarly, familiarisation with the strategies to be taught may be facilitated if teachers themselves try them out and judge which are the most effective for them.

Acceptance of learning strategy training, by both teachers and students, can be facilitated if some concrete evidence can be provided of the utility of such training. In the area of vocabulary learning, for example, a simple word test can be given to see how well students have retained items both with and without the use of different strategies and the two results compared.

While this chapter and others have pointed to a large number of learning strategies that can be taught, if the task seems overwhelming then it should be remembered that learners can benefit from quite small changes in one's teaching approach. As O'Malley (1987) points out, teachers should be confident that there are a number of strategies 'which can be embedded into their existing curricula, that can be taught to students with only modest extra effort, and that can improve overall class performance . . . '. One of the most beneficial might include preparing learners for tasks such as listening comprehension, rather than just plunging straight into them, by activating students' prior knowledge of the topic and its vocabulary through questioning and brain-storming. Another involves reviewing after the task what students feel they have learnt. While several writers emphasise the importance of students knowing what strategies are called, so that they become more familiar with them, it is not necessary to use complicated terms, which might be offputting to some learners and teachers. For instance, 'inferencing' might become 'using clues'.

Above all, teachers should select for instruction those strategies with which they themselves feel most comfortable and confident. Reiterating an earlier argument, it is worth emphasising again that the most important change in approach lies in encouraging students to think about the strategies they use and how they might improve upon them.

Note

1.   Upper Sixth is a term sometimes used in schools in England and Wales for the second and final year of an A-level course.

6 Students in the Round: Looking at Individuals

Introduction

Previous chapters have tried to present the characteristics of A-level language students seen as a group, drawing out those learning behaviours felt to be typical of either effective or ineffective students. There is a danger in this, however, of overlooking the fact that students are individuals, each with a particular learning make-up. Something of this make-up is inevitably lost if it is fragmented by looking at particular language skills or learning strategies.

The following sections aim to complete the picture, by presenting case studies of four students and discussing their overall learning behaviour, its affective element included. The students were selected to give a balance of male and female learners and cover a range of ability. In addition, these students displayed characteristics that were felt to be interesting in their own right. As before, D (diary) and I (interview) indicate the source of quotations.

Furthermore, it is useful to look at how remedial learning strategy instruction might function in practice and in response to particular difficulties, even where students appear to be highly effective learners.

Student M (female)

Student M was a dual linguist, taking French, German and English at A-level. At the start of the project, she had been learning French for six years, German for three. In the present study, her learning behaviour in German only was investigated. She had spent some time in both countries on exchanges, although not an excessive amount. She had obtained a top grade (A) at GCSE level in both French and German and was predicted to do the same at A-level.

Student M sensed that she devoted more energy to German than most of her peers (particular to vocabulary learning, which she felt most pupils pretended not to need to learn!). Her teacher claimed that she was highly organised in her approach to her studies. Perhaps surprisingly, her commitment to the subject did not seem to arise from any integrative orientation and she admitted that she had only decided in the summer holidays after her GCSE examinations to study German further. Instead, she felt that her ability in and enjoyment of the language had prompted her choice.

Within the group of learners studied, Student M was unique in hypothesising that a firm grasp of vocabulary and grammar, particularly tenses, together with spending time in the foreign country, lay behind successful language learning — most students mentioned only the latter component. This philosophy was largely borne out by her approach to vocabulary acquisition. She claimed to review new vocabulary regularly, thus showing a degree of self-direction (such tasks were not set by her teacher) and although she used many of the more common strategies such as self-testing and a degree of rote learning, she did not rely on these alone, combining them with transfer, repetition and, perhaps most importantly, creative re-combination, by making up 'some sentences using the new words to make sure I really understood them' (D). Such strategies may have contributed to her ability to recognise items rapidly in the think-aloud tasks.

Her control of grammar appeared to be equally secure and this was confirmed by her teacher. While she reported that structural manipulation, such as using the correct word order in subordinate clauses, now came naturally to her (as if it had become automatised), it was evident from the retrospective and think-aloud data that a clear knowledge of explicit rules underlay this ability, and that this knowledge had been gained easily at the GCSE stage — although grammatical knowledge did not appear to have been particularly emphasised by her teacher before A-level, according to the reports of other students from the same school.

Neither was this grammatical knowledge divorced from its application. Student M had a clear perception of form–function relationships and this facility, together with an appreciation of context factors, enabled her to sense instantly the item which would complete the gaps in the think-aloud cloze exercises. This approach is worth illustrating at length for what it shows about the proficient language learner:

> Es gibt auch eine Gruppe Schüler, ____ in ihrer Freizeit nichts ____ zu tun wissen [. . .] Sie gehört ____ Gruppe von Jungen und Mädchen an, ____ 'Clique'.

(There is also a group of pupils _____ don't have anything to do in their free time [. . .]They belong to _____ group of boys and girls, _____ 'clique'.)

. . . well, that'll be *'die'*, I think (writes *'die'*) . . . + . . . because, um, it's there's also a group of pupils who, which, who, so that'll be *'die'*, . . . *'nichts'* . . . *'sie gehört'* . . . I'm going to read it through, because I'm not quite sure . . . I think that's *'Sinnvolles'*, because that's nothing particularly useful to do, don't know anything to do (writes *'Sinnvolles'*) . . . um . . . they belong to a group . . . + . . . ah, it's *'einer'*, I'm thinking it's got to be she belongs to a group, and . . . so it'll be *'einer'*, because it's dative, and group is feminine.

Here, the student picked up the 'clues' to meaning given by the syntactic arrangement of such items as 'nichts _____ zu tun wissen', perceiving that an adjectival noun was required, and with the help of reading on as soon as a lack of comprehension was registered, selected an item in harmony not just with the local context, but with the context of the passage as a whole.

Interestingly, Student M attributed her greater (although still minor) difficulties in French to the fact that she had not learnt French grammar 'as enthusiastically earlier in the school as German grammar' (I). This enthusiasm was also apparent in her expressed desire to learn more about the conditional, a tense which she had found out something about but was keen to study further.

This initial 'rule-forming' approach, however, did not mean that Student M was lacking in the more communicative, meaning-based skills in which 'data gatherers' might be expected to be stronger. In some respects, it seemed that her control of form left her free to concentrate on such aspects. As her teacher stated, 'she's incredibly fluent, both orally and written. She can respond immediately to my questions'. The student herself emphasised the importance of speaking as much as possible in class and of actually producing orally the vocabulary that she had learnt, to the extent that she reported in her first interview and diaries saying new items out loud while learning them, so that she was using them orally from the beginning. Although she felt she did participate more in class than others (confirmed by her teacher), this was not without some reservations on her part, from the point of view of not wanting to stand out because of the frequency of her contributions. Interestingly, this nervousness was not perceived by her teacher, who described her as having plenty of self-confidence, 'a bit too much for some of the class'.

Such confidence was also apparent in the student's completion of the written think-aloud exercise, where her composition appeared to flow almost automatically (although there was also a degree of accuracy monitoring). This was true of other students, but whereas for them this seemed to occur in the use of formulaic phrases learned for GCSE level, Student M's production went beyond this in the form of sentences that were both syntactically and semantically more complex. Indeed, one of the qualities praised by her teacher was not just the formal quality of her German, 'but also the ideas that she can express'. This breadth of thought may also be reflected in the fact that of all the students of German who worked on the think-aloud cloze exercise, she was the only one who knew in English the meaning of 'clique'.

In reading and listening, automaticity, in the form of the word-recognition displayed in the think-aloud tasks, was again an underlying characteristic, as was the ability to identify and make use of syntactic groupings. The student's diaries, however, also showed her to be quite meticulous in looking up unknown words while reading and listening, something which is sometimes associated with weaker students. It may be that this was less detrimental to her overall reading comprehension than for others, in that even when searching for individual items, she was still able to consider words as part of sense groupings, as was suggested by her think-aloud performance. She also noted in her diary that she was able to cope without a dictionary, for example by using word-analysis, and that any checking was usually done *after* the main gist had been grasped. In several effective students the desire to pursue uncertainties was noticeable. This trait may rather ironically be called an 'intolerance of ambiguity', being a characteristic often associated in a negative sense with less effective learners (cf. Naiman *et al.*, 1978). One might alternatively borrow Johnstone's (1989) term, who describes learners who pursue many paths in their efforts to comprehend as 'achievers'.

Yet one is perhaps struck most by Student M's ability to stand back from her own learning and to reflect upon it. This she showed especially in her diary entries, which were highly detailed and analytical from the start. They indicate a deep level of thought about how one learns and also a strong degree of self-control. This is perhaps most evident in her reflections on listening comprehension:

> I found it was much easier if I didn't 'half-listen'; that is when I listen to a bit in German and try and work out at the same time what it is in English; I get behind if I do that. Instead I try and actually understand what they're saying as they say it instead of translating. . . . I've learnt that . . . you need to be v. disciplined not to just the stop the tape straight away as soon as you get stuck — that way you lose the gist and it'd never work like that in an exam.(D)

None of these thoughts appear to have been prompted by her teacher, whose main suggestion to pupils when listening was to repeat the tape over and over. Rather, Student M seemed to have enough insight to have discovered independently a highly effective mode of learning at an early stage, a quality which may be an essential feature of what is commonly referred to as aptitude. There are, however, problems with this term in that it suggests that effective language learners are somehow 'born' and not 'made'. The advantage of viewing highly able linguists as students who have independently discovered effective learning strategies is that 'aptitude' is no longer seen as something that is innate but as an ability that can be learned. This theme will be reconsidered in later paragraphs in relation to less effective learners.

Thus Student M seems to have few language learning difficulties. There is the sense, however, that her enjoyment of work in class was being somewhat inhibited by the concern about appearing more proficient than her peers. This is something that could be partially resolved by adopting some of the strategies proposed in Chapter 4. More extensive pair-work, possibly with another voluble student, would give her greater freedom to speak out, without fear of being judged aversely by other members of the group. At the same time, however, we need to address the issue of females feeling unwilling to display their abilities, for fear of appearing immodest. This is something that requires a cross-curricular approach if female confidence is to be increased effectively. It is possible, however, within one area such as the foreign language classroom, to promote a more healthy attitude to positive achievement. If all students are encouraged to evaluate their performance using some of the methods discussed in Chapter 4, then the tendency towards self-comparison with others and negatively competitive attitudes might be lessened.

Student P (female)

Student P was taking French, Chemistry and English at A-level. At the start of the project, she had been learning French for six years. She had been on an exchange to France and had participated in other visits. At GCSE level, she had gained a grade B and was predicted a grade B or C at A-level.

Student P used many positive learning strategies. Her vocabulary learning techniques included a wide range of strategies that went beyond rote learning and she was reported by her teachers to be able to use a wide range of lexis in her written work. She also noted in her diary the resolve to 'practice [sic] writing small examples of French text' in a form of creative recombination in order to improve her range of vocabulary. Orally, she was keen to participate and recognised the benefits of this, but she experienced a degree of anxiety about being seen to talk too much, claiming 'I always seem to be saying something, because all I want to do is talk really' (I). This nervousness went hand in hand with an element of perfectionism and general concern that she was not performing well enough. Her worries were not perceived by her teachers who described her as 'over-confident'.

This student did not on the surface seem to be highly motivated to pursue French to A-level and her choice was made on the basis of it being 'more something where I thought it would help me with some . . . help me with the subjects later on'. She did, however, express an interest and enjoyment in French as a language *per se*. Having chosen the subject, she showed strong commitment to it, believing that she worked harder than her peers, spending six hours a week on French private study and organising her time very effectively.

She showed a very high degree of self-direction and self-diagnosis/prescription and constantly supplemented her allotted homework by watching French films, reading round the subject and seeking to overcome gaps in her knowledge of grammar by completing exercises in a self-study course book. The latter was not without its problems, however, and her command of grammar was described by her teachers at the end of her first year as being 'still very weak'. Indeed, this weakness was attributed in part to her independence in trying to overcome her difficulties and reluctance to take advice:

> Because she works so much on her own, she gets the wrong idea into her head, learns the wrong thing and it's virtually impossible to get that idea out of her head.

It thus seems that for some students self-direction needs to be tempered with a degree of teacher guidance. During the think-aloud cloze exercises, Student P referred to both the meaning of the passage and to explicit rules, but it was clear that her knowledge of the latter was insecure, particularly with regard to basic verb endings. While the explanation from her teacher for her problems may account for some of her difficulties, it is also possible that she was trying to do too much at once, that is, gaining and reusing a wide range of vocabulary and concentrating on formal correctness. She admitted that a concern for the latter was something new to her, that 'I haven't got most of the grammar base . . . I didn't realise I wasn't making it [written French] accurate, until now' (I). While Student M's control of form from her earlier work at GCSE level appeared to allow her sufficient processing space to develop a wide range of vocabulary, Student P seemed to be divided by the demands of both form and content.

This may also account for her additional difficulties in writing — her teacher claimed that she 'thinks in English and translates from English into French and makes utter gibberish, utter gibberish!' It must be admitted, however, that this translation tendency was not greatly apparent from the student's diaries or think-aloud interview, in so far as she did undertake a degree of planning in the foreign language. She did, however, make frequent attempts to make her writing stylistically complex and it may be that she was stretching herself beyond her capabilities.

It is arguable, however, whether Student P would have achieved as much without her striving to do better and her willingness to take matters into her own hands. In her think-aloud reading comprehension at least, and in the grade that she was predicted, she appeared to have progressed more than many other students who had commenced A-level work with a higher grade at GCSE level than she did. Her autonomous approach to her work can be summed up best in her own complex metaphor, when describing the transition to A-level:

> It's a shock, it's like being thrown into the deep end, you've been swimming in the shallow end of the swimming pool and you thought, 'That's it, I'm getting there, I can swim', and then you get to A-level and you think, 'I can't swim, I've just been chucked in the deep end!' and that's just . . . how you feel and then a few weeks on you're thinking, 'Well, it's a challenge, I'm getting there', . . . at the beginning I felt as if I was just wading through mud, there was a river just floating across my head and I was just drowning in it, but I'm getting there eventually. You eventually manage to swim to the surface and you manage to float along with it. (I)

Perhaps all that was needed in this student's case was a willingness to accept a little help in swimming to the other side. This might be easier to achieve in a classroom where critically reviewing one's learning strategies, in collaboration with the teacher or with other learners, was an accepted practice. It might have helped Student P had she considered whether any of the strategies used by other members of the class could be more appropriate than her own, for example in the area of grammar learning. Rather than working doggedly at grammar exercises in the void, a more profitable strategy might involve giving these new grammatical structures a context by incorporating them into her written work. Furthermore, a think-aloud interview with the class teacher would provide the opportunity for a demonstration of how it is often more effective to remain within the limits of one's knowledge of the L2, rather than trying to translate one's thoughts directly from the mother tongue.

The comments made in relation to the affective concerns of Student M apply equally in this case, if not more so. This is true particularly where the problem of perfectionism and inadequate self-appraisal is concerned. Furthermore, the fact that Student P's teacher was unaware of her lack of confidence, indeed thought that the opposite was true, suggests a need for greater openness in the classroom on both sides.

Student F (male)

In addition to German, Student F was taking Maths and Further Maths at A-level. He had been studying German for four years when the project commenced. He had never been to Germany but had some contacts with the country through his uncle who was married to a German. He had gained a grade B in German at GCSE level and his predicted grade at A-level was C.

To a much greater extent than was the case for the previous two students, this learner's motivation to choose German as a subject to pursue at A-level was not readily apparent. Indeed, he admitted that although he had enjoyed learning the language it had not been his 'first third choice' and that he would have preferred to have taken Sport, which was not possible at his school. That German seemed to be less of a priority than his other subjects is reflected in his teacher's comments on his ability to work to deadlines, that 'German rates below Maths, so if there isn't too much to do for Maths, then homework comes in on time'. He also seemed to spend less time on German private study than other effective learners, two to three hours per week, and he displayed fewer signs in his retrospective interview or diaries of self-directed learning. Similarly, he reported that on receiving corrected work he did not always review it, 'just put it away', and that normally he did not evaluate written work before handing it in.

Motivational forces are of further interest in the case of Student F, in so far as he was the only learner in the project to claim that the relative 'masculinity' of German had influenced his decision to study the language, rather than French, at least to GCSE level. As suggested in Chapter 4, this stereotypical view of subjects being 'masculine' or 'feminine' may have been a product of the student's attending a co-educational school, where gender-based judgements about academic subjects are often more pronounced. In other respects, there was evidence of the effect of stereotypical views of appropriate male behaviour, particularly as far as affective responses to learning a language are concerned. On the one hand, Student F's teacher saw him as 'a very confident boy', largely because of his involvement and ability in sport, 'so he gets a certain amount of approbation from his peers', and reported that he was able to spring back from criticism and use it as a spur to further efforts (this is also suggested by some of his diary entries). He himself, like so many other male students interviewed, claimed that German caused him little anxiety. On the other hand, when pressed further about how he felt about speaking in front of the other members of the class (all but one of whom were female), he admitted that 'it makes me feel quite nervous sometimes' (I), mainly because of a desire not to look foolish or to invite a negative comparison — 'if I'm not that sure what to say, you don't know whether they know . . . they know exactly what to say, and it's me that doesn't, or if they don't know either' (I). This contradiction is possibly an indication of the male tendency to try and project a confident self-image in spite of inner concerns.

Still in the area of motivation, Student F's teacher believed that his interest in the language sprang from the rather 'logical' nature of its structure. Aware that he had been advised to choose a third A-level subject which would 'expand his horizons a bit', she felt this aspect of the subject appealed to him as a mathematician, and that his thinking could be summed up in the following words: 'good old German, there's an awful lot of precision work in there isn't there, so we'll do that!' As such, he was reported to enjoy and find easy the grammatical explanations presented by his teacher, usually in the manner of a formula (cf. the teacher interview, Chapter 5). He also claimed to find it straightforward learning such items as adjectival endings, using a method based on chanting. The application of such knowledge in written work, however, was problematic for him, as if, in the words of his teacher, 'the two were not connected at all . . . there's two separate tracks in his mind . . . he still doesn't seem to have got any of the little warning things in his head, you know, is this the right gender'. This inability to marry formal and communicative aspects was shown in the student's diary entries and his performance on the think-aloud cloze exercises. The former recorded his procedure while writing a narrative piece:

> When I was writing the narrations the sentences just flowed out [. . .] At that time I thought I was writing the right things. But once it was corrected I had found that I had all the tenses confused and mixed up. (D)

By contrast, he approached the cloze exercise almost entirely from a grammatical point of view, becoming involved (not always successfully) in the analysis of clauses into subject and object and trying to refer back to declensional tables in his mind. As such, the actual meaning of the passage tended to be overlooked and his completion of the tasks impeded.

Similar contradictory tendencies can also be detected in Student F's approach to reading comprehension. On the one hand, his teacher reported that he adopted a methodical approach to such tasks. Indeed, while working on the think-aloud reading passage, he often successfully employed the strategy of determining the main verb of a sentence and of using the syntax to guide him in his interpretation. He checked many items in the dictionary (a strategy also reported in his diary entries). On the other hand, this was not always done very carefully and sometimes the first definition given was selected, even if it did not convey a suitable meaning. Furthermore, the practice of looking at individual items (narrow focus) led in more difficult areas of the passage to limited comprehension.

Even though by the end of the first year of A-level work, Student F had achieved a moderate degree of proficiency (as suggested by his teacher's comments and grade prediction), it may be that he would have benefited from being shown how to employ strategies in a more flexible manner, for example, monitoring form and content in equal measure, rather than one or the other. His reaction to the suggestion of strategy training at the start of the A-level course also indicates a certain unwillingness to consider alternative modes of learning:

> I wouldn't think I'd like that much, because you like to do things how you like it and then for some things the way other people learn them isn't that good for you. (I)

Possibly, however, the objective appraisal of his current strategies and an analysis of how they could be improved upon might have helped him to achieve even more and, perhaps more importantly, encouraged him to take more active control over his learning than appears to be the case. Where students are resistant to the idea of reviewing and changing their learning strategies, it is important that persuasion rather than force is used to try to alter their attitudes. If strategy training takes place in group sessions, where everyone is sharing their ideas about the best way to tackle learning tasks, then reluctant students might be more willing to participate in such a review of learning approaches. Once possible alternative strategies have been discussed and demonstrated, the chance to try them out in a controlled situation, where evaluation and discussion of their effectiveness can take place, may make it more likely that they will be taken up and used in the long term. As suggested in Chapter 5, concrete evidence of how different strategies can help learning, perhaps in the form of some kind of test with and without the strategy, may convince the sceptical student. Similarly, structured, group activities within class involving the evaluation of corrected work may have helped this student to develop a more reflective and positive approach to errors.

On the other hand, Student F might have benefited from individual strategy training with regard to reading comprehension. Hosenfeld (1984) outlines how such remedial sessions might function within a classroom, with the rest of the class working on another activity while individual students spend time with the teacher on learning some of the reading strategies successful students use. The teacher prompts the individual student to ask a series of questions about unknown words, for example, what kind of word is it (verb, noun?), is it like an English word, given the context of the passage and/or my knowledge of the world, what would I expect it to mean in this sentence? Such questions seem particularly appropriate for Student F, to encourage him to turn less often to the dictionary; at the same time, *effective* dictionary skills could be taught, by asking him to think about whether the meaning he had selected really fitted the context of the sentence or passage.

By thus giving this student greater personal control over his performance on language tasks, one might also improve his motivation in the subject and likewise lessen his anxiety. At the same time, this further example of a teacher misreading a student's apparent confidence and the student's own reluctance to admit to any worries about language work, underlines again the need for classroom activities that will help open up communication, making students, male and female, better able to express their feelings and hence realise that they are not alone in their anxieties.

Student H (male)

Student H's A-level subjects were German, English and Religious Education. He had been studying German for four years at the start of the project but had never been to a German-speaking country. He had obtained a grade C for German at GCSE level and was predicted a D/E at A-level.

In many respects, this student seemed to display several of the characteristics traditionally associated with the good language learner. The reasons for his decision to pursue German to A-level were largely integrative, a desire to learn about 'the way people live and like getting to know other people from different countries' (I). His motivation in the sense of perseverance was also extremely high, his teacher commenting, 'where he finds the motivation to keep going, I don't know'. She also marvelled at his 'painstakingly meticulous' preparation of work and his 'ability to sit down, plan work and study'. This degree of conscientiousness was matched by the reliability and degree of commitment that characterised his participation in the research project. Furthermore, his retrospective interview suggested that he was engaged in a significant amount of self-directed learning and self-diagnosis.

Several of these attributes might also be felt to be those typically associated with female students and indeed Student H seemed to have more in common with the girls involved in the project than the boys, in terms of affective characteristics and study habits. Interestingly, and unlike most other boys, he himself remarked that languages seemed to be more typically 'girls' subjects', that this was true of all three of the subjects he was taking at A-level. He added, 'I think I prefer subjects where there are more girls in, I don't know why!' Like several female subjects, and perhaps to an even greater extent than most of them, he frequently expressed anxiety concerning his progress in German and in doing so did not shy away from using vocabulary that is noticeably absent from the interviews and diaries of other male students. Anxiety was particularly associated with listening comprehension and the forthcoming final A-level examination:

> [Under section headed 'How do I feel?']
> HOPELESS! I felt as if I will never pass my A-level German. I feel very concerned about my listening aspects of German. (D)

Although this entry was made early in the term, similar ones were made throughout the diary-keeping session, together with ones that indicated a high degree of negative self-comparison. It has already been mentioned in Chapter 4 that Student H was alone in seeming not to gain in confidence during the project and that this might be attributable to his inability to perceive any progress commensurate with the effort that he was devoting to his studies. His teacher also commented that he appeared to have grown used to 'failure', remarking that 'H's assumption is that it's going to be wrong, "because it always is"'.

Indeed, in spite of the potentially effective strategies mentioned earlier, Student H continued to experience considerable difficulties throughout his first year of A-level work, although he did make progress. Again, as suggested in Chapter 4, this may be because aspects of his learning approach, such as meticulous preparation, can be labour-intensive, giving relatively little return on the effort expended. The student's diaries suggest that he was unable to think of alternative solutions which might have proved more effective. Under the heading of 'What should I do now?', his most frequent comment was 'Practise'. Other strategies, as suggested by his think-aloud interview, were used inappropriately or inflexibly. His over-reliance on context in reading and listening and tendency towards the so-called 'perseverative text processing strategy' (Kimmel & MacGinitie,

1984), have already been discussed in detail in Chapter 3 and are indicative of this ineffective use of reading strategies.

Furthermore, to an even greater extent than Student F, Student H seemed unable to perceive any link between the grammar rules he had been taught and the role structure plays in meaning. His think-aloud interview in the cloze exercises indicates that he was following procedures outlined by his teacher (further evidence of this was obtained from the teacher interview), in analysing sentences into, for example, subject, verb, object, but without really understanding the functions they perform. It is worth citing at length his comments made while deciding what to put on the end of 'unser' ('our') in the first gap of Text A, after he had used the dictionary to determine the gender of 'Gemeinde' ('community'):

> In unserer Klasse stellten wir uns die Frage, wie Jugendliche in ____ (unser) Gemeinde ihre Freizeit ____ (verbringen).
> (In our class we asked each other about how young people in ____ (our) community ____ (spend) their free time.)

In your class stands the question what young people in your community do with their free time . . . in your . . . in your . . . so it's not . . . it's not going to be in the nominative case, cos that's the subject . . . it could be . . . well, it's not the genitive, cos that's possession, so I've got three more to choose from, nominative, accusative or dative . . . in your . . . and I'm doing I'm being asked the question, so accusative . . . I think it's the accusative, so feminine accusative, '*ein', 'eine', '*einen' . . . . (writes '*unsere') . . . is that right? . . . it doesn't look right to me . . . + . . . this is in the . . . this is in its, um, in its form before it's affected by anything (pointing to 'unser'), and I know that's feminine ('Gemeinde'), and I've got to work out the case it's in, and I know it's not in the genitive case, cos . . . to me that's the easiest one to work out, cos it's not possession, and I don't belong to the class, as I'm not connected with it, and then I've got the nominative, accusative and dative . . . between the nominative, accusative and dative — the dative I always get confused cos it's . . . one's having the verb done to you and one's doing the verb, and I don't think it's the nominative case cos I'm not nearer the front . . . '

This convoluted explanation suggests the accumulation of a discrete set of 'rules', almost completely divorced from the actual meaning of the sentence. It highlights some of the dangers that may arise in teaching structures in an analytical, 'grammarian' form to students who are not by nature disposed to such an approach.

It might be argued, however, that this student's difficulties were simply the result of a lack of what might be called language aptitude. This was the view of his teacher, who in spite of her admiration for his tenacity, felt that:

> He's got, bless his heart, but he's got no linguistic ability whatsoever, he really hasn't . . . there is innate linguistic ability, isn't there, and he hasn't got any.

In some respects, her supposition appears to be borne out if one compares some of the student's difficulties with aspects of the standard definition of linguistic aptitude provided by Carroll, as recorded in various works (e.g. Carroll, 1981). Student H was described by his teacher as being unable, in listening comprehension, to match sounds and symbols and thus seemed to have a low level of phonetic coding ability. This was also observed in the think-aloud exercise, as was his difficulty in identifying the various syntactic roles played by items in a sentence (akin to Carroll's grammatical sensitivity). Similarly, his inductive learning ability, the capacity to identify patterns, rules and relationships within language was observed to be poor.

For all these indications of low aptitude, however, it seems unduly pessimistic to conclude that the difficulties of learners such as Student H are beyond resolution. While aptitude may be regarded by some as innate and thus immutable, learning strategies are more amenable to refinement (cf. comments by McLaughlin, 1990). This is suggested by the fact that weaker learners like Student H *do* use many of the same strategies as their more successful peers, if ineffectively. How they might be helped to modify their learning behaviour is the question. As before, Student H would have benefited from an extensive review of his learning strategies and how he applied them. Individual strategy training would seem more appropriate here than group sessions, perhaps with his teacher modelling effective techniques and asking him to imitate them immediately afterwards. Areas to concentrate on in reading and listening would include the need to move away from an almost exclusive reliance on inferencing from context, checking initial predictions made about the meaning of a passage based on its presumed context, in the light of how the text progresses. This would involve using strategies to complement inferencing from context, including looking for cognates; in reading, moving backwards and forwards in the text to reconsider original interpretations (double-check monitoring), trying a variety of alternative interpretations to find the best fit (substitution). More effective use of a dictionary would also have helped Student H; in his think-aloud interview he demonstrated how, even when he did stop to check the meaning of words, his resourcing strategies were adversely affected by inferencing and world elaboration:

> *Zumindest behauptet [. . .] Professor Horst Opaschowski, daß bereits 79 Prozent der 14- bis 19jährigen über zu wenig Nachtruhe klagen . . .*
> *(Professor Horst Opaschowski at least claims that already 79% of 16 to 19 year olds are suffering from too little sleep.)*
>
> Well, it's a new area, and um, where young people can go which is free from stress, and, um, the professor has said that 79% of the 14 to 19 year olds . . . and that's . . . I think that's to go out at night (pointing to 'Nachtruhe') I'll look that up (does so) . . . 'night rest', yeah, how they spend their evenings out of school.

Here, one might show him the need to check that the meaning found fits in with items immediately preceding and following the word and not just the presumed overall context.

This strategy training would need to be combined with tasks such as diary keeping that would encourage Student H to evaluate the effectiveness of the new strategies employed and the extent to which they were helping him to make progress. In this way, it would be hoped that he would develop greater insight into his own learning behaviour, feel more in control of the situation and lose some of the sense of hopelessness that came across so strongly during the project.

7 Conclusion

Introduction

What picture, then, has emerged of language learning at A-level? This is best answered by returning to the original questions posed in Chapter 1 and summarising what has emerged in relation to each.

What difficulties are faced by A-level learners within the foreign languages classroom?

Written and oral comments from students largely supported the anecdotal evidence referred to in Chapter 1 concerning the wide gap between the demands of GCSE French and German programmes and those of A-level work — although naturally the degree to which difficulties were experienced varied between individual learners within different schools and colleges. Moreover, some students obviously enjoyed the challenge of work which they felt was more 'authentic'. The nature of the difficulties experienced, however, was not entirely predictable. While *reading* was frequently cited as a strength in the open section of the questionnaire, responses to the closed section indicated that many students were heavily dependent on resourcing in comprehending texts. Views on *vocabulary learning* were equally mixed, although a sizeable number of students reported feeling overwhelmed by the amount they had to learn (or were expected to know). In the area of *grammar*, while some students welcomed more explicit explanations of structure, or worked confidently within the framework of a thorough and largely explicit revision of grammar that seemed to prevail in many establishments, others indicated that they found problematic the application of grammar in written and oral work, the greater emphasis placed on the matter compared with earlier periods of language learning, the apparently sudden increase in demands made by teachers in terms of accuracy, and the use of grammatical terminology. Some factors, such as a greater emphasis on accuracy, applied also to *written work*, with length and the complexity of topics to be discussed causing additional problems. On the other hand, where teachers provided support in the form of asking students to write on familiar topics or within familiar narrative frameworks, the difficulties were less acute.

The same applied to *oral work*. As a skill much emphasised at GCSE level, this appeared to cause more problems than might have been anticipated, even though a large number of respondents cited it as a strength. It was viewed positively largely where students were involved in oral work of a basic interpersonal and communicative skills type, such as role-plays. Where they were asked to perform at a higher, cognitive/academic language proficiency level, in class discussions involving the expression of opinions, then oral work was felt to be very difficult. Additional factors contributing to students' difficulties in this area were concerns about accuracy, fluency, pronunciation, accent and a limited vocabulary.

The most obviously problematic area, however, appeared to be *listening comprehension*, in so far as it was mentioned by many respondents to the questionnaire as a weakness but by relative few as a strength (especially in French). Students were not only troubled by the speed and linguistic complexity of authentic French and German, but by problems with word-recognition and maintaining concentration. Once again, listening is frequently assumed to be a 'communicative' skill and therefore one with which students should be familiar from earlier stages in their language learning. Clearly, this is far from being the case.

What are the learning strategies employed by students to overcome the difficulties they experience?

Both the retrospective and the think-aloud interviews confirmed that the students involved in the project had developed potentially conscious strategies by which they sought to acquire, retrieve and utilise language and that they were able to describe them. The number and range of strategies were found to be less important than the manner and combination in which they were employed, which was often inappropriate. In *reading* and *listening comprehension*, effective students were more likely to use a multi-pronged approach to comprehending the text, balancing strategies such as inferencing from context with those that looked more closely at the meaning of individual words, involving, for example, the use of cognates or prefixes or suffixes to decode the item. Weaker students relied heavily on inferencing because of a limited ability in rapid word-recognition and in identifying the syntactic role of items. While students employed some of the learning strategies identified in earlier studies as beneficial to language comprehension (e.g. comprehension monitoring and double-check monitoring), these key metacognitive strategies were employed less frequently by all students than might have been expected. This was most apparent for weaker students, whose failure to take appropriate action when comprehension breakdowns were signalled was often apparent, with many seeming to adopt a 'perseverative text processing strategy' (Kimmel & MacGinitie, 1984) whereby an initial interpretation was adhered to despite contradictory evidence. In reading, resourcing emerged as an important strategy for most students, although it was not always a helpful one.

Turning specifically to *listening comprehension*, it was noted that students of all abilities claimed to listen out for 'key items' (selective attention). More effective students made better use of this strategy, because they were more often able to identify words which were 'key' items in the true sense of the word, i.e. important as far as the central meaning of a phrase was concerned, and to establish how these items fitted in with the other elements of the phrase. They were better able to do this partly because the items they recognised were more numerous and identified more rapidly than was the case for less effective students, who were more inclined to identify perhaps one word and then failed to see what role this played in the phrase as a whole.

In the area of *grammar learning* and *grammatical manipulation*, the strategies used by students were in concordance with the supposition made from the questionnaire results, namely that the teaching and learning of explicit grammatical rules was more widespread than might be expected in view of the generally communicative approach adopted at earlier stages of language learning. Both interviews suggested that many students made frequent reference to formal rules and patterns within their language work. The retrospective interview further indicated that this was accompanied by resourcing, rote learning of conjugation and/or declension tables. In contrast, a small but sizeable group claimed to rely mainly on what might be called instinct (visual or auditory monitoring) in their judgement of grammaticality, with a sub-group indicating that they depended on guessing.

Within the framework of the think-aloud cloze exercises, few students used form- and meaning-based strategies in an effective combination. Indeed, such harmony was achieved by only a small number of highly effective students. Many either adhered doggedly to grammatical rules which they thought applied, without checking if this was in keeping with the meaning of the text, or selected items which fitted from the point of view of meaning but which were grammatically not feasible. On the one hand, this appears to be an indication of a lack of training in using strategies effectively, on the other, it may suggest that at the start of an A-level course, students, although all at the same point in their academic career, are at different stages in their grammatical development, both in their ability to analyse language and in their ability to perceive the essential link between grammatical forms and the functions in terms of meaning which they perform.

In the learning of *vocabulary*, the main factor identified was the extent to which language students at this level were reliant on a small range of strategies, with the inclusion of very few which involve active enhancement of the material to be retained (such as mnemonic devices).

Important strategies identified in the skill of *writing* included planning, drafting, monitoring one's production from the point of view of accuracy, meaning, language repertoire, style and sophistication, using either auditory or visual monitoring, or reference to rules or patterns, production evaluation, substitution, translation, resourcing and circumlocution/paraphrase. Creating practice opportunities, mainly in the form of writing to penfriends, was reasonably common, but chiefly among girls.

A qualitative consideration of two main strategy categories, planning and monitoring again brought important insights into how students use strategies when writing. Regarding the first of these, few students seemed to make detailed plans or to plan in the foreign language (except a few very effective learners). The extent to which students appeared to generate their ideas in the L1 and then to translate these into the L2 — in the case of weaker students, almost verbatim, using transfer in the form of borrowing L1 structures — was striking.

While some effective students did plan in the L1, they seemed to be less inclined to translate their ideas word-for-word and used language repertoire monitoring more effectively (although not more often) than weaker students. Monitoring for accuracy (together with pattern/rule application) emerged in the think-aloud interview, almost paradoxically, as a strategy more widely used by less effective students, but several important points in this respect were noted. First, these students were inconsistent in how they applied accuracy monitoring, checking some items and not others, and were often hampered by the fact that their knowledge and command of the patterns/rules to which they were referring was weak. Second, in some cases monitoring appeared as an impediment to the flow of composition, resulting in writing which was fragmentary and lacking in style. Third, monitoring seemed to be restricted to surface errors, such as genders, while sentences where the meaning was nearly totally obscured by inappropriate syntax or vocabulary choice were accepted by students. This seemed on occasions to be caused by their inability to stand back from their writing and see that the sense of what they were trying to say, although clear to them because the idea was firmly implanted in their mind, might be less clear to others.

Effective students, on the other hand, both in drafting and in monitoring, seemed more aware of the need to consider one's audience and monitored additionally for style and sophistication. Some very effective students were observed to delay monitoring for accuracy until they had got their ideas down on paper, in order not to interrupt the flow of their composition.

Two major points of observation emerged concerning *oral skills*. On the one hand, it was observed that the transition to A-level work had allowed students to employ several of the strategies normally associated with communicative language teaching: creating practice opportunities, naturalistic practice, circumlocution/paraphrase, cooperation and risk-taking. As might be expected, there were variations in the form in which certain of these were employed. The most effective students not only took advantage of visits to the foreign country but also created practice opportunities in this country by seeking out native speakers, speaking in the L2 to family or friends, or deliberately re-using in class newly learnt expressions. On the other hand, the incidence of planning, translation and silent rehearsal was taken as a reflection of some of the difficulties students reported in discussing higher-level ideas, a skill with which they were unlikely to be familiar from earlier work.

How do these learner difficulties and learning strategies relate to gender and affective factors, such as anxiety and motivation?

Oral work appeared as a central issue in this respect. All sources of information from students found that comments relating to difficulties in this area (including worries about 'performance' factors such as accent and pronunciation) were significantly more frequent among girls, as were those relating to worrying about one's work in general and keeping up with the other members of the class. In some instances it seemed as if oral performance (particularly in whole-class situations) was bound up in these students' minds with how they were viewed as a person, with class group dynamics appearing to influence the situation. Negative self-comparison with others, or with an idealised image of the self (a form of perfectionism) were also involved in certain cases. It was suggested that such feelings might well be detrimental to oral work, in so far as a strategy commonly mentioned as a way of dealing with these anxieties was to avoid speaking out in class where possible.

Girls further seemed worried at the prospect of being the only class member not to understand some aspect of the language. It was suggested that while boys seemed more aware of the commonality of their difficulties, girls were less able to assess the situation objectively, even if they were performing at a high level. It was also observed, however, that the degree of anxiety witnessed in the male participants might be an underestimation of the truth, in that their reactions to questions about their feelings suggested an unwillingness to admit to worrying about their work or speaking out in class.

In more general aspects of their language work, a tendency towards conscientiousness on the part of girls was in evidence. For example, they appeared to plan more carefully in written work. While the 'female' strategies just mentioned may be viewed negatively in that they are perhaps indicative of low-self esteem (frequently at the root of conscientiousness), others appear as more positive within the framework of language learning. In both listening and oral work, girls seemed better able to respond to the 'human' element of the task, in the former, using inferencing from tone to aid their comprehension, in the latter, displaying greater evidence of cooperation strategies. They were also more likely to have developed contacts with native speakers.

It was observed that there were certain links between motivation, learning strategies, anxiety and gender. Boys appeared to be more likely to establish their own personal agenda for learning and to experience demotivation and frustration if this did not match the teaching agenda. Both sexes gave the impression that important factors in fostering high motivation and low anxiety included the setting of tasks which were neither above nor below their ability, and their teacher's acknowledgement of any improvement they had made in their performance.

Yet one of the most vital components of motivation is the ability to direct one's own learning, involving self-analysis of one's strengths and weaknesses, one's learning behaviour, and the adoption of suitable strategies to deal with any problems. More effective students appeared better able to do this, while for most it was an attribute that was still waiting to be fully developed. It was further argued, drawing on evidence from the learner diaries, that where students were encouraged to assess their own learning in terms of the strategies they had used and what they had achieved, greater self-esteem and lower anxiety were likely to result, as students perceived a link between effort and outcome over which they might have some control.

How do teachers perceive their students' learning difficulties and what steps do they take to resolve them?

Certain disparities between students' perceptions of their difficulties and those made by their teachers emerged from the questionnaire. It was observed that teachers were inclined to underestimate the difficulties students experienced in *oral work* and *listening comprehension*, together with those they anticipated facing in the future, and to emphasise instead their problems in *writing* and *grammar*. Weaknesses in study skills were also emphasised more heavily by teachers, with students showing few signs of concern about this aspect of their work. Comments made in the teacher interview went some way to reinforce those expressed in the questionnaire, with certain respondents underlining students' weaknesses in the area of independent, self-directed learning outside class.

Regarding steps taken to ease the transition, many teachers appeared to be tackling the BICS/CALP gap by presenting students at the start of the course with structured tasks within the framework of familiar topics. At the same time, much attention was devoted to the thorough revision (or teaching for the first time) of grammatical forms, often within separate grammar lessons. Certain teachers reported having taken steps to deal with affective problems and to develop students' self-confidence. Study skills, however, appeared to attract less attention than might have been expected in view of the concern expressed about them in earlier sections of the questionnaire.

While the findings are generally encouraging and offer many examples of good practice, the teacher interview indicated that few teachers took steps to encourage their students to become better learners in the sense of helping them to develop effective learning strategies. Indeed, it would seem that teachers had a limited understanding of the meaning or import of learning strategies, perhaps seeing their role as one of 'teaching language' rather than of developing learning skills. Pressures of time also appeared to be a factor in this respect. It was noted that many appeared to assume that their students knew how to study, or that it was their own responsibility, not that of the teacher, to develop these skills. Where certain strategies had been presented to students, such as in reading comprehension, this was often done in a sporadic fashion, with little real practice or follow-up work on how to put such strategies to most effective use.

The Way Forward

Previous chapters have already looked at possible solutions to the situation just outlined, but it is worth underlining these and presenting them in the form of a 'seven-point plan':

Get to know your students

This is not as obvious as it might first appear and involves the teacher developing an appreciation of those aspects of their learning that students find difficult, on both a cognitive and an affective level. It may not be readily apparent from students' performance on language tasks that they are experiencing problems. For example, a reading text prepared at home for discussion in class may seem, from students' ability to answer questions about it, to have caused few difficulties; yet this may well mask the fact that it took several hours of laboriously consulting the dictionary to arrive at comprehension. More openness between learners is especially important regarding affective concerns, where apparent student confidence, particularly on the part of highly able female learners, frequently conceals anxieties about speaking out and participating in class activities.

Review your materials

While the start of an A-level course almost inevitably brings new challenges for students, problems with demotivation and low morale can arise if these challenges are beyond them. Again, this may seem to be an obvious statement, but it is not something that all teachers take into account. Initial tasks presented to students need to be of a kind with which they are already familiar, structured and short. The content of early texts should similarly be within the limits of their experience. Grammar teaching must be carefully integrated into lessons, rather than taught as a separate entity, if the situation noted in previous chapters, where students fail to see the connection between structure and meaning, is to be avoided.

Focus on learning strategies

The central argument of previous chapters has been the importance of looking not only at *what* students are learning, but *how* they are learning. Furthermore, only a few able students are likely to develop on their own learning strategies that are appropriate to the given task and effectively implemented. Most will require detailed and structured guidance in this respect. Learning strategy training, however, as outlined in Chapter 3, needs to be integrated into students' regular classes if they are going to appreciate their relevance for language learning tasks; students need to constantly monitor and evaluate the strategies they develop and use; and they need to be aware of the nature, function and importance of such strategies.

This last point applies equally to teachers. One of the most vital factors in determining the success of learning strategy training appears to be an understanding and acceptance of learning strategies by instructors, and their confidence in being able to conduct strategy training in the classroom. All of this points to a need for more emphasis to be placed on the issue of learning strategies in general within programmes of initial teacher training and in-service course for practising teachers.

Encourage reflection

This again applies both to teachers and learners. Those teachers who have thought carefully about how they learned a language, about which strategies are most appropriate for which tasks, are more likely to be successful in developing 'strategic competence' in their students. For learners, a vital component of self-directed learning lies in the on-going evaluation of the methods they have employed on tasks and of their achievements within the A-level programme. This will have benefits for their progress in both a cognitive and an affective sense.

Strategy training is an on-going process

Most of the teachers I spoke to, if they did try to promote effective learning strategies in their students, did so in single, isolated sessions, often at the outset of the A-level course. However, research suggests that many strategies, which are themselves complex skills, take time and guided practice to acquire. As argued in Chapter 3, the time and effort spent on such activities is a good investment, in that it eventually fosters greater learner autonomy. This is at the centre of effective language learning, for, in the words of Ellis and Sinclair (1989: 2), 'those learners who are responsible for their own learning can carry on learning outside the classroom'.

Work as a team

Some of the problems noted earlier regarding hesitancy on the part of teachers to embark on strategy training might be avoided if it is an approach adopted across the language department. Not only can resources be pooled and information exchanged, but a joint venture may well heighten the motivation of teachers apprehensive about embarking on such a task. Opportunities for discussing difficulties and successes seem vital in this respect.

Furthermore, learning strategy training is an issue that has cross-curricular implications. While it is true that there are often problems in transferring skills learnt in one subject area to another, encouraging students to think about how they are learning now and how they could learn more effectively is of relevance to all aspects of the curriculum. Indeed, reflectiveness may well be the key transferrable skill.

Start them young

This book has concentrated on the learning difficulties and strategies of advanced language learners. Although there is some indication that the use of learning strategies develops with age, with cognitive strategies such as repetition being acquired earliest, there is also evidence that simple strategy training can be effective with pupils as young as 11 years of age (Grenfell & Harris, 1993, 1994). It seems probable that students who are encouraged from an early age to think about how they are learning stand a better chance of becoming 'strategically competent' as they grow older. Problems of transition can occur at various stages of one's language learning; Bagguley (1990), for example, illustrates how university foreign language students in the UK often find it hard to adjust to their new course. With a firmer emphasis on the development of such a competence these difficulties might be more readily overcome.

Final thoughts

In Chapter 1 it was suggested that one of the main goals of second language acquisition research is to shed light on the question of 'who learns how much of what language under what conditions' (Spolsky, 1989: 3). Although this book does not pretend to have had such lofty ambitions, it is hoped that insights have been gained into certain elements of this maxim, namely those concerning 'who' and 'under what conditions'. That is (and referring again to Spolsky, 1989), it has tried to uncover some of the differences that exist between individual learners and the learning behaviour that seems to facilitate effective language learning within the framework of A-level study. Above all, it is hoped that the study has illustrated the pressing need for teachers to actively *help* students take more responsibility for their own learning, by encouraging greater reflection about learning strategies. In the words of Norman (1980: 256):

It is strange that we expect students to learn yet seldom teach them anything about learning.

It is this access to the learning process which educators must provide, rather than merely assuming that all learners will discover it automatically for themselves.

Appendixes

A1: Glossary

affective Relating to emotional or psychological responses, feelings or attitudes towards particular situations or experiences.

A-level, Advanced Level, GCE (General Certificate of Education) An examination taken by pupils at 18 years of age in England, Wales and Northern Ireland. Traditionally, students follow courses in two or three subjects for two years before the final examination. At the beginning of the A-level course, students of foreign languages will typically have been learning their first foreign language for five years, their second foreign language for two to five years. Most will have taken the **GCSE** examination prior to entering an A-level programme of study. Pass grades awarded range from A (the highest) to E.

bottom–up processing A form of processing information in reading or listening comprehension whereby meaning is derived by analysing and decoding individual words.

GCSE, General Certificate of Secondary Education An examination taken by pupils at 16 years of age in England, Wales and Northern Ireland, and the principal means of assessing the **National Curriculum** at that stage. Learners of foreign languages generally take the examination after five years of study in their first foreign language, after two to five years in their second foreign language. The GCSE was introduced in 1986, with the first examination in the summer of 1988. It replaced the former GCE (General Certificate of Education) Ordinary Level (O-level) and CSE (Certificate of Secondary Education) examinations. Grades awarded range from A* (since 1994, the highest grade) to G.

cognitive Relating to knowledge or intellectual activities.

cognitive strategy A learning strategy that aids the comprehension, learning, handling or retention of material by means of direct mental manipulation or transformation of that material. An example would be

173

grouping together words to be learnt according to different categories. See also Appendix A.2.

cognitive theory, and language learning This views language acquisition as a complex cognitive skill that functions in the same way as other cognitive skills, based on the acquisition and storage of information in memory, first **short-term** and then **long-term memory**.

communicative competence The ability to speak and understand a language with due regard to its grammar, sociolinguistic or cultural aspects, and to be able to employ successfully **communication strategies** to overcome breakdowns in communication.

communication strategies Techniques employed by a speaker to overcome breakdowns in communication, particularly those arising from imperfect knowledge of or proficiency in the foreign language. Examples include paraphrase, gesture, mime. See also Appendix A.2.

interlanguage A language students' intermediate form of a second or foreign language, often a blend of his/her native language and the language being learned.

L1 The mother tongue.

L2 The foreign or second language.

learner diaries Journals in which students record information relating to their learning, for example, how they have attempted to learn something, what they feel they have achieved, their plans for future learning.

learning strategies Thoughts or behaviours that help students to understand, learn or retain new information.

long-term memory Memory that stores information and retains it over a long period. This information lies dormant until it is activated in **short-term memory**.

metacognitive strategy A **learning strategy** that involves reflection about the process of learning and the most appropriate way to approach it. Typically, metacognitive strategies entail planning for, monitoring or evaluating the success of learning activities. See also Appendix A.2.

metalanguage Terminology used for the description or analysis of language.

National Curriculum A compulsory national curriculum for maintained schools at primary and secondary levels in England, Wales and Northern Ireland. Programmes of study and attainment targets are set within each subject at four key stages, corresponding to ages 7, 11, 14 and 16. The **GCSE** is the main form of assessment at Key Stage Four.

perseverative text processing strategy A negative strategy employed by some students, mainly with regard to reading comprehension but also in listening comprehension, whereby an initial hypothesis is made concerning a text's meaning and then adhered to rigidly in spite of later evidence in the text that disconfirms it.

retrospective interview An interview in which learners are asked to look back and report on the learning strategies they generally use.

short-term memory The active working memory store that holds information for a brief period, with the individual being aware of the information stored in it.

social/affective strategy A **learning strategy** that may involve contact with others to aid learning, as in cooperation on tasks or exchanging information. Affective or emotional responses that may hinder learning can also be controlled or alleviated by social/affective strategies, such as thinking positively, sharing one's worries with others. See also Appendix A.2.

strategic competence The ability to use **communication strategies** to overcome breakdowns in communication, for example, using a paraphrase when an item of vocabulary is unknown. (ii) Making full and proficient use of learning strategies.

study skills Techniques, usually overt and visible, that aid learning. They are usually function at a lower level than **learning strategies**, which act as executive processes coordinating study skills. Study skills are often taught specifically to help students pass examinations and may include such techniques as writing essays under timed conditions.

think-aloud interview, thinking aloud Verbalising one's thought processes during a learning activity, performing a learning activity and reporting on the **learning strategies** being used at one and the same time.

top–down processing A form of processing information in reading or listening comprehension whereby prior experience or background knowledge is used to predict or infer the meaning of a text.

A2: Definitions of Learning Strategies Used by Students

The following taxonomy has been adapted from that of O'Malley and Chamot (1990: 137–139), and Oxford (1985, 1986). Strategies and quotations taken from these two sources are indicated as [1] and [2] respectively. Strategies (or aspects of these) observed in A-level students which were not felt to be covered by these earlier taxonomies are indicated by *. Terms used to identify and describe the strategies are therefore a combination of the language of these writers and my own. Examples given originate from the student interviews. (NB: A revised version of the O'Malley and Chamot (1990) taxonomy can be found in Chamot and O'Malley (1994: 62–3)).

Metacognitive strategies

Advance organisation[1,2]	Examining aspects of a forthcoming language task prior to embarking upon it proper (e.g. reading and thinking about the questions before hearing a listening passage or reading/listening to a text for gist comprehension before attempting to answer questions on it).
Creating practice opportunities[2]	Deliberately looking for or creating as many opportunities as possible to use the L2 (e.g. trying to participate as much as possible in class, finding penpals, buying L2 magazines).
Directed attention[1,2]	Prior to tackling a task, deciding to concentrate on it fully; during the task, maintaining concentration.
Drafting (L1/L2)*	Generating a preliminary version of the final composition, refining and editing it (e.g. writing a first version of an essay, in the L1 or L2, then rewriting it as the final L2 copy.

Evaluation

(i) Before correction:

Production evaluation (accuracy)*	Checking one's work when the task is finished from the point of view of grammatical accuracy (cf. production monitoring).
Production evaluation (delayed)*	Checking one's work after a period of time has elapsed (e.g. 'I'll leave it alone . . . . go back to it with a fresh mind, look through it again').
Production evaluation (meaning)*	Checking one's work when the task is finished from the point of view of the meaning conveyed (cf. production monitoring).
Strategy evaluation[1]	Assessing strategies used once the task is completed.

(ii) After teacher's corrections:

Amending errors*	Writing out/repeating orally the correct version.
Analysing errors*	Deciding why something is incorrect and how to correct it.
Assessing errors*	Judging the seriousness of errors made.
Attending to errors*	Making a mental note of the corrected version (e.g. telling oneself to avoid the error another time).
Reading through errors*	Looking to see where one has made mistakes.

Monitoring (during task completion):

Auditory monitoring[1]	'Using one's "ear" for the language (how something sounds) to make decisions' (e.g. when deciding on an adjective ending)[1].
Comprehension monitoring[1]	'Checking, verifying, or correcting one's understanding' [1], of a written or spoken text (e.g. realising that one's suggested interpretation of a sentence does not make sense).
Double-check monitoring[1]	Looking back over the task at decisions made or possibilities already considered (e.g. while reading, checking one's initial interpretation of a word in the light of its different use later in the passage).
* Language repertoire monitoring	During the task, assessing whether one knows enough of the L2 to complete it fully (e.g. 'I won't think up something too difficult that I know I won't be able to write down in French').
Production monitoring * (accuracy)	Checking or correcting one's language production from the point of view of grammatical accuracy (e.g. concentrating on correct subject/verb agreements).
Production monitoring * (meaning)	Checking or correcting one's language production from the point of the meaning conveyed (e.g. 'Am I expressing myself clearly? Am I covering all the points?').

* Sophistication monitoring	Checking that one's language production goes beyond basic requirements (e.g. 'You can write something that's not so boring as you've been learning for GCSE, you find something a bit more imaginative').
Strategy monitoring[1]	Assessing how well a strategy is working.
Style monitoring[1]	'Checking, verifying, or correcting based upon an internal stylistic register' [1] (e.g. at the phrase or sentence level).
Visual monitoring[1]	'Using one's "eye" for the language (how something looks) to make decisions' (e.g. when deciding on the spelling of a word).
Planning (L1/L2)[1]	Making plans for the completion or structure of a language task (e.g. jotting down the main ideas to be included in an essay, in the L1 or L2; outlining paragraphs and thinking about the sequence of ideas presented).
Problem identification[1]	Identifying elements of a task that hold the key to its successful completion (e.g. identifying words in a passage that are central to its comprehension).

Progress monitoring:

Comparison*	Comparing one's performance/understanding with that of others in the class.
Grade assessment*	Judging one's progress by referring to grades obtained.
Self-assessment[2]	Judging one's overall progress against one's own internal measure.
Reviewing*	Looking over work completed in class, including re-reading new vocabulary or grammar notes, following up areas covered to ensure they have been understood.

Scheduling/ organisation[2]	Drawing up and using suitable schedules for the regular and punctual completion of assignments, over an appropriate period of time (e.g. writing assignment submission dates in a diary; spreading work out over the week); managing one's time and work efficiently (e.g. prioritising tasks to be completed).
Selective attention[1]	Prior to tackling a task, deciding to focus on particular aspects of it; during the task, focusing on particular aspects of the task or the language involved in it (e.g. deciding to listen out for key words in a listening comprehension passage).
Self-diagnosis/ prescription[2]	Determining one's weaknesses in the L2 and deciding what ought to be done to deal with these.
Self- management/ *philosophising[1]	Understanding what helps one complete language tasks successfully and making sure that tasks are carried out in that manner; theorising about how a language works and the best way to learn it (e.g. 'I don't mind speaking in class, I think it's important that you speak as much as possible').

Cognitive strategies

* Cohesion markers	Referring to emphasis markers to assist completion of a task (e.g. locating key points in a passage from such phrases as 'It's important that . . . ').

Elaboration (relating new information to previously acquired knowledge, to comprehend, retain or produce language)[1]:

Academic elaboration[1]	'Using knowledge gained in academic situations'[1].
Between parts elaboration[1]	'Relating parts of the task to each other' [1] (e.g. using one's understanding of the first part of a text to help understand a later part).
Personal elaboration[1]	'Making judgements about or reacting personally to the material presented' [1].
Questioning elaboration[1]	'Using a combination of questions and world knowledge to brainstorm logical solutions to a task' [1].

World elaboration[1]	'Using knowledge gained from experience in the world'[1].
Formulaic phrases*	Making use of or noticing prefabricated chunks of language to comprehend or produce language (e.g. beginning an essay with a well-rehearsed phrase).
Highlighting[2]	Highlighting words, phrases, rules, perhaps by marking or underlining.
Hypothesising*	Suggesting possible meanings/solutions for a task.
Imitation[2]	Following the model of a native speaker or writer to improve one's own language performance.
Inferencing[1,2]	Making use of available information to guess the meanings or usage of unknown items
(a) By context	Guessing from the general context of the passage;
(b) By tone	Guessing from the tone of voice used by the speaker;
(c) By visual images	Guessing from pictures accompanying a text;
(d) 'Hearing in'*	Being so influenced by the general context of a listening passage that one imagines hearing certain vocabulary items that are in fact absent.
Interpretation[2]	Translating from one language to another in a non-verbatim manner (e.g. striving to produce an L1 version of an L2 passage that is stylistically acceptable).
Narrow focus*	Concentrating on the deciphering of a word, phrase or syllable (often to the detriment of overall comprehension).
Naturalistic practice[2]	Practising the L2 in authentic settings (e.g. watching films, reading magazines, talking to native speakers).
Note-taking[1,2]	Writing down key words and concepts during the language task to assist its completion.
Omission*	Skipping unknown L2 items (e.g. in a reading comprehension passage.)

Pattern/rule application[2]	Using grammatical rules and patterns in the L2 to complete a task (e.g. referring back to previously learnt rules about tense usage when writing); thinking logically about grammatical elements of the L2 (e.g. deciding which case a preposition takes and from this choosing an appropriate adjective ending).
Pattern/rule search[2]	Looking for patterns and rules in the L2 to assist learning (e.g. learning verb conjugations in a paradigmatic fashion).
* Pot luck	Making a wild guess about the meaning or use of a word, selecting a grammatical form at random.
* Reading in L1/L2	In think-aloud reading comprehension/cloze tasks, reading a sentence aloud using a mixture of both languages.
* Reading in L2	In think-aloud reading comprehension/cloze tasks, reading a phrase aloud in the L2.
* Reading on	Reading the next sentence/paragraph in a passage to aid comprehension of unknown parts.
Recombination[2]	Creating a phrase or sentence by combining items previously learnt in a new way.
Repetition * (oral)	Repeating a chunk of language in order to learn it.
Repetition * (aural)	Listening to a chunk of language several times to aid retention or understanding.
Resourcing[1,2]	Using reference sources containing information on the L2 (e.g. dictionaries, textbooks, grammar books, previously completed work).
Rule exercises[2]	Practising grammatical rules through oral or written language exercises.
Sentence analysis*	Breaking sentences down into grammatical units to aid comprehension or formal accuracy (e.g. determining whether a noun is the subject or the object of the sentence).
Substitution[1]	Trying out alternative approaches or solutions, selecting different words or phrases to accomplish a language task.

Summarisation[1,2]   Making a mental or written summary of language and information set out in a task.

Test-taking*   Using one's knowledge of how tests/tasks are laid out/formulated to complete them successfully.

Transcription*   Understanding listening tasks by writing down verbatim chunks of language, often in a phonetic manner.

Transfer[1,2]   Using previously acquired L1 or L3 linguistic knowledge to assist in the completion of an L2 language task (e.g.using one's knowledge of cognates to comprehend a vocabulary item).

Translation[1,2]   Giving a word-for-word translation from one language to another.

Vocabulary retention strategies:

Contextual-isation[2]   Remembering new L2 items by creating a context for them or recalling the context in which they were first presented.

Imagery[2]   Remembering a word by creating a mental image of it.

List-making[2]   Drawing up a list of new L2 material to be remembered without grouping related items.

Listing by attribute[2]   Drawing up a list of new L2 material to be remembered and forming groups, e.g. according to common attributes (e.g. verbs) or opposites (e.g. black-white).

Loci[2]   Memorising L2 information by recalling its position on the page, or in the form of a mental picture.

*** Masking**   Memorising a word by covering up alternatively the L1 and L2 side of a vocabulary list and looking at the opposite side.

*** Novel associations**   Relating new items to other concepts by means of strange associations.

Rote-learning[2]   Memorising by heart a word or phrase, or rule, without understanding why or how it is used (e.g. reading a list of new words over and over in a mechanical fashion).

Rhymes/ rhythms[2]	Focusing on the sound of L2 items when trying to remember them (e.g. learning declensions by making up a chant based on them).
* Self-testing	Reproducing the L2 item in response to the L1 prompt, or vice versa.
Situationalism[2]	Linking a new word with the situation in which it was first heard or read.
Word analysis*	Finding the meaning of an L2 word by breaking it down into small components.

Social/affective strategies

Anxiety reduction[2]	Reducing anxiety by such means as joking, relaxation techniques.
Avoidance*	Avoiding a task or experience that makes one feel anxious or discouraged.
Clarification[2]	Seeking the clarification, repetition or explanation of an item or task from a teacher, native speaker or peer.
Cooperation[1, 2]	Working together with other learners to complete a language task, perhaps by pooling information, checking work or providing comments on each other's oral or written work.
Perseverance[2]	Maintaining one's efforts in language study, in spite of the difficulty of the material or one's earlier performance.
Problem-sharing*	Discussing one's difficulties or worries about the L2 with others.
Risk-taking*	Being prepared to risk looking foolish or being incorrect in one's use of the L2.
Self-encouragement[2]/ self-talk[1]	Repeating positive statements to oneself in order to gain more confidence in one's L2 performance.
Silent rehearsal*	In oral work, silently repeating a word or phrase to one's self before producing it.

Verification[2]   Asking a teacher, native speaker or peer for
                        verification of an item, asking if an utterance is
                        correct, if a rule fits a certain example.

Communication strategies

Circumlocution/   Compensating for a lack of L2 knowledge by
paraphrase*   rephrasing one's message.

* Code switch   Using the L1 to bridge communication gaps.

Appendix B: Research Instruments

B1 The student questionnaire

I am interested in finding out how students view their A-level French
and/or German studies, so that we might be able to ease the transition from
GCSE to advanced work. I would be very grateful if you would help me by
completing the following questionnaire. Your replies will remain completely anonymous.

Thank you.

Mrs S Graham, Research Student, School of Education, University of Bath.

Before you start, please answer the following questions:

1. Are you male __ or female __? (please tick)

2. State the language(s) you are studying at A-level _____
   and the grade(s) you got for them at GCSE: _____

3. How easy was it for you to get these grades?

a) French: very easy _ ; quite easy _ ; quite hard _ ; very hard _ (tick one)

b) German: very easy _ ; quite easy _ ; quite hard _ ; very hard _ (tick one)

4. How long have you been studying (a) French _____
   (b) German _____ (from scratch)?

SECTION A — FRENCH

Please write a few brief sentences about French at A-level under the
following headings:

1. *Things that I have found easy so far in A-level French (e.g. specific language
skills or grammar points):*

2. *Things that I think I will enjoy during the course*:

3. *Things that I have found difficult so far in A-level French (e.g. specific language skills or grammar points)*:

4. *Difficulties that I may have later in the course*:

SECTION B — GERMAN

Please write a few brief sentences about German at A-level under the following headings:

1. *Things that I have found easy so far in A-level German (e.g. specific language skills or grammar points)*:

2. *Things that I think I will enjoy during the course*:

3. *Things that I have found difficult so far in A-level German (e.g. specific language skills or grammar points)*:

4. *Difficulties that I may have later in the course*:

SECTION C — FRENCH

Below are some areas of language learning which have, in the past, caused students difficulties during the first term of a French A-level course. **Please put a tick next to all statements which refer to things you are finding difficult** *at this stage of your course.* If you are also studying German at A-level, please complete Section D as well. If you wish to comment on any of the statements, please do so in the space provided.

I am having difficulties in: *Comments*

1. Coping with the amount of vocabulary I have to learn.

2. Using new vocabulary appropriately.

3. Expressing my ideas in spoken French.

4. Knowing when to use different tenses.

5. Using the right verb form.

6. Writing accurately in French.

7. Applying what I learned for GCSE to A-level work.

8. Understanding grammar.
   (Give examples of specific grammar points if necessary).

9. Adjusting to the sort of topics we study now.

10. Expressing my ideas in written French.

11. Reading a text without a dictionary.

12. Using French when discussing texts.

13. Constructing sentences in French.

14. Improving my writing skills.

15. Following class discussions in French.

16. Answering quickly in oral work.

17. Writing essays in French.

18. Knowing what to note down in class.

19. Working on my own initiative.

20. Organising my work.

21. Coping with the speed of listening assignments.

22. Concentrating on listening assignments.

23. Using grammar correctly.
    (Give examples of specific grammar points if
    necessary).

24. Getting adjective agreements right.

25. Remembering the gender of words.

26. Studying literary texts.

27. Keeping up with the others in the group.

28. Working without worrying.

29. Coping with the amount of work set.

Thank you!

SECTION D — GERMAN

Below are some areas of language learning which have, in the past, caused students difficulties during the first term of a German A-level course. **Please put a tick next to all statements which refer to things you are finding difficult** *at this stage of your course.* If you wish to comment on any of the statements, please do so in the space provided.

I am having difficulties in: *Comments*

1. Coping with the amount of vocabulary I
   have to learn.

2. Using new vocabulary appropriately.

3. Expressing my ideas in spoken German.

4. Knowing when to use different tenses.

5. Using the right verb form.

6. Writing accurately in German.

7. Applying what I learned for GCSE to
   A-level work.

8. Understanding grammar.
   (Give examples of specific grammar points if
   necessary).

9. Adjusting to the sort of topics we study
   now.

10. Expressing my ideas in written German.

11. Reading a text without a dictionary.

12. Using German when discussing texts.

13. Constructing sentences in German.

14. Improving my writing skills.

15. Following class discussions in German.

16. Answering quickly in oral work.

17. Writing essays in German.

18. Knowing what to note down in class.

19. Working on my own initiative.

20. Organising my work.

21. Coping with the speed of listening assignments.

22. Concentrating on listening assignments.

23. Using grammar correctly.
    (Give examples of specific grammar points if necessary).

24. Using cases correctly.

25. Remembering the gender of words.

26. Studying literary texts.

27. Keeping up with the others in the group.

28. Working without worrying.

29. Coping with the amount of work set.

Thank you!

B2: The teacher questionnaire

LANGUAGE LEARNING POST-GCSE — QUESTIONNAIRE FOR TEACHERS CURRENTLY TEACHING FRENCH AND/OR GERMAN TO A YEAR 12/LOWER SIXTH A-LEVEL GROUP

I am a research student at the University of Bath and I am investigating the process of transition from GCSE to A-level for students of French and/or German. The project begins with a survey among Year 12/Lower Sixth A-level students in eight counties, which requests information regarding any difficulties they are experiencing in the first term of their A-level course. This will be followed by detailed studies of 24 students as they progress through their first year. The purpose of this is to monitor the learning strategies employed by students to cope with the difficulties identified, with a view to gaining an insight into effective modes of learning. It is hoped that the project will lead to recommendations in terms of teaching and learning strategies, assessment and syllabus design, which will help students to make the transition to advanced level work more successfully.

In addition, I should like to gather teachers' opinions on the nature of their students' learning difficulties. I should be grateful if you would assist me in this task by answering the questions on the following pages, with reference to your current Year 12/Lower Sixth A-level students. All replies will remain completely anonymous and are required solely for the purpose of this research.

Thank you.

Mrs Suzanne Graham, Research Student, School of Education, University of Bath.

INTRODUCTION

Before going on to the main part of the questionnaire, please answer the following questions:

1. Are you male __ or female __ ? (please tick)

2. Which languages are you currently teaching at A-level?

   (please tick): French ___ German ___

3. How many years' teaching experience do you have? ___

4. How many students do you have in your current First Year A-level group?
   (i) French ___ (ii) German ___

5. How many hours of homework a week (on average) do you set students during the first term of the A-level course?
   (i) French _____ (ii) German _____

6. Which A-level examination syllabus are you preparing First Year A-level students for?
   (i) French _____ (ii) German _____

7. Which A-level text book(s) do you use with students?

   (i) French _____

   (ii) German _____

Please tick here if you do not use a text book: French __ German __

If you are teaching *French only* at A-level, please now complete Sections A and C; *German only*, Sections B and D; *both French and German*, Sections A, B, C and D.

SECTION A — FOR THOSE TEACHING FRENCH AT A-LEVEL

1. Which aspects of the A-level course have your students coped well with so far?

2. Which aspects have they found difficult?

3. Where do you think their strengths will lie as the A-level course progresses?

4. What difficulties may they have later in the course?

5. Regarding the process of transition from GCSE to A-level in Modern Languages, please comment on
a) how you personally try to ease your students into A-level work:

b) any other suggestions for possible strategies to ease the transition.

SECTION B — FOR THOSE TEACHING GERMAN AT A-LEVEL

1. Which aspects of the A-level course have your students coped well with so far?

2. Which aspects have they found difficult?

3. Where do you think their strengths will lie as the A-level course progresses?

4. What difficulties may they have later in the course?

5. Regarding the process of transition from GCSE to A-level in Modern Languages, please comment on
   a) how you personally try to ease your students into A-level work:

   b) any other suggestions for possible strategies to ease the transition.

SECTION C — FRENCH

Below are some areas of language learning which have, in the past, caused students difficulties during the first term of a French A-level course. **Please put a tick next to all statements which refer to areas where** *the majority of your present students are having difficulties* *at this stage of their course.* If you are also teaching German at A-level, please complete Section D as well. If you wish to comment on any of the statements, please do so in the space provided.

The majority of my students are having difficulties in: Comments

1. Coping with the amount of vocabulary they have to learn.

2. Using new vocabulary appropriately.

3. Expressing their ideas in spoken French.

4. Knowing when to use different tenses.

5. Using the right verb form.

6. Writing accurately in French.

7. Applying what they learned for GCSE to A-level work.

8. Understanding grammar.
   (Give examples of specific grammar points if necessary)

9. Adjusting to the sort of topics studied at A-level.

10. Expressing their ideas in written French.

11. Reading a text without a dictionary.

12. Using French when discussing texts.

13. Constructing sentences in French.

14. Improving their writing skills.

15. Following class discussions in French.

16. Answering quickly in oral work.

17. Writing essays in French.

18. Knowing what to note down in class.

19. Working on their own initiative.

20. Organising their work.

21. Coping with the speed of listening assignments.

22. Concentrating on listening assignments.

23. Using grammar correctly.
    (Give examples of specific grammar points if necessary).

24. Getting adjective agreements right.

25. Remembering the gender of words.

26. Studying literary texts.

27. Working without worrying.

28. Coping with the amount of work set.

Thank you!

SECTION D — GERMAN

Below are some areas of language learning which have, in the past, caused students difficulties during the first term of a German A-level course. **Please put a tick next to all statements which refer to areas where** *the majority* **of your present students are having difficulties** *at this stage of their course.* If you wish to comment on any of the statements, please do so in the space provided.

The majority of my students are having difficulties in: *Comments*

1. Coping with the amount of vocabulary they have to learn.

2. Using new vocabulary appropriately.

3. Expressing their ideas in spoken German.

4. Knowing when to use different tenses.

5. Using the right verb form.

6. Writing accurately in German.

7. Applying what they learned for GCSE to
    A-level work.

8. Understanding grammar.
    (Give examples of specific grammar points if
    necessary):

9. Adjusting to the sort of topics studied at
    A-level.

10. Expressing their ideas in written German.

11. Reading a text without a dictionary.

12. Using German when discussing texts.

13. Constructing sentences in German.

14. Improving their writing skills.

15. Following class discussions in German.

16. Answering quickly in oral work.

17. Writing essays in German.

18. Knowing what to note down in class.

19. Working on their own initiative.

20. Organising their work.

21. Coping with the speed of listening
    assignments.

22. Concentrating on listening assignments.

23. Using grammar correctly.
    (Give examples of specific grammar points if
    necessary):

24. Using cases correctly.

25. Remembering the gender of words

26. Studying literary texts.

27. Working without worrying.

28. Coping with the amount of work set.

Thank you!

B3: The learner diary

Date ___

1. *Activity and situation (in class/outside class).*

2. *Things I found easy/things I found difficult.*

3. *How I dealt with the task.*

4. *What have I learned/what have I achieved?*

5. *How do I feel?*

6. *What should I do now?*

Appendix C: Materials Used in the Think-Aloud Interview

C1: Listening comprehension

(i) French

During the following task I would like you to listen to an interview about holidays and answer the questions which follow. Throughout the task, I would like you to tell me everything that is going through your mind as you try to understand the passage: for example, what you understand and what you don't; how you are trying to work out the meaning of the parts you don't understand. The tape will be paused to give you time to think aloud.

(Transcript of passage):

Interviewer Et les jeunes Français, veulent-ils partir en vacances en famille? M. Laurent a remarqué que par rapport à il y a une quinzaine d'années il y a un changement notable.

M. Laurent La grande tendance des jeunes Français c'est de vouloir partir seuls, seuls, c'est-à- dire sans les parents, mais en groupe, en bande d'amis, eventuellement en stop, là où on s'amuse, c'est-à-dire plus particulièrement sur les côtes, et également sillonner l'Europe, ou même les pays pas trop lointains d'Afrique. On peut dire que pour les adolescents en France les vacances sont certainement un temps fort où on peut, peut-être encore davantage que dans l'année, se retrouver entre soi.

Interviewer Qu'est-ce qu'on peut donc offrir aux jeunes qui veulent partir en groupe?

Second Interviewee Nous organisons des randonnées à bicyclette, avec un système de camping, c'est-à-dire que les jeunes partent en faisant plusieurs haltes tous les soirs, dans des endroits différents. Au cours de chaque journée, en fonction d'où ils se trouvent, ils pratiquent une activité différente, c'est-à-dire s'ils s'arrêtent près d'un lac, ils font un petit peu de voile, s'ils s'arrêtent près d'une colline, une montagne, une rocher, ils peuvent s'initier à l'escalade. S'ils s'arrêtent près d'une rivière, ils peuvent s'initier au kayak.

(BBC, *Voix de France. Les Français et leurs vacances*, reprinted with permission)

1. What is said about how young people spend their holidays?
2. What do they seem to want out of a holiday?
3. What sort of holidays and activities for young people are mentioned?

(ii) German

During the following task I would like you to listen to a passage on young people and leisure and answer the questions which follow. Throughout the task, I would like you to tell me everything that is going through your mind as you try to understand the passage: for example, what you understand and what you don't; how you are trying to work out the meaning of the parts you don't understand. The tape will be paused to give you time to think aloud.

(Transcript of passage):

First speaker: Astrid

Ich bin die Astrid, und ich bin 17 Jahre alt, gehe in Rheinbach auf ein Mädchengymnasium und werde nächstes Jahr Abitur machen. Mir persönlich ist eigentlich wichtig, daß ich teils eine sinnvolle Freizeitgestaltung habe und anderseits aber auch nicht zu sehr ausgefüllt bin mit Freizeit, daß ich auch für mich freie Zeit habe; daß ich das also ein bißchen einteilen kann.

Second speaker: Andreas

Ich heiße Andreas, bin 20 Jahre alt, und ich mache zur Zeit noch eine Lehre als Radio- und Fernsehtechniker, bin jetzt aber auch bald fertig. Ja, und mir ist wichtig an der Freizeit, daß sie halt sinnvoll ausgestattet ist, aber daß sie halt nicht in Streß ausartet, also daß man eine wohlgewogene Mischung aus Tätigkeiten, sinnvollen Tätigkeiten hat und aber auch gleichzeitig Zeit für sich und seine Freunde hat, und das ist mir wichtig. [...] Nach der Arbeit gehe ich einmal in der Woche Basketball spielen, ein anderes Mal laß ich mir einfach offen, um eher zu mir selbst zurückzufinden, also jetzt um Fernsehen zu gucken oder zu lesen. [....] Und dann am Wochenende gehe ich auch öfters zu Konzerten oder mache mit paar Freunden so Fotosafaris, also besichtige Nachbarstädte und fotografiere da einfach los.

(Inter Nationes, *Jugend bei uns. Teil 4*)

1. What does Astrid say is important as far as her free time is concerned?
2. What is important for Andreas?
3. How does Andreas spend his free time after work?
4. What does he do at weekends?

C2: Reading comprehension

(i) French

Your task is to read the passage below in order to understand it. As you do this, tell me everything that is going through your mind, e.g. tell me when you come to something you don't understand, when you lose track of the passage, and what you are doing to overcome these problems.

JEUNES RENNAIS
UN COUP DE POUCE POUR VOS VACANCES

L'an dernier, de jeunes Rennais obtenaient une bourse de la Fondation de France pour réaliser des vacances actives. Vous aussi, vous pouvez préparer un projet de vacances un peu fou.

Emmanuelle M. a passé trois semaines à Djenne au Mali en août 1987. Elle a participé à la construction de salles de classe en briques de banco dans la tradition du pays. Rencontres enrichissantes, confrontation avec les réalités, elle a pu se faire une vraie idée d'un pays du tiers-monde. « Les gens respirent le bonheur malgré leurs problèmes » dit-elle. Cinq autres jeunes avaient, eux, choisi la découverte des marais de Guérande. Ils sont incollables sur la description d'une saline, le ramassage du sel, la formation d'un marais, les outils du paludier.

Vous avez entre 16 et 21 ans, vous voulez vous évader en réalisant un projet de vacances cet été, en Europe, seul ou en petit groupe, mais vous avez peu de moyens. Ne baissez pas pour autant les bras car la Fondation de France peut vous aider à réaliser vos rêves, en vous attribuant une bourse "Jeune Découverte Européenne" ou "Jeune Solidarité Européenne" (1500 F maximum par personne).

Exemples de projets aidés en 1987 : raid équestre de quinze jours, découverte des marais de Guérande, voyage en Laponie, participation à la construction d'une école au Mali... Dépôt des dossiers : 15 mai au plus tard, sélection des projets : début juin.

(French text from University of Oxford Delegacy of Local Examinations, 1989)

(ii) German

Your task is to read the passage below [see p. 200] in order to understand it. As you do this, tell me everything that is going through your mind, e.g. tell me when you come to something you don't understand, when you lose track of the passage, and what you are doing to overcome these problems.

(German text from Goethe-Institute, 1990)

C3: Writing

(i) French

Write a paragraph on the following subject, again, thinking aloud as you do so. Remember to tell me everything that goes through your mind.

Quelles seraient pour toi les vacances idéales? Explique ta réponse.

(ii) German

Write a paragraph on the following subject, again, thinking aloud as you do so. Remember to tell me everything that goes through your mind.

Was bedeutet das Wort „Freizeit" für dich?

Die große Angst, etwas zu verpassen

Studie: Junge Leute stöhnen unter dem Freizeitstreß

Hamburg – Eine neue Art von Anstrengung raubt jungen Leuten den Schlaf: Der Freizeitstreß. Zumindest behauptet der Hamburger Erziehungswissenschaftler und Professor Horst Opaschowski, daß bereits 79 Prozent der 14- bis 19jährigen "über zu wenig Nachtruhe klagen – weil sie einfach zu viele Freizeitangebote haben.

Das entnimmt der Wissenschaftler einer Repräsentativuntersuchung des BAT-Freizeit-Forschungsinstituts, in der 2000 Jugendliche ab 14 Jahren befragt wurden. Fast 60 Prozent gaben zu, daß sie

"schlicht zu viele Freizeitinteressen" hätten und sich am Feierabend und am Wochenende "zu viel vornehmen". Opaschowski sieht hier eine Parallele zum Berufsstreß: "Im Beruf ist es die Angst, zu versagen. In

der Freizeit die Angst, etwas zu verpassen."

Die neue Freizeitformel, die allem den Stempel der Hektik aufdrücke, laute: "Mehr tun in gleicher Zeit." Alles, was länger als zwei Stunden dauere, sei bei

jungen Leuten out. "Die Jugendlichen, so Opaschowski, "wollen dauernd etwas Neues erleben."

Ohne sich zu lange bei einer Beschäftigung aufzuhalten, springen sie von einem Freizeitprogramm zum anderen. In den USA wurde bereits ein neuer Begriff für den selbstverordneten Freizeitstreß geprägt: Hopping. Es gebe TV-Hopping, Party-Hopping, oder Sport-Hopping. Opaschowski: "Weil sie nirgends einen Ruhepunkt finden, droht die Gefahr, daß die Jungendlichen die Kontrolle über sich selbst verlieren."

Freizeitstreß beim Windsurfen: Bei diesem schnellen, anstrengenden Sport kommen Hektiker auf ihre Kosten.
Foto: Strub

C4: Cloze exercies

(i) French

1a) Here you have another passage, also on the theme of holidays.In the first part of the exercise, fill in the gaps using the words in brackets. You may need to change the form of these words before inserting them in the gaps.

Pour réussir vos vacances, _____ (éviter) l'isolement. Ne vous coupez pas de votre réseau de soutien, famille et amis. Il faut que vous partiez avec ceux que vous _____ (connaître) bien, car la cohabitation peut vous _____ (agacer). Quand vous venez d'arriver et que vous voulez sortir, _____ (se méfier) des mondanités (excessif) dans les clubs, cela _____ (pouvoir) vous coûter.

1b) In the second part of the exercise, the passage continues. Fill in the gaps by choosing a word from the list (you will not use all of them).

Vous profiterez _____ de vos vacances si vous avez _____ toutes les questions en suspens (notes, factures) avant de partir. Fixez-vous de _____ objectifs personnels. Cela vous _____ du bien. Mais, attention! En un jour de surmenage physique ce bénéfice peut être _____ . Cependant, si vous êtes habitué à un train de vie trépidant, ne _____ pas un endroit trop tranquille.

choisissait	ferait	nouvelle	réglé
choisissez	meilleur	parti	toutes
fait	mieux	perdre	vieux
fera	nouveaux	perdu	

(Adapted from the Northern Examinations and Assessment Board, 1989, with permission)

(ii) German

1a) Here you have another passage on the theme of leisure: in the first part of the exercise, fill in the gaps using the words in brackets. You may need to change the form of these words before inserting them in the gaps.

Wie verbringst du deine Freizeit?

In unserer Klasse stellten wir uns die Frage, wie Jugendliche in _____ (unser) Gemeinde ihre Freizeit _____ (verbringen). Wir _____ (finden) viele_____ (interessant) Beobachtungen wie Modellbau, Pferdepflege usw. Der Fernsehapparat spielt aber eine recht _____ (wichtig) Rolle in der Freizeitgestaltung _____ (viel).

1b) In the second part of the exercise, the passage continues. Fill in the gap by choosing a word from the list (you will not use all of them).

Es gibt auch eine Gruppe Schüler, _____ in ihrer Freizeit nichts _____ zu tun wissen, wie zum Beispiel die 14 jährige Katja. Sie gehört _____ Gruppe von Jungen und Mädchen an, _____ „Clique", die sich am allerliebsten noch am frühen Abend _____ , um ein bißchen mit dem Mofa _____ .

das	getroffen	ihrer	sinnvoll	wegfahren
die	herumzufahren	Neues	Sinnvolles	zurückkam
einer	hat	seiner	trifft	

Appendix D: Subjects Involved in the Study

The following tables give details of the respondents to the student questionnaire.

Table D1 Number of respondents according to sex, and language studied

Female French	162	Male French	122
Female German	87	Male German	59

Table D2 Number of respondents according to educational sector (MC, maintained comprehensive school; MS, maintained selective school; I, independent school; FE, further education/sixth form college)

Female French								*Male French*							
MC	104	MS	26	I	6	FE	26	MC	40	MS	52	I	20	FE	10
Female German								*Male German*							
MC	52	MS	13	I	3	FE	19	MC	23	MS	18	I	9	FE	9

Table D3 GCSE grade obtained for the language studied at A-level (% of respondents)

Female French								*Male French*							
A	71%	B	20%	C	7%	D	2%	A	85%	B	12%	C	2%	D	1%
Female German								*Male German*							
A	71%	B	20%	C	7%	D	2%	A	66%	B	24%	C	9%	D	1%

Table D4 Perceptions of how easily this grade was obtained (% of respondents)

	very easy	quite easy	quite hard	very hard	blank
Female French	15%	53%	29%	2%	1%
Male French	45%	36%	17%	—	—
Female German	15%	51%	31%	2%	1%
Male German	20%	54%	24%	—	2%

Tables D5 and D6 give details of the respondents to the teacher questionnaire. The mean average for years of teaching experience was 15, and the examination board most widely used was the University of Oxford Local Delegacy.

Table D5 Number of respondents according to sex, and subject taught at A-level

Female French	26	Male French	17
Female German	14	Male German	16

Table D6 Number of respondents according to educational sector (MC, maintained comprehensive; MS, maintained selective; I, independent; FE, further education/sixth form college)

Female French								Female German							
MC	16	MS	4	I	1	FE	5	MC	10	MS	2	I	0	FE	2
Male French								Male German							
MC	8	MS	4	I	5	FE	0	MC	8	MS	3	I	4	FE	1

Table D7 gives details of the students participating in the interviews and diary study.

Table D7

Student	Language[a]	Sex	Effective/less effective
A	Ger	M	Effective
B	Fr, *Ger*	M	Effective
C	Fr, *Ger*	M	Effective
D	Fr, *Ger*	M	Effective
E	Ger	M	Effective
F	Ger	M	Effective
G	Ger, *Fr*	M	Less effective
H	Ger	M	Less effective
I	Ger	M	Less effective
J	Fr	M	Less effective
K	Ger	M	Less effective
L	Fr	M	Less effective
M	Ger, *Fr*	F	Effective
N	Fr, *Sp*	F	Effective
O	Fr, *Ger*	F	Effective
P	Fr	F	Effective
Q	Fr	F	Less effective
R	Fr, *Ger*	F	Less effective
S	Ger	F	Less effective
T	Fr	F	Effective
U	Fr	F	Effective
V	Ger	F	Effective
W	Ger	F	Less effective
X	Fr	F	Less effective[b]

[a] Where students were taking two languages at A-level, the second language, not examined in the project, is given in italics (Fr ≡ French; Ger ≡ German; Sp ≡ Spanish)
[b] Student X did not take part in the think-aloud interview.

Appendix E: Results

E1: Results from the student questionnaire — Sections A/B

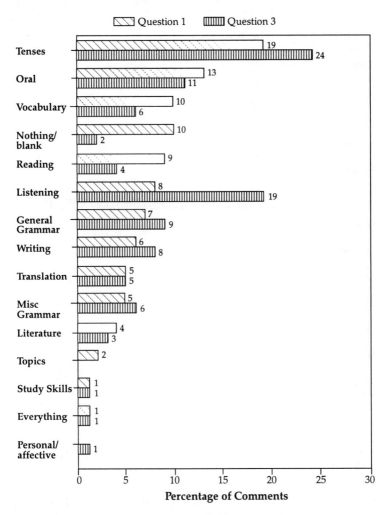

Note: Figures shown represent a percentage of the total number of comments made by respondents of each sex.

Histogram E1 French question 1: Things that I have found easy so far in A-level French; compared with French question 3: Things that I have found difficult so far in A-level French. Question 1, $N = 468$ comments; Question 3, $N = 510$ comments

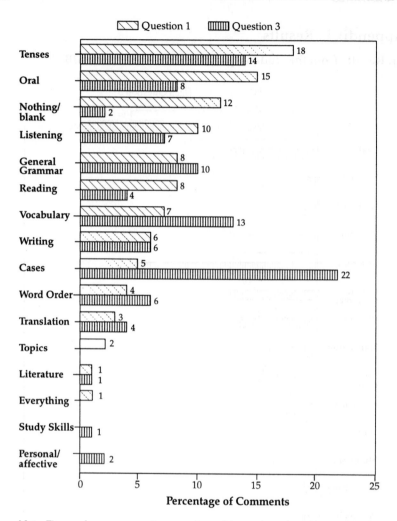

Note: Figures shown represent a percentage of the total number of comments made by respondents of each sex.

Histogram E2 German question 1: Things that I have found easy so far in A-level German; compared with German question 3: Things that I have found difficult so far in A-level German. Question 1, N = 240 comments; Question 3, N = 301 comments

E2: Results from the student questionnaire — gender differences, Sections A/B

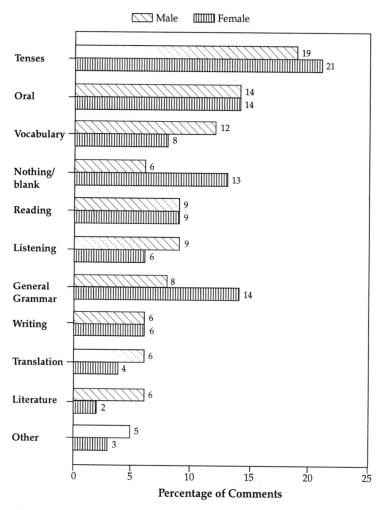

Note: Figures shown represent a percentage of the total number of comments made by respondents of each sex.

Histogram E3 French question 1, male and female compared. Male: $N = 213$ comments; Female: $N = 253$ comments

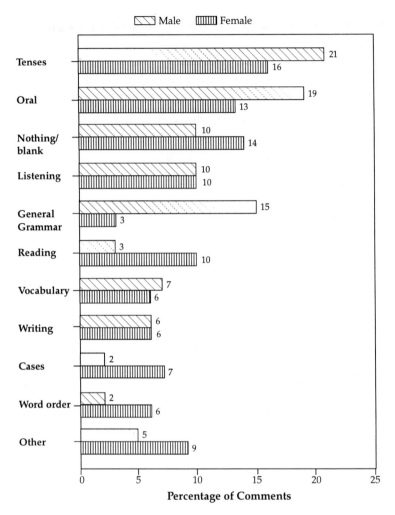

Note: Figures shown represent a percentage of the total number of comments made by respondents of each sex.

Histogram E4 German question 1, male and female compared. Male: N = 97 comments; Female: N = 143 comments

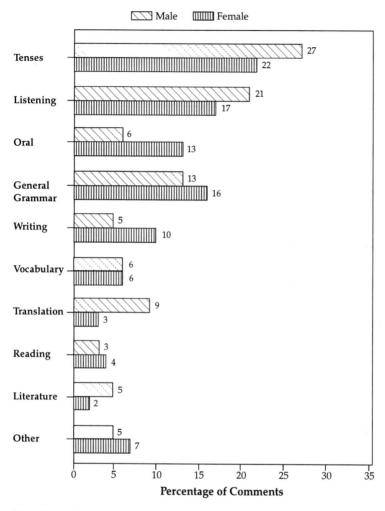

Note: Figures shown represent a percentage of the total number of comments made by respondents of each sex.

Histogram E5 French question 3, male and female compared. Male: $N = 191$ comments; Female: $N = 319$ comments

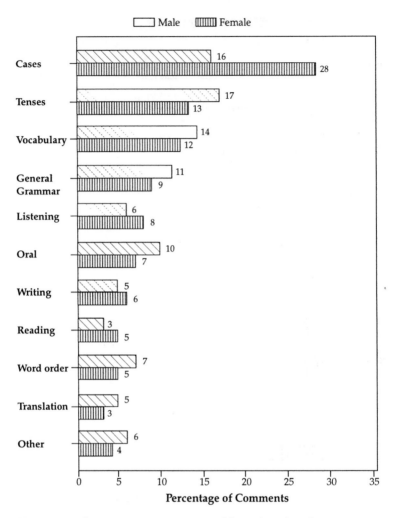

Note: Figures shown represent a percentage of the total number of comments made by respondents of each sex.

Histogram E6 German question 3, male and female compared. Male: N = 133 comments; Female: N = 168 comments

E3: Results from the student questionnaire — Sections C/D

Table E3.1 Section C, all French respondents, $N = 284$ (Note: Figures represent the number and percentage of respondents indicating that they have had difficulties with these items. Percentages have been rounded up).

	No.	%
1. Coping with the amount of vocabulary I have to learn	99	35
2. Using new vocabulary appropriately	64	23
3. Expressing my ideas in spoken French	178	63
4. Knowing when to use different tenses	124	44
5. Using the right verb form	92	32
6. Writing accurately in French	168	59
7. Applying what I learned for GCSE to A-level	48	17
8. Understanding grammar	106	37
9. Adjusting to the sort of topics we study now	43	15
10. Expressing my ideas in written French	105	37
11. Reading a text without a dictionary	189	67
12. Using French when discussing texts	125	44
13. Constructing sentences in French	67	24
14. Improving my writing skills	71	25
15. Following class discussions in French	63	22
16. Answering quickly in oral work	121	43
17. Writing essays in French	104	37
18. Knowing what to note down in class	34	12
19. Working on my own initiative	39	14
20. Organising my work	45	16
21. Coping with the speed of listening assignments	178	63
22. Concentrating on listening assignments	111	39
23. Using grammar correctly	111	39
24. Getting adjective agreements right	94	33
25. Remembering the gender of words	108	38
26. Studying literary texts	65	23
27. Keeping up with the others in the group	54	19
28. Working without worrying	95	33
29. Coping with the amount of work set	63	22

Table E3.2 Section D, all German respondents. $N = 146$

	No.	%
1. Coping with the amount of vocabulary I have to learn	72	49
2. Using new vocabulary appropriately	41	28
3. Expressing my ideas in spoken German	82	56
4. Knowing when to use different tenses	55	38
5. Using the right verb form	50	34
6. Writing accurately in German	98	67
7. Applying what I learned for GCSE to A-level	22	15
8. Understanding grammar	71	49
9. Adjusting to the sort of topics we study now	23	16
10. Expressing my ideas in written German	67	46
11. Reading a text without a dictionary	105	72
12. Using German when discussing texts	48	33
13. Constructing sentences in German	44	30
14. Improving my writing skills	37	25
15. Following class discussions in German	30	21
16. Answering quickly in oral work	60	41
17. Writing essays in German	44	30
18. Knowing what to note down in class	18	12
19. Working on my own initiative	11	8
20. Organising my work	18	12
21. Coping with the speed of listening assignments	65	45
22. Concentrating on listening assignments	31	21
23. Using grammar correctly	74	51
24. Using cases correctly	88	60
25. Remembering the gender of words	101	69
26. Studying literary texts	34	23
27. Keeping up with the others in the group	26	18
28. Working without worrying	38	26
29. Coping with the amount of work set	26	18

E4: Results from the student questionnaire — gender differences, Sections C/D

Table E4.1 Section C, male and female French compared. Female N = 162 Male N = 122 (F = female; M = male;)

	F.No.	F (%)	M.No.	M (%)	χ^2
1. Coping with the amount of vocabulary I have to learn	50	31	49	40	2.65
2. Using new vocabulary appropriately	47	29	17	14	*9.06
3. Expressing my ideas in spoken French	115	71	63	52	*11.14
4. Knowing when to use different tenses	80	49	44	36	*5.02
5. Using the right verb form	62	38	30	25	*5.95
6. Writing accurately in French	103	64	65	53	3.06
7. Applying what I learned for GCSE to A-level	38	24	10	8	*11.54
8. Understanding grammar	64	40	42	34	0.77
9. Adjusting to the sort of topics we study now	26	16	17	14	0.24
10. Expressing my ideas in written French	75	46	30	25	*14.07
11. Reading a text without a dictionary	115	71	74	61	3.34
12. Using French when discussing texts	82	51	43	35	*6.67
13. Constructing sentences in French	42	26	25	21	1.14
14. Improving my writing skills	44	27	27	22	0.94
15. Following class discussions in French	42	26	21	17	3.06
16. Answering quickly in oral work	78	48	43	35	*4.74
17. Writing essays in French	66	41	38	31	2.76
18. Knowing what to note down in class	21	13	13	11	0.35
19. Working on my own initiative	24	15	15	12	0.37
20. Organising my work	28	17	17	14	0.59
21. Coping with the speed of listening assignments	100	62	78	64	−0.14
22. Concentrating on listening assignments	68	42	43	35	1.32
23. Using grammar correctly	70	43	41	34	2.70
24. Getting adjective agreements right	59	36	35	29	1.88
25. Remembering the gender of words	69	43	39	32	3.33
26. Studying literary texts	38	24	27	22	0.07
27. Keeping up with the others in the group	39	24	15	12	*6.27
28. Working without worrying	73	45	22	18	*22.84
29. Coping with the amount of work set	47	29	16	13	*10.19

Note: * indicates that the difference is significant at the $p < 0.05$ level.
A minus signs indicates that the difference is in the direction of male respondents.

Table E4.2 Section D, male and female German compared. Female $N = 87$ Male $N = 59$ (F = female; M = male)

	F.No.	F (%)	M.No.	M (%)	χ^2
1. Coping with the amount of vocabulary I have to learn	43	49	29	49	0.00
2. Using new vocabulary appropriately	24	28	17	29	–0.03
3. Expressing my ideas in spoken German	50	57	32	54	0.15
4. Knowing when to use different tenses	37	43	18	31	2.16
5. Using the right verb form	30	34	20	34	0.00
6. Writing accurately in German	59	68	39	66	0.05
7. Applying what I learned for GCSE to A-level	15	17	7	12	0.79
8. Understanding grammar	46	53	25	42	1.55
9. Adjusting to the sort of topics we study now	16	18	7	12	1.13
10. Expressing my ideas in written German	43	49	24	41	1.08
11. Reading a text without a dictionary	61	70	44	75	–0.35
12. Using German when discussing texts	33	38	15	25	2.49
13. Constructing sentences in German	26	30	18	31	–0.01
14. Improving my writing skills	20	23	17	29	–0.63
15. Following class discussions in German	19	22	11	19	0.22
16. Answering quickly in oral work	36	41	24	41	0.00
17. Writing essays in German	24	28	20	34	–0.67
18. Knowing what to note down in class	8	9	10	17	–1.96
19. Working on my own initiative	7	8	4	7	0.08
20. Organising my work	8	9	10	17	–1.96
21. Coping with the speed of listening assignments	44	51	21	36	3.19
22. Concentrating on listening assignments	20	23	11	19	0.40
23. Using grammar correctly	46	53	28	47	0.41
24. Using cases correctly	61	70	27	46	*8.71
25. Remembering the gender of words	60	69	41	69	0.00
26. Studying literary texts	20	23	14	24	–0.01
27. Keeping up with the others in the group	16	21	8	14	1.22
28. Working without worrying	26	30	12	20	1.66
29. Coping with the amount of work set	18	21	8	14	1.15

Note: * indicates that the difference is significant at the $p < 0.05$ level.
A minus signs indicates that the difference is in the direction of male respondents.

Table E4.3 Sections C and D, all male and female compared. Female N = 249, Male N = 181 (F = female; M = male)

	F.No.	F %	M.No.	M %	χ^2
1. Coping with the amount of vocabulary I have to learn	93	37	78	43	−1.44
2. Using new vocabulary appropriately	71	29	34	19	*5.38
3. Expressing my ideas in spoken French/German	165	66	95	52	*8.32
4. Knowing when to use different tenses	117	47	62	34	*6.99
5. Using the right verb form	92	37	50	28	*4.12
6. Writing accurately in French/German	162	65	104	57	2.57
7. Applying what I learned for GCSE to A-level	53	21	17	9	*10.88
8. Understanding grammar	110	44	67	37	2.22
9. Adjusting to the sort of topics we study now	42	17	24	13	1.05
10. Expressing my ideas in written French/German	118	47	54	30	*13.46
11. Reading a text without a dictionary	176	71	118	65	1.46
12. Using French/German when discussing texts	115	46	58	32	*8.72
13. Constructing sentences in French/German	68	27	43	24	0.69
14. Improving my writing skills	64	26	44	24	0.11
15. Following class discussions in French/German	61	24	32	18	2.87
16. Answering quickly in oral work	114	46	67	37	3.30
17. Writing essays in French/German	90	36	58	32	0.78
18. Knowing what to note down in class	29	12	23	13	−0.11
19. Working on my own initiative	31	12	19	10	0.39
20. Organising my work	36	14	27	15	−0.02
21. Coping with the speed of listening assignments	114	58	99	55	0.42
22. Concentrating on listening assignments	88	35	54	30	1.44
23. Using grammar correctly	116	47	69	38	3.06
24. **					
25. Remembering the gender of words	129	52	80	44	2.43
26. Studying literary texts	58	23	41	23	0.02
27. Keeping up with the others in the group	57	23	23	13	*7.18
28. Working without worrying	99	40	34	19	*21.58
29. Coping with the amount of work set	65	26	24	13	*10.54

Note: * indicates that the difference is significant at the $p < 0.05$ level.
A minus signs indicates that the difference is in the direction of male respondents.
** Question 24 has been omitted as the wording is not common to both French and German.

References

Allwright, D. (1984) Why don't learners learn what teachers teach? The interaction hypothesis. In D.M. Singleton and D.G. Little (eds) *Language Learning in Formal and Informal Contexts* (pp. 3–18). Dublin: IRAAL.
— (1988) *Observation in the Language Classroom*. London: Longman.
Anderson, L.W. and Burns, R.B. (1989) *Research in Classrooms: The Study of Teachers, Teaching and Instruction*. Oxford: Pergamon.
Askew, S. and Ross, C. (1988) *Boys Don't Cry: Boys and Sexism in Education*. Milton Keynes: Open University Press.
Assessment of Performance Unit. (1985) *Foreign Language Performance in Schools* (Report on 1985 Survey of French). London: Department of Education and Science.
Atkinson, T. (1992) Le hamster a mangé mon pneu: Creative writing and IT. *Language Learning Journal* 6, 68–72.
Au, S.Y. (1988) A critical appraisal of Gardner's social psychological theory of second-language (L2) learning. *Language Learning* 38, 75–100.
Bachman, L.F. (1990) *Fundamental Considerations in Language Testing*. Oxford: Oxford University Press.
Bacon, S.M. (1992) The relationship between gender, comprehension, processing strategies, and cognitive and affective response in foreign language listening. *Modern Language Journal* 76, 160–77.
Bagguley, P. (1990) From school to university — 'Rites de passage'. *Francophonie* 1, 4–7.
Bailey, K.M. (1983) Competitiveness and anxiety in adult second language learning: Looking at and through the diary studies. In H.W. Seliger and M.H. Long (eds) *Classroom Oriented Research in Second Language Acquisition* (pp. 67–102). Rowley, MA: Newbury House.
Bailey, K.M. and Ochsner, R. (1983) A methodological review of the diary studies: Windmill tilting or social sciences? In K.M. Bailey, M.H. Long and S. Peck (eds) *Studies in Second Language Acquisition: Series on Issues in Second Language Research* (pp. 188–98). Rowley, MA: Newbury House.
Batters, J.D. (1988) Pupil and teacher perceptions of foreign language learning and teaching. PhD thesis, University of Bath.
BBC (No date) *Voix de France: Les Français et leurs vacances*. London: BBC.
Beebe, L.M. (1983) Risk-taking and the language learner. In H.W. Seliger and M.H. Long (eds) *Classroom Oriented Research in Second Language Acquisition* (pp. 39–65). Rowley, MA: Newbury House.
Berryman, C.L. (1980) Attitudes toward male and female sex-appropriate and sex-inappropriate language. In C.L. Berryman and V.A. Eman (eds) *Communication, Language and Sex* (pp. 195–216). Rowley, MA: Newbury House.

Bialystok, E. (1988) Psycholinguistic dimensions of second language proficiency. In W. Rutherford and M. Sharwood Smith (eds) *Grammar and Second Language Teaching* (pp. 31–50). New York: Newbury House

Black, J.H. (1993) Learning and reception strategy use and the cloze procedure. *Canadian Modern Language Review* 49, 418–45.

Block, E. (1986) The comprehension strategies of second language readers. *TESOL Quarterly* 20/ 3, 463–94.

Bonadona, M. (1990) Students' diaries as an evaluation tool for language instruction. M Phil thesis, University of Salford.

Brown, A.L. and Palincsar, A.S. (1982) Inducing strategies learning from texts by means of informed, self-control training. *Topics in Learning and Learning Disabilities* 2, 1–17.

Burstall, C., Jamieson, M., Cohen, S. and Hargreaves, M. (1974) *Primary French in the Balance*. Slough: NFER.

Byram, M. and Esarte-Sarries, V. (1991) *Investigating Cultural Studies in Foreign Language Teaching*. Clevedon, Avon: Multilingual Matters.

Canale, M. (1983) From communicative competence to communicative language pedagogy. In J.C.Richards and R.W. Schmidt (eds) *Language and Communication* (pp. 2–27). London: Longman.

— (1984) A communicative approach to language proficiency assessment in a minority setting. In C. Rivera (ed.) *Communicative Competence Approaches to Language Proficiency Assessment: Research and Application* (pp. 107–22). Clevedon, Avon: Multilingual Matters.

Canale, M. and Swain, M. (1980) Theoretical bases of communicative approaches to second language teaching and testing. *Applied Linguistics* 1(1), 1–47.

Carrell, P.L. (1988) Some causes of text-boundedness and schema interference in ESL reading. In P.L. Carrell, J. Devine and D.E. Eskey (eds) *Interactive Approaches to Second Language Reading* (pp. 101–13). Cambridge: Cambridge University Press.

Carroll, J.B. (1975) *The Teaching of French as a Foreign Language in Eight Countries*. Stockholm: Almqvist & Wiksell.

— (1981) Twenty-five years of research on foreign language aptitude. In K.C. Diller (ed.) *Individual Differences and Universals in Language Learning Aptitude* (pp. 83–118). Rowley, MA: Newbury House.

Chambers, G.N. (1989) A-level syllabuses in the post-GCSE era. Have they changed? MA thesis, London University Institute of Education.

Chamot, A.U. (1987) The learning strategies of ESL students. In A. Wenden and J. Rubin (eds) *Learner Strategies in Language Learning* (pp. 71–83). Englewood Cliffs, NJ: Prentice-Hall.

Chamot, A.U. and Küpper, L. (1989) Learning strategies in foreign language instruction. *Foreign Language Annals* 22, 13–24.

Chamot, A.U. and O'Malley, J.M. (1994) *The CALLA Handbook: Implementing the Cognitive Academic Language Learning Approach*. Reading, MA: Addison Wesley.

Chesterfield, R. and Chesterfield, K.B. (1985) Natural order in childrens' use of second language learning strategies. *Applied Linguistics* 6/1, 45–59.

Chomsky, N. (1965) *Aspects of the Theory of Syntax*. Cambridge, MA: MIT Press.

Clark, A. (1993) Bridging the gap: GCSE to 'A' level. *Language Learning* 8, 66–8.

Clarke, M.A. (1980) The short circuit hypothesis of ESL reading. *Modern Language Journal* 64, 203–9.

218   EFFECTIVE LANGUAGE LEARNING

Coates, J.C. (1986) *Women, Men and Language: A Sociolinguistic Account of Sex Differences in language*. New York: Longman.
Cohen, A. (1984) Studying second language learning strategies: How do we get the information? *Applied Linguistics* 5(2), 101–11.
— (1987) Student processing of feedback on their compostitions. In A. Wenden and J. Rubin (eds) *Learner Strategies in Language Learning* (pp. 57–69). Englewood Cliffs, NJ: Prentice-Hall.
Cohen, L. and Manion, L. (1989) *Research Methods in Education*, 3rd edn. London: Routledge.
Crookall, D. and Oxford, R. (1992) Dealing with anxiety: Some practical activities for language learners and teacher trainees. In E.K. Horwitz and D.J. Young (eds) *Language Anxiety. From Theory and Research to Classroom Implications* (pp. 141–51). Englewood Cliffs, NJ: Prentice-Hall.
Crookes, G. and Schmidt, R.W. (1991) Motivation: Reopening the research agenda. *Language Learning* 41, 469–512.
Crossan, B. (1992) GCSE to A level. The Essex cohort study 1989–91. AEB Seminar, May 1992.
Cummins, J. (1979) Cognitive/academic language proficiency, linguistic interdependence, the optimal age question and some other matters. *Working Papers on Bilingualism*, 19, 197–205.
— (1980) The cross-lingual dimensions of language proficiency: Implications for bilingual education and the optimal age issue. *TESOL Quarterly*, 14(2), 175–87.
— (1981) Empirical and theoretical underpinnings of bilingual education. *Journal of Education* 163, 16–29.
— (1984) *Bilingualism and Special Education. Issues in Assessment and Pedagogy*. Clevedon, Avon: Multilingual Matters.
Cummins, J. and Swain, M. (1986) *Bilingualism in Education*. London: Longman.
Curran, C.C. (1976) *Counseling-Learning in Second Languages*. Apple River, Ill: Apple River Press.
Dale, R.R. (1974) *Mixed or Single-Sex Schools?* Vol. III. London: Routledge & Kegan Paul.
Deaux, K. and Farris, E. (1977) Attributing causes for one's own performance: The effects of sex, norms and task outcome. *Journal of Research in Personality* 11, 59–72.
Delamont, S. (1980) *Sex Roles and the School*. London: Methuen.
Department of Education and Science/Welsh Office (DES/WO) (1985) *GCSE. General Certificate of Education. National Criteria. French*. London: HMSO.
— (1991) *Modern Foreign Languages in the National Curriculum*. London: HMSO.
Dickinson, L. (1987) *Self-instruction in Language Learning*. Cambridge: Cambridge University Press.
— (1992) *Learner Training for Language Learning*. Dublin: Authentik Language Learning Resources Ltd.
Dörnyei, Z. and Thurrell, S. (1991) Strategic competence and how to teach it. *ELT Journal* 45(1), 16–23.
Dulay, H., Burt, M. and Krashen, S. (1982) *Language 2*. New York: Oxford University Press.
Dweck, C.S. and Bush, E.S. (1976) Sex differences in learned helplessness: I. Differential debilitation with peer and adult evaluators. *Developmental Psychology* 12, 147–56.

Dweck, C.S., Goetz, T.E. and Strauss, N.L. (1980) Sex differences in learned helplessness: IV. An experimental and naturalistic study of failure generalization and its mediators. *Journal of Personality and Social Psychology* 38, 441–52.

Eastman, J.K. (1987) Remedial training in listening comprehension. *System* 15, 197–201.

Ehrman, M. and Oxford, R. (1988) Effects of sex differences, career choice, and psychological type on adult language learning strategies. *Modern Language Journal* 72, 253–65.

Ellis, R. (1990) *Instructed Second Language Acquisition: Learning in the Classroom.* Oxford: Basil Blackwell.

— (1992) *Second Language Acquisition and Language Pedagogy.* Clevedon, Avon: Multilingual Matters.

Ellis, G. and Sinclair, B. (1989) *Learning to Learn English. A Course in Learner Training.* Cambridge: Cambridge University Press.

Ely, C.M. (1986) An analysis of discomfort, risktaking, sociability, and motivation in the L2 classroom. *Language Learning* 36, 1–25.

Ericsson, K.A. and Simon, H.A. (1980) Verbal reports as data. *Psychological Review* 87, 215–51.

Eskey, D.E. (1988) Holding in the bottom: An interactive approach to the language problems of second language readers. In P.L. Carrell, J. Devine and D.E. Eskey (eds) *Interactive Approaches to Second Language Reading* (pp. 93–100). Cambridge: Cambridge University Press.

Filmer-Sankey, C. (1993) OXPROD: A summative account. *Language Learning Journal* 7, 5–8.

Foss, K.A. and Reitzel, A.C. (1988) A relational model for managing second language anxiety. *TESOL Quarterly* 22(3), 437–54.

Fotos, S. and Ellis, R. (1991) Communicating about grammar: A task-based approach. *TESOL Quarterly* 25(4), 605–29.

Gardner, R.C. (1985) *Social Psychology and Second Language Learning: The Role of Attitudes and Motivation.* London: Edward Arnold.

Gardner, R.C. (1988) The socio-educational model of second language learning: Assumptions, findings, and issues. *Language Learning* 38, 101–26.

Gardner, R.C. and Lambert, W.E. (1972) *Attitudes and Motivation in Second Language Learning.* Rowley, MA: Newbury House.

Gardner, R.C. and MacInytre, P.D. (1993) A student's contributions to second-language learning. Part II: Affective variables. *Language Teaching* 26, 1–11.

Gass, S. and Varonis, E. (1986) Sex differences in NNS/NNS interactions. In R. Day (ed.) *Talking to Learn: Conversation in Second Language Acquisition* (pp. 327–51). Rowley, MA: Newbury House.

Genesee, F. and Hamayan, E. (1980) Individual differences in second language learning. *Applied Psycholinguistics* 1, 95–110.

Gillette, B. (1987) Two successful language learners. An introspective account. In C. Faerch and G. Kasper (eds) *Introspection in Second Language Research* (pp. 268–79). Clevedon, Avon: Multilingual Matters.

Glisan, E.W. (1988) A plan for teaching listening comprehension: Adaptation of an instructional reading model. *Foreign Language Annals* 21, 9–16.

Goethe-Institut. (1982) *Texte zur Landeskunde im Unterricht. Schule und Freizeit, I.* Munich: Goethe-Institut.

Goethe-Institut. (1990) *AZ-Journal 2/90. Aktuelle Texte aus der Abendzeitung.* Munich: Goethe-Institut.

Graham, S. (1994) Foreign language learning processes in post-compulsory education. PhD thesis, University of Bath.

Grenfell, M. (1991) Communication: Sense and nonsense. *Language Learning Journal* 3, 6–8.

Grenfell, M. and Harris, V. (1993) How do pupils learn? (Part 1) *Language Learning Journal* 8, 22–5.

— (1994) How do pupils learn? (Part 2) *Language Learning Journal* 9, 7–11.

Guidelines for Written French at A level. (1986) London: Published jointly by the Standing Conference on University Entrance and the Council for National Academic Awards.

Harris, V. and Frith, A. (1990) Group work in the modern languages classroom. *Language Learning Journal* 1, 71–4.

Hatch, E. (1974) Second language learning — universals. *Working Papers on Bilingualism* 3, 1–18.

Haynes, M. (1984) Patterns and perils of guessing in second language reading. In J. Handscombe, R.A. Orem and B.P. Taylor (eds) *On TESOL '83: The Question of Control* (pp. 163–76). Washington: TESOL.

Heafford, M. (1993) What is grammar, who is she? *Language Learning* 7, 55–8.

Heald, D. (1991) Untranslatables, particles and pitfalls in German.Practical problems in the classroom. *UEA Papers in Linguistics (Norwich)* 32, 27–36.

Hedge, T. (1988) *Writing.* Oxford: Oxford University Press.

Heyde, A.W. (1977) The relationship between self-esteem and the oral production of a second language. In H.D. Brown, C.A. Yario and R.H. Crymes (eds) *On TESOL '77: Teaching and Learning English as a Second Language. Trends in Research and Practice* (pp. 226–40). Washington DC: TESOL 1977.

— (1979) The relationship between self-esteem and the oral production of a second language. PhD thesis, University of Michigan, Ann Arbor.

Heyde Parsons, A.W. (1983) Self-esteem and the acquisition of French. In K.M. Bailey, M.H. Long and S. Peck (eds) *Studies in Second Language Acquisition: Series on Issues in Second Language Research* (pp. 175–87). Rowley, MA: Newbury House.

HM Inspectors. (1985) *Modern Languages in the Sixth Form.* Stanmore: Department of Education and Science.

Hingley, P. (1983) Modern languages. In J. Whyld (ed.) *Sexism in the Secondary Curriculum* (pp. 99–110). London: Harper and Row.

Holmes, J. (1991) Language and gender. *Language Teaching* 17, 207–20.

Hooper, J. (1989) The role of grammar in the contemporary foreign language classroom. MA (Ed.) thesis, University of Southampton.

Horwitz, E.K. (1991) Preliminary evidence for the reliability and validity of a foreign language anxiety scale. In E.K. Horwitz and D.J. Young (eds) *Language Anxiety. From Theory and Research to Classroom Implications* (pp. 37–39). Englewood Cliffs, NJ: Prentice-Hall.

Horwitz, E.K., Horwitz, M.B. and Cope, J. (1986) Foreign language classroom anxiety. *Modern Language Journal* 70, 125–32.

Hosenfeld, C. (1979) Cindy: A learner in today's foreign language classroom. In W. Borne (ed.) *The Foreign Language Learner in Today's Classroom Environment* (pp. 53–75). Montpelier, Vermont: Northeast Conference on the Teaching of Foreign Languages.

— (1984) Case studies of ninth grade readers. In J.C. Alderson and A.H. Urquhart (eds) *Reading in a Foreign Language* (pp. 231–49). London: Longman.

Howell-Richardson, C. and Parkinson, B. (1988) Learner diaries: possibilities and pitfalls. In P. Grunwell (ed.) *Applied Linguistics in Society. Papers from the Twentieth Anniversary Meeting of the British Association for Applied Linguistics. University of Nottingham, September 1987* (pp. 74–79). London: CILT for BAAL.

Hulstijn, J. H. (1993) When do foreign language readers look up the meaning of unfamiliar words? The influence of task and learner variables. *Modern Language Journal 77*, 13–147.

Hurman, J. (1992) Performance in the A-level speaking test by candidates with GCSE training: Oral examiners' views. *Language Learning Journal 5*, 8–10.

Inter Nationes (No date) *Jugend bei uns. Teil 4*. Bonn-Bad Godesberg: Inter Nationes.

Johnstone, R. (1989) *Communicative Interaction: A Guide for Language Teachers.* London: CILT.

Keller, J.M. (1983) Motivational design of instruction. In C.M. Reigeluth (ed.) *Instructional Design Theories and Models* (pp. 386–433). Hillsdale, NJ: Erlbaum.

Kelly, A. (1985) The construction of masculine science. *British Journal of Sociology of Education 6*, 134–54.

Kenning, M-M. (1992) The joint languages diversification model: Aspects of a case study. *Language Learning Journal 5*, 2–5.

Kimmel, S. and MacGinitie, W.H. (1984) Identifying children who use a perservera-tive text processing strategy. *Reading Research Quarterly 19*, 162–72.

Klapper, J. (1993) Practicable skills and practical constraints in FL reading. *Language Learning Journal 7*, 50–4.

Knapman, D. (1982) *School-Associated Anxieties. A Report Based on the Results of a Local Survey*. Psychological Service, Somerset Education Department.

Krashen, S.D. (1985) *The Input Hypothesis*. London: Longman.

Lado, R. (1961) *Language Testing: The Construction and Use of Foreign Language Tests. A Teacher's Book*. London: Longman.

LaFrance, M. (1991) School for scandal: Different educational experiences for females and males. *Gender and Education 3*, 3–31.

Langer, I., Schulz v. Thun, F. and Tausch, R. (1974) *Verstandlichkeit in Schule, Verwaltung, Politik und Wissenschaft*. Munich: Reinhardt

Larsen-Freeman, D. and Long, M.H. (1991) *An Introduction to Second Language Acquisition Research*. London: Longman.

Leki, I. (1990) Coaching from the margins: Issues in written response. In B. Kroll (ed.) *Second Language Writing: Research Insights for the Classroom* (pp. 57–68). Cambridge: Cambridge University Press.

Lennon, P. (1993) The advanced learner: Affective, social and motivational factors. *Language Learning Journal 8*, 39–43.

Lewcowicz, J. and Moon, J. (1985) Evaluation: A way of involving the learner. In J.C. Alderson (ed.) *Evaluation. Lancaster Practical Papers in English Language Education, Volume 6* (pp. 45–80). Oxford: Pergamon Press.

Licht, B.G. and Dweck, C.S. (1983) Sex differences in achievement orientations: Consequences for academic choices and attainments. In M. Marland (ed.) *Sex Differentiation and Schooling* (pp. 72–97). London: Heinemann.

Licht, B.G. and Shapiro, S.H. (1982) Sex differences in attributions among high achievers. Paper Presented at the Meeting of the American Psychological Association, Washington, D.C.

Loulidi, R. (1990) Is language learning really a female business? *Language Learning Journal* 1, 40–3.

Low, G. (1991) Bridging the A' level gap. *Education* 177/21, 425.

Lukmani, Y. (1972) Motivation to learn and learning proficiency. *Language Learning* 22, 261–73.

Maccoby, E.E. and Jacklin, C.N. (1974) *The Psychology of Sex Differences*. Stanford: Stanford University Press.

MacDonald, M. (1980) Schooling and the reproduction of class and gender relations. In L. Barton, R. Meighan and S. Walker (eds) *Schooling, Ideology and the Curriculum* (pp. 29–49). London: Falmer.

MacIntyre, P.D. and Gardner, R.C. (1989) Anxiety and second language learning: Toward a theoretical clarification. *Language Learning* 9, 251–75.

Mann, S.J. (1982) Verbal reports as data: A focus on retrospection. In S. Dingwall and S.J. Mann (eds) *Methods and Problems in Doing Applied Linguistic Research* (pp. 87–104). Lancaster: Department of Linguistics and Modern English Language, University of Lancaster.

McLaughlin, B. (1990) The relationship between first and second languages: Language proficiency and language aptitude. In B. Harley, P. Allen, J. Cummins and M. Swain (eds) *The Development of Second Language Proficiency* (pp. 158–74). Cambridge: Cambridge University Press.

Metcalfe, P., Laurillard, D. and Mason, R. (1995) The decline in written accuracy in pupils' use of French verbs. *Language Learning Journal* 12, 47–50.

Mitchell, R. (1988) *Communicative Language Teaching in Practice*. London: CILT.

Mitchell, R. and Hooper, J. (1990) Teachers' views of language knowledge. *CLE Working Papers, University of Southampton* 1, 18–26.

Murphy-O'Dwyer, L. (1985) Diary studies as a method for evaluating teacher training. In J.C. Alderson (ed.) *Evaluation. Lancaster Practical Papers in English Language Education, Volume 6* (pp. 97–128). Oxford: Pergamon Press.

Naiman, N., Fröhlich, M., Stern, H.H. and Todesco, A. (1978) *The Good Language Learner*. Ontario: The Ontario Institute for Studies in Education. Reprinted (1996) Clevedon, Avon: Multilingual Matters Ltd.

Nicholls, J.G. (1975) Causal attributions and other achievement-related cognitions: Effects of task outcome, attainment value, and sex. *Journal of Personality and Social Psychology* 31, 379–89.

Nisbet, J. and Shucksmith, J. (1986) *Learning Strategies*. London: Routledge and Kegan Paul.

Norman, D.A. (1980) Cognitive engineering and education. In D.T.Tuma and F. Reif (eds) *Problem Solving and Education* (pp. 97–107). Hillsdale, NJ: Erlbaum.

Northern Examinations and Assessment Board. (1989) *General Certificate of Education. French Advanced Paper II. Friday 9 June 1989*. Manchester: Northern Examinations and Assessment Board.

— (1991) *General Certificate of Education. French Advanced Paper II. Friday 14 June 1991*. Manchester: Northern Examinations and Assessment Board.

— (1992) *GCE Examiners' Reports 1991. Modern Foreign Languages*. Manchester: Northern Examinations and Assessment Board.

Nuttall, C. (1982) *Teaching Reading Skills in a Foreign Language*. London: Heinemann.

Nyikos, M. (1990) Sex-related differences in adult language learning: Socialization and memory factors. *Modern Language Journal* 74, 273–87.

Oller, J. and Perkins, K. (1978) Intelligence and language proficiency as sources of variance in self-reported affective variables. *Language Learning* 28, 85–97.

O'Malley, J. (1987) The effects of training in the use of learning strategies on learning English as a second language. In A. Wenden and J. Rubin (eds) *Learner Strategies in Language Learning*. London: Prentice-Hall.

O'Malley, J.M. and Chamot, A.U. (1990) *Learning Strategies in Second Language Acquisition*. Cambridge: Cambridge University Press.

O'Malley, J.M., Chamot, A.U. and Küpper, L. (1989) Listening comprehension strategies in second language acquisition. *Applied Linguistics* 10, 418–37.

Omerod, M.B. (1975) Subject preference and choice and educational and single-sex secondary schools. *British Journal of Educational Psychology* 45, 257–67.

Oxford, R. (1985) *A New Taxonomy of Second Language Learning Strategies*. Washington, DC: ERIC Clearinghouse on Languages and Linguistics.

— (1986) Development and psychometric testing of the strategy inventory for language learning. Army Research Institute Technical Report. Alexandria, VA: US Army Research Institute for the Behavioural & Social Sciences.

— (1989) *Language Learning Strategies: What Every Teacher Should Know*. New York: Newbury House/Harper & Row.

Oxford, R., Crookall, D., Cohen, A., Lavine, R., Nyikos, M. and Sutter, W. (1990) Strategy training for language learners — six situational case studies and a training model. *Foreign Language Annals* 23, 197–216.

Oxford, R. and Nyikos, M. (1989) Variables affecting choice of language learning strategies by university students. *Modern Language Journal* 73, 291–300.

Oxford, R.L., Nyikos, M., and Ehrman, M. (1988) Vive la différence? Reflections on sex differences in use of language learning strategies. *Foreign Language Annals* 21, 321–29.

Palincsar, A.S. and Brown, A.L. (1984) Reciprocal teaching of comprehension-fostering and comprehension-monitoring activities. *Cognition and Instruction* 1, 117–75.

Paris, S.G. (1988) Fusing skill and will: The integration of cognitive and motivational psychology. Paper presented at the annual meeting of the American Educational Research Association, New Orleans, LA., April 1988.

Parkinson, B. and Howell-Richardson, C. (1989) Learner diaries. In C. Brumfit and R. Mitchell (eds) *Research in the Language Classroom* (pp. 128–40). London: Modern English Publications/British Council.

Parsons, J.E., Ruble, D.N. Hodges, K.L. and Small, I. (1976) Cognitive-developmental factors in emerging sex differences in achievement-related expectancies. *Journal of Social Issues* 32, 47–61.

Peck, A. (1988) *Language Teachers at Work: A Description of Methods*. Hemel Hempstead: Prentice Hall.

Perl, S. (1979) The composing processes of unskilled college writers. *Research in the Teaching of English* 13, 317–336.

Phillips, E.M. (1992) The effects of language anxiety on students' oral test performance and attitudes. *Modern Language Journal* 76, 14–26.

Pickard, N. (1995) Out-of-class language learning strategies: Three case studies. *Language Learning Journal* 12, 35–7.

Powell, R.C. (1986a) Towards a better understanding of the foreign language education of boys and girls in comprehensive schools with particular reference to sex-differences and the drop-out problem. PhD thesis, University of Bath.

— (1986b) *Boys, Girls and Languages in School*. London: CILT.

Powell, R.C., Barnes, A. and Graham, S. (1996) The assessment of writing skills at GCSE 1995 and 1998. A review of current and future practice. Unpublished report for the School Curriculum and Assessment Authority.

Powell, R.C. and Littlewood, P. (1982) Foreign languages: The avoidable options. *British Journal of Language Teaching* 20, 153–59.

Rees, F. and Batters, J. (1988) Cherchez les garçons. *Teachers' Weekly* 14 November, 18–19.

Rees, P.F. (1995) Reading in French from GCSE to 'A' level: The student perspective. In M. Grenfell (ed.) *Reflections on Reading From GCSE to 'A' Level*. London: CILT.

Reiss, M.A. (1985) The good language learner: Another look. *Canadian Modern Language Review* 41, 511–23.

Rock, D. (1990). A'level language papers: Aims, objectives and tactics. *German Teaching* 2, 18–24.

Rubin, J. (1975) What the 'good language learner' can teach us. *TESOL Quarterly* 9/1, 41–51.

— (1981) Study of cognitive processes in second language learning. *Applied Linguistics* 11(2), 117–31.

Rubin, J. and Thompson, I. (1982) *How to Be a More Successful Language Learner*. Boston, MA: Heinle & Heinle.

School Curriculum and Assessment Authority (SCAA) (1993) *GCE A/AS Subject Cores for Modern Foreign Languages*. London: SCAA.

Schultz, J.M. (1991) Writing mode in the articulation of language and literature classes: Theory and practice. *Modern Language Journal* 75(iv), 411–17.

Schulz, R.A. (1981) Literature and readability: Bridging the gap in foreign language reading. *Modern Language Journal* 65 (Spring), 43–53.

Schumann, J.H. (1978) Social and psychological factors in second language acquisition. In J.C. Richards (ed.) *Understanding Second and Foreign Language Learning* (pp. 163–78). Rowley, MA: Newbury House.

Scovel, T. (1978) The effect of affect on foreign language learning: A review of the anxiety research. *Language Learning* 28, 129–42.

Seliger, H.W. (1977) Does practice make perfect? A study of interaction patterns and L2 competence. *Language Learning* 27, 263–78.

— (1983) The language learner as linguist: Of metaphors and realities. *Applied Linguistics* 4/3, 179–91.

Selinker, L. (1972). Interlanguage. *International Review of Applied Linguistics* 10, 209–31.

Sharwood-Smith, M. (1981) Consciousness-raising and the second language learner. *Applied Linguistics* 11(2), 159–68.

Skehan, P. (1989) *Individual Differences in Second-Language Learning*. London: Edward Arnold.

— (1991) Individual differences in second language learning. *Studies in Second Language Acquisition* 13, 275–98.

Skutnabb-Kangas, T. (1984) *Bilingualism or Not, the Education of Minorities*. Clevedon, Avon: Multilingual Matters.

Smith, E.R. and Miller, F.D. (1978) Limits on perception of cognitive processes: A reply to Nisbett and Wilson. *Psychological Review* 85, 355–62.

Spender, D. (1980). *Man Made Language*. London: Routledge and Kegan Paul.

— (1982) *Invisible Women: The Schooling Scandal*. London: Writers and Readers Publishing Cooperative.

Spolsky, B. (1989) *Conditions for Second Language Learning. Introduction to a General Theory.* Oxford: Oxford University Press.

Stern, H.H. (1975) What can we learn from the good language learner? *Canadian Modern Language Review* 31, 304–18.

— (1983) *Fundamental Concepts of Language Teaching.* Oxford: Oxford University Press.

Stipek, D.J. and Hoffman, J.M. (1980) Children's achievement-related expectancies as a function of academic performance histories and sex. *Journal of Educational Psychology* 72, 861–65.

Sutherland, M.B. (1981) *Sex Bias in Education.* Oxford: Basil Blackwell.

— (1983) Anxiety, aspirations and the curriculum. In M. Marland (ed.) *Sex Differentiation and Schooling* (pp. 60–71). London: Heinemann.

Swain, M. and Burnaby, B. (1976) Personality characteristics and second language learning in young children: A pilot study. *Working Papers on Bilingualism* 11, 76–90.

Tannen, D. (1987) *That's Not What I Meant! How Conversational Style Makes or Breaks Your Relations With Others.* London: J.M. Dent and Sons Ltd.

Thomas, K. (1990) *Gender and Subject in Higher Education.* Buckingham: The Society for Research into Higher Education and Open University Press.

Thorogood, J. and King, L. (1991) *Bridging the Gap: GCSE to 'A' Level.* London: CILT.

University of Oxford Delegacy of Local Examinations. (1989) *Advanced Supplementary Level Summer Examination, May 1989. French. Paper I.* Oxford: University of Oxford Delegacy of Local Examinations.

van Ek, J.A. (1979) The threshold level. In C.J.Brumfit and K. Johnson (eds) *The Communicative Approach to Language Teaching* (pp. 103–16). Oxford: Oxford University Press.

Wallach, M.A. and Kogan, N. (1959) Sex differences and judgement processes. *Journal of Personality* 27, 555–64.

Walmsley, R. (1990) Poorly translated ideals. *Times Educational Supplement* 10 August, 10.

Weinrich-Haste, H. (1981) The image of science. In A. Kelly (ed.) *The Missing Half, Girls and Science Education* (pp. 216–29). Manchester: Manchester University Press.

Wenden, A. (1987) Incorporating learner training in the classroom. In A. Wenden and J. Rubin (eds) *Learner Strategies in Language Learning* (pp. 159–68). Englewood Cliffs, NJ: Prentice-Hall.

White, P. (1980). Limitations on verbal report of internal events. *Psychological Review* 87, 105–12.

Whyte, J. (1984). Observing sex stereotypes and interactions in the school lab. and workshop. *Educational Review* 36, 75–86.

Widdowson, H.G. (1990). *Aspects of Language Teaching.* Oxford: Oxford University Press.

Zamel, V. (1983) The composing processes of advanced ESL students: Six case studies. *TESOL Quarterly* 17/2, 165–87.

Index

Subjects

academic elaboration 65, 179
accuracy
— demands of A-level 9, 16-8, 122
— monitoring for 63, 65, 66, 68, 144, 149-50, 152, 155, 165-6
— students' difficulties with 1-2, 10, 19, 21, 27, 127, 155, 162, 169
— oral work 70, 71, 106
— versus content 152
— versus fluency 39
active engagement in learning 38, 39, 91, 98, 99, 112, 121
activating prior knowledge 87, 88, 146
advance organisation 50, 81, 134, 135, 176
affective factors and responses
— definition 92, 173
— influence on language learning 4, 92-7, 119, 154
— learner diaries and 46, 104, 110-11, 118-21, 123, 158
— learning strategies and 5, 41, 42, 119, 166-7, 170
— management of 39, 116-7, 128, 136-7, 151, 154, 168, 169
— oral work and 29, 40, 69, 104-8, 110-11, 119, 120-1, 152
affective filter 93
age, and learning strategy use 40-1, 171
A-level, Advanced Level
— anxiety and 95, 101-9, 116, 123
— assessment and 11, 16-18, 132
— compared with GCSE 18-19, 144, 162
— definition 1, 9, 173
— demands of 1-3, 9, 16-19, 20-30, 162, 205-6

— gender differences and 28-30, 101-3, 117
— grammatical development and 74-5, 165
— individual students and 147, 151, 154, 155, 157, 158
— learning strategies and 37, 48-83, 91, 171
— learning strategy instruction and 83-5, 129, 139, 143, 156
— managing change at 77-9, 169
— motivation and 97-9, 111-16, 122, 152, 154, 155
— strategic awareness and 85-6, 170
— students' difficulties 3, 5-6, 162-3, 171, 211
— study skills and 2, 126-28, 136, 145, 168
— transition from GCSE 1-2, 16-36, 95, 98, 122, 125, 127-30, 138-42, 153, 162, 166
ambiguity
— intolerance of 150
— tolerance of 38, 39
antagonism 107
anxiety
— communicative 95
— debilitating 94, 102
— facilitating 94, 102, 119
— gender differences and 94-5, 102-10, 117, 151, 152, 158, 166-7
— influence on language learning 4, 83, 92-5, 118-19, 149, 154
— language 93, 105
— learner diaries and 46, 104, 110-11, 118-21, 123, 158

— learning strategies and 5, 7, 110-11, 118-19, 120, 166-8
— listening comprehension and 158
— management of 39, 116-17, 128, 136-7, 151, 154, 168, 169
— motivation and 97, 114, 157
— oral work and 24, 29, 69, 71, 89, 104-8, 110-11, 119-21, 149, 152, 155, 166
— reduction 123, 161, 183
— reflection and 118-19, 161
— state 93
— trait 93
application of patterns and rules 63, 65, 66, 72, 74, 81, 152, 164, 165, 181
aptitude 4, 80, 97, 151, 160
assessment by grade 79, 178
association, learning vocabulary by means of 90, 182
attitude to language learning 4, 92, 96, 98, 99, 100, 103, 111, 112
Attribution Theory 97
audiolingual/audiovisual method 11
auditory monitoring 63, 66, 72, 81, 164, 165, 177
autonomy, learner 31, 32, 40, 83, 86, 97, 98, 138, 145, 153, 170
avoidance 106, 111, 116, 166, 183

Behaviourism 11, 12
bottom-up processing 52, 53, 57, 58, 87, 88, 134, 173
bravado, male 102

CALP (Cognitative/Academic Language Proficiency) 18, 19, 27, 33, 141, 163, 168
case system 27, 28, 29, 46, 72, 73, 75, 125
circumlocution/paraphrase 184
— oral work and 81, 89, 130-1, 143, 166
— written work and 63, 68, 165
clarification 42, 71, 183
classroom observation 39, 43
cloze exercises 46, 74-77, 82, 148, 150, 152, 155, 159, 164
code switch 184
cognates (transfer) 40, 53, 54, 61-3, 64, 67, 87, 89, 134-5, 160, 165, 182
cognitive strategies 42, 64, 173, 179-83

cognitive theory, language learning and 4, 173
cohesion markers 50, 82, 88, 179
communication apprehension 30, 94, 105
communicative competence 7, 10, 11, 12, 13, 14, 79, 127, 174
communication, lack of 110, 115, 139, 154, 157
communication strategies 16, 142, 174
communicative language ability 13
comparison, progress monitoring and 178
competitiveness 94, 103, 109, 151
comprehensible input 101, 130, 141
comprehension monitoring 50, 51, 54-6, 87, 149, 163, 177
consciousness-raising 35
contextualisation 182
control, language learning and 117-20, 122-3, 156, 157, 161, 167
cooperation 71, 81, 83, 121, 143, 166, 167, 183
creating practice opportunities 49, 53, 63, 70, 72, 80, 82, 165, 166, 176
creative re-combination 148, 151

data gatherers 73, 149
demotivation 2, 30, 33, 113, 114, 115, 122, 141, 142, 145, 167, 169
dictionary 42, 74, 150, 165, 181
— grammatical rules and 72, 159
— instruction in using 87-88, 128, 135, 136, 157, 160-1
— reliance on 26, 54, 63, 64, 156, 162, 169
— students' difficulties with 40, 58-61, 164
differentiation of tasks 115, 122
directed attention 50, 65, 81, 176
discussion work 69, 101, 120, 121, 126, 127, 130, 140, 163, 166
double-check monitoring 51, 54, 61, 62, 67, 74, 87, 160, 163, 177
drafting 63, 88, 89, 132, 143, 165, 166, 176

elaboration 51, 52, 82, 141, 144, 179
— academic 65, 179
— between-parts 179
— personal 179
— questioning 179

— world 53, 56, 57, 180
emphasis markers 50, 179
equal opportunities 117, 121
errors 89, 144, 165
— amending 69, 131, 177
— analysing 69, 144, 157, 177
— assessing 69, 144, 157, 177
— attending to 177
— reading through 177
essays 1, 17, 27, 33, 88-9, 131, 132, 143
essay planning 88, 131, 132, 143
ethnocentricity 99
evaluation 64, 65, 68, 69, 78, 81, 84, 86,
   139, 143, 144
— peer 94, 106, 107, 110, 117, 151
— production 176
— strategy 80, 84, 119, 153, 156, 169,
   170, 176
— teacher's 94, 106, 109
extrinsic motivation 98, 116

fear of negative evaluation 94, 105, 106
flashcards 90
Flexible Learning Project 40
formal practice 41-2
form/function relationship 74-7, 148,
   155, 159, 164, 165
formulaic phrases 70, 130, 131, 142,
   150, 180

GCSE, General Certificate of
   Secondary Education
— assessment and proficiency and
   15-16
— definition 1, 9, 173
— formulaic phrases and 41, 70, 150
— gender differences and 102
— grades 118, 147, 151, 153, 154, 157
— grammar and 73, 148
— oral work 105, 131
— reading 138
— study habits 77
— transition to A-level 1-2, 16-36, 95,
   98, 122, 125, 127-30, 138-42, 153,
   162, 166
— writing 66, 88-9
gender
— anxiety 94-5, 102-10, 117, 151, 152,
   158, 166-7

— control of learning 122-3
— definition 99
— differences in attitudes to language
   learning 100
— differences in language learning 3,
   28-30, 92, 99-103
— differences in learning strategy use
   5, 7, 41-2, 81-3
— gender-based judgements about
   academic subjects 100, 154, 158
— motivation and 99-100
grammar, grammatical
— accuracy 11, 17
— acquisition 31, 32, 34, 35, 71-7, 78,
   80, 90, 132-4, 140, 144, 153, 155, 164
— appropriateness 13-4
— awareness 2, 21
— competence, proficiency 12, 16, 79,
   148, 149, 160
— exercises 114, 153
— gender differences and 28-9, 81-2
— grammatical development 75, 165
— learning strategies 31, 32, 34, 71-7,
   90, 101, 132-4
— learning strategy instruction and
   32, 144
— manipulation 46, 71-7, 159, 164
— monitoring 66, 67
— motivation and 113-4, 122
— students' difficulties 2, 10, 15, 21-4,
   31, 67, 125-6, 138, 152, 162, 168
— teaching 24, 32, 63, 73, 80, 114,
   125-8, 130, 132-4, 138, 144, 155, 159,
   164, 168, 169
grammar-translation method 11, 35
grammatical competence, and
   communicative competence 12-13
group dynamics 108, 120, 128, 166
grouping words/phrases 90, 133

Hawthorne Effect 46
hesitation fillers 89, 143
High-Input Generators 70
highlighting 180
hypothesising 180

illocutionary competence 14, 17
imagery 182
imitation 180

inductive learning ability 160
inferencing 180
— by context 50, 51, 52-3, 56-9, 62, 74,
   87, 88, 134, 136, 139, 141, 144, 146,
   157, 158, 160, 163, 180
— by tone 50, 88, 167, 180
— by visual images 180
— hearing-in 50, 52, 53, 180
Input Hypothesis 130
integrative orientation 96-8, 111, 113,
   148, 157
instrumental orientation 96, 97, 98,
   100, 112, 113
interlanguage 12, 75, 76, 174
interpretation 54, 62, 74, 180
intrinsic motivation 98, 116
introspection 43, 44, 45, 119
interest, and motivation 98, 113

key words 50, 51, 56, 88, 134, 164
keyword method 90

language competence 13
language philosophy 79, 80
language repertoire monitoring 63,
   131, 142, 143, 153, 165, 177
learner diaries
— definition 174
— learning strategy training and 84, 161
— recording anxiety 104, 110-11,
   118-21, 123, 158
— recording motivation 99, 113,
   114-15, 121-3, 155
— recording learning strategies 74, 78,
   149-56
— reflection and 80-1, 139, 150, 167
— strategic awareness and 85-6, 167
— research tool 46-8
learning strategies
— A-level students and 5-7
— anxiety and 95, 102-3, 119, 166-8
— aptitude and 151, 160
— autonomy and 32
— cognitive theory and language
   learning 4
— control over one's learning and 117,
   123
— definition 3, 174
— gender differences and 41-2, 81-3

— grammar learning, manipulation
   and 71-7, 90-1
— listening comprehension and 49-53,
   88-9, 164
— motivation and 116, 122, 167
— oral work and 69-71, 89
— reading comprehension and 53-63,
   87-8
— recording 43-48
— reflection and 121
— response to learning difficulties
   163-66
— study habits 77-81
— teachers' views of 128-9, 132-46, 168
— vocabulary learning and 89-91, 165
— writing and 63-9, 165
learning strategy instruction 32, 34,
   83-91, 119, 122, 128-30, 132, 135,
   136, 139, 141, 144-6, 153, 157, 161,
   164-5, 168-71
listing by attribute 182
list-making 77, 182
listening, comprehension
— A-level assessment and 17
— anxiety and 94
— data gatherers/rule formers and 73
— gender differences and 29, 81-2,
   101-2, 167
— language philosophy and 79
— learning strategies and 49-53, 88-9, 164
— learning strategy instruction and
   32, 144
— motivation and 114
— students' difficulties and 2, 7, 25,
   33-4, 163
— teachers' approaches to 134-6, 139
— teachers' views of 125-7
literary work 1, 5, 31, 109, 113, 114, 116
   131, 134, 140, 142
loci 90, 182
long-term memory 44, 174
Low-input Generators 82

masking 77, 182
metacognitive strategies 42, 43, 50, 54,
   64, 78, 84, 163, 174, 176-9
mnemonic devices 77, 90, 91, 165, 182-3
monitoring 50, 54, 65, 69, 72, 78, 81, 84,
   88, 143, 144, 166, 177

— for accuracy 63, 65, 68, 165, 166, 177
— auditory 63, 66, 72, 81, 164, 165, 166, 177
— comprehension 50, 51, 54-6, 87, 149, 163, 177
— double-check 51, 54, 61, 62, 67, 74, 87, 160, 163, 177
— for meaning expressed 63, 64, 68, 156, 165, 177
— of production 63, 67, 74, 165, 177
— progress 47, 78, 79, 86, 137, 178
— for the style and sophistication of language used 63, 64, 66, 165, 166, 178
— strategy 54, 55, 82, 84, 169, 178
— visual 63, 66, 72, 164, 165, 178
motivation
— A-level students and 111-16
— anxiety and 94-5
— control over one's learning and 157
— definition 96, 98
— gender-based views of subjects and 154
— gender differences and 99-100
— influence on language learning 4, 39, 92, 93, 96-9, 113-16
— influence on learning strategy use 5, 7, 91, 102, 166-8
— reflection and 121-3
— teachers and 170
— topics studied and 129, 130
Myers-Briggs Type Indicator 41

narrow focus 50, 54, 88, 156, 180
National Criteria, and GCSE 15
National Curriculum 15, 36, 174
naturalistic practice 49, 53, 70, 82, 166, 180
NEEDS Project 2
negative evaluation, fear of 94, 105, 106
negative self-comparison 29, 79, 107, 109, 120, 137, 158, 166
note taking 128, 180
novel associations 182

omission 54, 74, 82, 180
oral work
— anxiety and 40, 89, 93-5, 151-2, 166
— communicative competence and 12
— data gatherers/rule formers and 73, 149

— formulaic phrases and 70, 142
— fluency 35
— gender differences and 28-9, 42, 81, 101, 117, 166
— learning strategies and 69-71, 89
— learning strategy instruction and 143
— motivation and 96
— students' difficulties 2, 7, 24-5, 33
— students' strengths in 24
— teachers' approaches to 130, 136-7
— teachers' views of 125-7
organisational competence 13, 17
organisational/scheduling strategies 78, 128, 136, 145, 148, 152, 179

pair-work 120, 121, 137, 151
pattern/rule application 63, 65, 66, 72, 74, 81, 152, 164, 165, 181
pattern/rule search 181
peer-group evaluation 94, 106, 107, 110, 117, 151
perfectionism 106, 109, 152, 154, 166
perseverance 110, 116, 122, 157, 183
perseverative text processing strategy 56, 158, 164, 175
personal agenda 32, 98, 99, 115, 121, 123, 167
phonetic coding ability 160
planning 63-5, 69, 81, 88, 131, 153, 157, 165-7, 178
pot luck 59, 76, 181
pragmatic competence 14, 17
problem identification 50, 54, 74, 82, 178
problem-sharing 51, 183
production
— evaluation 63, 165, 176
— monitoring 63, 67, 74, 165, 177
progress monitoring 47, 78, 79, 86, 137, 178
proficiency, notions of 7, 10-19
psychophysiological competence 13, 14

questioning elaboration 179

rational cloze exercises 46
reading, comprehension
— A-level assessment and 17
— cloze exercises and 74
— gender differences and 28, 82-3

— learning strategies and 53-63, 87-8, 79
— learning strategy instruction and
    32, 144, 169
— motivation and 114
— reading in L1/L2 181
— reading in L2 54, 74, 181
— reading on 181
— students' difficulties 2, 7, 26, 31, 33,
    34, 156, 157, 160, 168
— students' strengths in 26, 150
— teachers' approaches to 127, 134-6,
    140-2
— teachers' views of 126
reciprocal teaching 144
recombination 148, 151, 181
rehearsal, silent 70, 81, 106, 166, 183
relevance, and motivation 99, 114, 115
remedial learning strategy instruction
    147, 153, 156
repetition 136, 148, 171, 181
resourcing 42, 74, 150, 165, 181
— grammatical rules and 72, 133, 159
— instruction in using 87-88, 128, 135,
    136, 157, 160-1
— reliance on 26, 54, 63, 65, 156, 162,
    169
— students' difficulties with 40, 58-61,
    164
retrospection 43, 44
retrospective interview
— definition 45, 175
— grammar learning and
    manipulation 71
— listening comprehension 49-50
— oral work 69-71
— reading comprehension 53
— recording anxiety 104, 111, 113
— recording gender differences 82
— recording motivation 99, 113, 115
— research tool 43, 45-6
— Student F and 154-7
— Student H and 157-61
— Student M and 147-51
— Student P and 151-4
— study habits 77-80
— vocabulary learning 77
— writing 64-9
reviewing 78, 146, 178
rhymes/rhythms 183

risk-taking 71, 83, 92, 93, 97, 103, 108,
    110, 166, 183
role-plays 1, 15, 17, 24, 33, 69, 130, 131,
    163
rote learning 72, 77, 89, 119, 132, 148,
    151, 164, 182
rule exercises 90, 181
rule formers 73, 149

School Curriculum and Assessment
    Authority 16, 17
scheduling/organisation 78, 128, 136,
    145, 148, 152, 179
selection, of reading passages 142
selective attention 50, 54, 134, 164, 179
self-analysis 121, 167
self-assessment 8, 79, 111, 118, 120,
    137, 151, 154, 178
self-comparison 151
— negative 29, 79, 107, 109, 120, 137,
    158, 166
— overt 109
self-diagnosis/prescription 71, 80, 133,
    152, 158, 179
self-directed learning 31, 78, 79, 83, 85,
    86, 98, 121, 123, 137, 140, 144, 148,
    152, 154, 158, 167, 168, 170
self-encouragement/self-talk 111,
    183
self-esteem 7, 8, 71, 92, 93, 95, 97, 102,
    103-10, 111, 116, 117
self-image 94, 109, 110, 117, 119, 166
self-management/philosophising 41,
    49, 70, 73, 80, 179
self-testing 77, 133, 148, 183
sentence analysis 54, 74, 134, 155, 159, 181
short-term memory 44, 45, 175
silent rehearsal 70, 81, 106, 166, 183
situationalism 183
social/affective strategies 42, 71, 91,
    175, 183
sociolinguistic competence 12-14, 17
strategic competence 12-14, 17, 170,
    171, 175
strategy evaluation 80, 84, 119, 153,
    156, 169, 170, 176
strategy monitoring 54, 55, 82, 84, 169,
    178
stereotyping 99, 100, 101, 112, 117, 154

study skills 2, 37, 126-8, 136, 145, 168,
    175
substitution 54, 160, 165, 181
summarisation 74, 182
syntax 59-63, 139, 150, 156, 160, 163,
    165

teacher's agenda 115, 167-8
teaching strategies 5, 7, 8, 35, 36, 113,
    125, 127, 129-32, 134-8, 141, 143
tenses 23, 25, 29, 32, 35, 46, 72, 125,
    133, 148
test taking 182
think-aloud interview, thinking aloud
— anxiety and 83
— definition 43, 175
— diagnostic tool 85
— grammar learning and
    manipulation 71, 74-7
— learning strategy instruction and 84
— listening comprehension 50-3,
    138
— reading comprehension 53-63, 78,
    138
— recording motivation 99, 113, 115
— reflection and 85
— research tool 43, 45-6
— Student F and 154-7
— Student H and 157-61
— Student M and 147-51
— Student P and 151-4
— tasks used 196-202
— writing 63-9
tolerance of uncertainty 38
top-down processing 52, 57, 58, 87, 175
topics studied at A-level 7, 20, 28, 30,
    33, 114, 121, 127, 129, 130, 141, 162,
    168
transcription 51, 182
transfer, use of cognates 40, 53, 54,
    61-4, 67, 87, 89, 134-5, 160, 165,
    182
translation 1, 11, 29, 54, 63, 64, 65, 67,
    69, 74, 82, 88, 121, 142, 153, 165, 166,
    182

uncertainty, tolerance of 38
Universal Grammar 12

verification 184
visual monitoring 63, 66, 72, 164, 165,
    178
vocabulary
— activating prior to listening or
    reading 87, 88
— anxiety and 94, 95
— communication strategies and 143
— gender differences and 29
— language philosophy and 79, 148
— learning strategies and 34, 77-8,
    141, 149, 165, 182
— learning strategy instruction and
    32, 87-90, 146
— range 13, 58, 64, 69, 94, 121
— reworking 142
— motivation and 113
— students' comprehension
    difficulties 25, 49-51
— students' learning difficulties 2, 7,
    26, 27, 162
— teaching approaches 33, 132-3, 135,
    136, 138
— teachers' views of 126

word analysis 54, 59, 61-2, 74, 82, 87,
    134-5, 150, 183
world elaboration 53, 56, 57, 180
writing
— A-level assessment and 17
— compared with listening
    comprehension 25
— fluency and 35, 54, 149, 155
— formulaic phrases and 142
— gender differences and 28-9, 81-82,
    100-1
— grammatical accuracy and 27, 72
— learning strategies and 46, 63-9,
    165
— learning strategy instruction and
    33, 88-9
— students' difficulties 2, 7, 27, 33,
    153, 155, 162
— students' strengths in 24
— teachers' approaches to 33, 130-1,
    143
— teachers' views of 168, 126, 127
— vocabulary range and 151

Authors

Allwright, D. 70, 98, 99, 115
Anderson, L.W. 5
Askew, S. 82
Assessment of Performance Unit (APU) 99, 100
Atkinson, T. 89
Au, S.Y. 96

Bachman, L.F. 13, 14, 17
Bacon, S.M. 102
Bagguley, P. 171
Bailey, K.M. 47, 94, 109
Batters, J.D 3, 29, 101, 113
BBC x, 196
Beebe, L.M. 93, 97
Berryman, C.L. 101
Bialystok, E. 34
Black, J.H. 46
Block, E. 54
Bonadona, M. 47, 86
Brown, A.L. 84, 144
Burnaby, B. 93
Burns, R.B. 5
Burstall, C. 97, 98, 99, 100
Bush, E.S . 101
Byram, M. 100

Canale, M. 12, 13, 14
Carrell, P.L. 57
Carroll, J.B. 99, 100, 160
Chambers, G.N. 19
Chamot, A.U. x, 3, 19, 42, 43, 48, 65, 71, 84, 91, 129, 132, 144, 175, 176
Chesterfield, K.B. 40
Chesterfield, R. 40
Chomsky, N. 12
Clark, A. 35
Clarke, M.A. 141
Coates, J.C. 42
Cohen, A. 43, 68
Cohen, L. 6, 46
Crookall, D. 120
Crookes, G. 98, 113, 114, 116
Crossan, B. 2
Cummins, J. 18, 19, 33, 126, 141
Curran, C.C. 97

Dale, R.R. 100
Deaux, K. 110
Delamont, S. 99
Department of Education and Science/ Welsh Office (DES/WO) 15
Dickinson, L. 84, 86
Dörnyei, Z. 143
Dulay, H. 93
Dweck, C.S. 101, 102, 109

Eastman, J.K. 88
Ehrman, M. 41
Ellis, G. 37, 84, 86, 170
Ellis, R. 35, 75, 76
Ely, C.M. 93, 108, 117
Ericsson, K.A. 44, 45
Esarte-Sarries, V. 100
Eskey, D.E. 52

Farris, E. 110
Filmer-Sankey, C. 100
Foss, K.A. 120, 137
Fotos, S. 35
Frith, A. 40, 95

Gardner, R C. 4, 92, 93, 95, 96, 97
Gass, S. 101
Genesee, F. 93
Gillette, B. 138
Glisan, E.W. 88
Goethe-Institut 199
Graham, S. 23
Grenfell, M. 22, 40, 41, 83, 95, 141, 171

Hamayan, E. 93
Harris, V. 40, 41, 83, 95, 141, 171
Hatch, E. 73
Haynes, M. 58, 62
Heafford, M. 35
Heald, D. 58
Hedge, T. 64
Heyde, A.W. 93
Heyde Parsons, A.W. 93
HM Inspectors 2
Hingley, P. 100, 101
Hoffman, J.M. 102
Holmes, J. 3, 101

Hooper, J. 35, 128
Horwitz, E.K. 30, 93, 94, 105
Hosenfeld, C. 52, 56, 58, 85, 157
Howell-Richardson, C. 86
Hulstijn, J. H. 87
Hurman, J. 2

Inter Nationes 197

Jacklin, C.N. 42, 101, 103
Johnstone, R. 18, 141, 150

Keller, J.M. 98, 113, 114, 116
Kelly, A. 105
Kenning, M-M. 100
Kimmel, S. 56, 158, 164
King, L. 2, 35
Klapper, J. 87, 88
Knapman, D. 94
Kogan, N. 103
Krashen, S.D. 92, 130
Küpper, L. 3, 43, 65, 71, 132

Lado, R. 11
LaFrance, M. 108
Lambert, W.E. 4, 96
Langer, I. 142
Larsen-Freeman, D. 5, 92
Lennon, P. 96
Leki, I. 68
Lewcowicz, J. 86
Licht, B.G. 101, 102, 109
Littlewood, P. 105
Long, M.H. 5, 92
Low, G. 2
Loulidi, R. 99
Lukmani, Y. 96

Maccoby, E.E. 42, 101, 103
MacDonald, M. 102
MacGinitie, W.H. 56, 158, 164
MacIntyre, P.D. 92, 93, 95
McLaughlin, B. 80, 160
Manion, L. 6, 46
Mann, S. J. 43
Metcalfe, P. 19
Miller, F.D. 45
Mitchell, R. 14, 128
Moon, J. 86

Murphy-O'Dwyer, L. 86
Naiman, N. 38, 43, 71, 150
Nicholls, J.G. 101
Nisbet, J. 37
Norman, D.A. 171
Northern Examinations and
    Assessment Board x, 201
Nuttall, C. 88
Nyikos, M. 41, 77

Ochsner, R. 47
Oller, J. 47
O'Malley, J.M. x, 19, 42, 48, 50, 52, 83,
    84, 91, 144, 175, 176
Omerod, M.B. 100
Oxford, R. x, 41, 42, 48, 83, 84, 90, 101,
    115, 120, 175

Palincsar, A.S. 84, 144
Paris, S.G. 91
Parkinson, B. 86
Parsons, J.E. 109
Peck, A. 35, 88
Perkins, K. 47
Perl, S. 64, 66, 68
Phillips, E.M. 93, 95
Pickard, N. 54
Powell, R.C. 3, 89, 99, 105

Rees, F. 29, 113
Rees, P.F. 26
Reiss, M.A. 77
Reitzel, A.C. 120, 137
Rock, D. 17
Ross, C. 82
Rubin, J. 38, 40, 43, 84, 86, 90, 93

School Curriculum and Assessment
    Authority 16, 17
Shucksmith, J. 37
Schmidt, R.W. 98, 113, 114, 116
Schultz, J.M. 19, 33, 140, 143
Schulz, R.A. 141, 142
Schumann, J.H. 92
Scovel, T. 94, 102
Seliger, H.W. 44, 70, 82
Selinker, L. 12
Shapiro, S.H. 102
Sharwood-Smith, M. 35

Simon, H.A. 44, 45
Sinclair, B. 37, 84, 86, 170
Skehan, P. 6
Skutnabb-Kangas, T. 18, 19
Smith, E.R. 45
Spender, D. 103, 108
Spolsky, B. 4, 171
Stern, H.H. 4, 10, 40, 92
Stipek, D.J. 102
Sutherland, M.B. 100, 102
Swain, M. 12, 13, 14, 18, 93

Tannen, D. 42, 110
Thomas, K. 100
Thompson, I. 84, 90
Thorogood, J. 2, 35

Thurrell, S. 143
University of Oxford Delegacy of
　Local Examinations x, 198

van Ek, J.A. 14
Varonis, E. 101

Wallach, M.A. 103
Walmsley, R. 19
Weinrich-Haste, H. 100
Wenden, A. 83
White, P. 45
Whyte, J. 108
Widdowson, H.G. 76

Zamel, V. 64